£ 2.50

# KILLER IN CLOWNTOWN

Martin Dillon was born in Belfast, and after an early career in print and broadcasting journalism, became a producer with BBC Northern Ireland, where he initiated some of Ulster's most controversial radio and television programmes. In 1973 he co-authored *Political Murder in Northern Ireland*, long considered the definitive study of political assassination there. He also co-authored *Rogue Warrior of the SAS*, a biography of the World War II hero, Blair Mayne. His plays have been performed on BBC radio and television. *Killer in Clowntown* is the third in a series of investigative studies of Ireland since the current 'troubles' began in 1968, the first two being *The Shankill Butchers* and *The Dirty War*.

*By the same author*

ROGUE WARRIOR OF THE SAS

POLITICAL MURDER IN NORTHERN IRELAND

THE SHANKILL BUTCHERS

THE DIRTY WAR

# KILLER IN CLOWNTOWN

## Joe Doherty, the IRA and the Special Relationship

*Martin Dillon*

ARROW BOOKS

Arrow Books Limited
20 Vauxhall Bridge Road, London SW1V 2SA

An imprint of the Random Century Group

London Melbourne Sydney Auckland
Johannesburg and agencies throughout
the world

First published by Hutchinson in 1992

This edition published in 1992 by Arrow Books

© Martin Dillon 1992

Printed and bound in Great Britain by
Cox & Wyman Ltd., Reading, Berkshire

ISBN 0 09 919571 2

I dedicate this book to Kathy, Crawford and Nadia for their constant love and support while I write about the nature of conflict.

# Contents

# Acknowledgements

There are people within secret establishments and organisations who assisted me by providing information for this book on the understanding they should not be named. The writer of conflict is always in the position of not being able to name some of his sources but is able to name those people who were central to providing the creative and technical support required.

Others: Frank Delaney is a friend and fellow writer who has always encouraged me. His encouragement and advice were invaluable. Brian McLaughlin spent many hours transferring my written material to computer discs and was a constant source of support. He was a discreet and welcome companion during many hours of correcting the script. My agent, Anthony Harwood of Curtis Brown, was a calming influence during the writing of a difficult book. Linda Nee provided excellent typing skills for correcting the final manuscript. I am forever indebted to my wife Kathy and our children, Crawford and Nadia, for persevering with me while I write about conflict in a dangerous society. Kathy was always a creative source who offered the necessary appraisals of my efforts.

Finally in writing my books there are friends and colleagues who deserve mention because their presence in my life or within its confines are a constant source of creative inspiration. They include my parents, Gerard and Maureen Dillon, my sister, Ursula McLaughlin, Susan Collier Delaney, Dr Conor Cruise and Maura O'Brien, Patrick O'Brien, Ian and Cecilia Kennedy, my mother-in-law, Maureen Bannon, Sam and Shirley, Brian, Anne and Paula Turley, Professor Simon Lee and his wife Patricia, Ronnie and Shoshana Appelton, Fidelma McVeigh, Michael Lavery QC,

Michael Lynch LLB, Brian and Kate Garrett, Colin and Jane Lewis, Ivor Oswald, David and Janet Ross, Moore and Sandra Sinnerton, Don and Rosie Anderson, David Malone, Chris Moore and John Bach, who lectures in criminology in Northern Ireland.

I reserve special thanks for Gladys Shelley, whose song about New York, 'Clowntown', inspired the title of this book and who made my stay in New York one of the most memorable.

Linden Stafford, David Sykes and Crispin Avon remain dear friends who are part of an interesting world.

While writing this book I moved home to Buckinghamshire and the transition was made easier by colleagues such as Roy Davies, Head of History at BBC Elstree, and *Timewatch* producer, Ken Kirby. They provided the creative conversation which is necessary to every writer and particularly one who moved to a new environment. In Buckinghamshire, Cecil and Diane, June, Mick and Rita and others in my village illustrated that living without the constant presence of violence and death is a necessary prerequisite even in the life of a writer who chronicles it.

In the world of journalism there are two people who have always been willing to answer my queries. Jim Campbell is a wealth of information who continues to write despite attempts to kill him, and David McKittrick of the *Independent* provides fascinating insights for those living beyond the violence of Northern Ireland. The two historians who remain and offer balanced perceptions of the conflict are A. T. Q. Stewart and Paul Bew.

# Prologue:
# An Unfolding Story

On Saturday 24 August 1990 I was sitting in my home outside Belfast when I received a phone call from my employers, the British Broadcasting Corporation. I was told that a senior official at the British Government's Northern Ireland Office had been in contact with the BBC switchboard seeking my telephone number. In keeping with BBC policy the official had been refused my number because it was ex-directory; as a writer on terrorism, I preferred my number and address to remain confidential. I phoned the Northern Ireland Office, located the Government official and was told that he was contacting me on behalf of Douglas Archard, the US Consul-General in Belfast. I was puzzled by the means being used to locate me and wondered why Archard should have resorted to such a circuitous route when he could as easily have telephoned the BBC. In any case, I knew him personally, and was intrigued that he should find it necessary to employ the resources of a British Government department to locate me unless discretion was essential. Maybe he was concerned that phoning my employers would compromise him.

I lost little time in ringing Douglas Archard, and quickly discovered there was a sensitive matter which he wished to discuss with me. It concerned a court hearing in New York involving Joseph Doherty, an IRA man who had been incarcerated in the United States for over seven years. Douglas made it clear he was representing a request from the US Administration that I assist them with the Doherty case. He told me that I was regarded as the foremost authority on Irish terrorism and that my most recently published book, *The Dirty War*, was considered to be the definitive study of the conflict in Ireland.

As our conversation developed it became apparent that he was only a conduit for the request to enlist my help and did not wish to be drawn into any arrangements I might choose to make with his superiors. I advised him that, if I was being asked to confirm details of material in my books, I would favourably consider such a request. A writer naturally feels obliged to defend his work; and *The Dirty War* contained the IRA's 'Green Book', the only published and up-to-date edition of the organisation's rules, constitution and objectives. I told Archard I required more detailed information regarding the request before I was prepared to continue our discussion. He replied that he would pass the matter to the office of the United States Attorney for the Southern District of New York.

After the phone call I retrieved a file on Joseph Doherty which contained newspaper clippings on his life as a terrorist and his court battles in the United States. I kept a file on him because I intended at a future date to include him in a study of hitmen; now I needed to acquaint myself with his history. I reflected on my conversation with Douglas Archard and the manner in which it had taken place. As a writer I was familiar with delivering lectures but this was the first time I was faced with a possible use of my material in a courtroom, and I was worried whether I was being sought as a prosecution witness to damage Doherty's testimony. The prospect of being presented as an opponent of Doherty engendered a feeling of insecurity. I knew only too well that the IRA viewed prosecution witnesses as legitimate targets and I could place my family and myself in danger. I decided to wait for the telephone call from the US Attorney's Office before making a firm decision.

The next day I was contacted by Claude Millman, an assistant attorney to the US Attorney for the Southern District, Otto Obermaier. Millman explained his professional duties before reaching the crux of the matter. He informed me about Doherty's history of litigation and stressed that a habeas corpus hearing scheduled for 4 September was crucial to US Government interests. He and Obermaier represented the Attorney-General, Richard L. Thornburgh, against Doherty, and they required an expert witness to testify about the nature of IRA membership to disprove Doherty's claim that he had resigned from the organisation in 1982 before fleeing to the US. They believed I was qualified to prove that he could not have resigned and that he posed a threat to the interests of the US if released on bond (bail).

My fears about the role I was being asked to fulfil were suddenly realised. It was clear that I was being put forward as a leading witness to destroy Doherty's testimony. I told Millman I needed two things: time to consider his request, and the complete file on the Doherty case. He used a special courier service, and within twenty-four hours I was in possession of all the briefs from both legal camps and masses of legal documents. They made several days of voracious reading, and the transcripts of the many hearings were astounding, both in the nature of the case and in the strategy used by both sides. I wondered why Doherty attracted such intense interest from successive US Administrations. And how had the US judicial process become so steadily compromised in the pursuit of one man? My increasing fascination with the case did not, however, obscure the risk to myself if I agreed to be a leading witness.

I asked several contacts in the security forces in Northern Ireland if they believed the American request constituted a danger to me. Each of them agreed that as an author I was entitled to defend my work but if I stepped outside those parameters I might as well 'buy myself a brown box'.

Accordingly I phoned Millman and told him that in principle I could not act as a witness within his terms of reference, though I was prepared to explain to him, not a court, my own writing on the history of the conflict: he would have to decide whether that would prove valuable. Next day he telephoned and said he wished me to travel to New York where I could view other material relevant to the case; he added that he respected my decision and my right to talk privately about matters connected with my published work. I asked him who had recommended me to Otto Obermaier, but he could not tell me. He offered to pay all my expenses, plus the fee I would normally receive for lectures, and suggested I travel to New York as soon as possible.

On 31 August I met Claude Millman at my hotel in the centre of Manhattan. He explained he was one of many assistant attorneys involved with the case over a seven-year period, and that was proving a major problem. As attorneys left the Southern District, others less intimate with Doherty's facts were obliged to wade through the myriad documents. Now he was just another of those young attorneys who had found themselves faced with learning the intricacies of one of the longest-running legal sagas in US judicial history. We arranged to meet the following morning at the

US Attorney's building in lower Manhattan, where I would be free to examine the complete file.

While I was at the US Attorney's Office, FBI Special Agent Frank Schulte arrived. Schulte was head of a counter-terrorist task force which specialised in combating Irish terrorism, and he was the most experienced of its undercover agents, with ten years in the field. His work concentrated mainly on the IRA and its attempts to buy hi-tech weaponry in the United States. He believed the IRA was using the US as a safe haven for terrorists fleeing British justice, and much of his covert activity included surveillance on Irish-Americans and other US citizens who supported the Irish republican cause. Schulte had travelled to Northern Ireland on several occasions to liaise with British intelligence, and operatives within covert groups similar to his own; namely Special Branch and E4A, a specialist police unit which was involved in many controversial shootings. He had called in to rehearse with Millman the testimony he hoped to give in court three days later. Millman stressed to Schulte the importance of his convincing the court of his anti-terrorist experience before talking directly about Joseph Doherty. This implied awkwardnesses: Schulte clearly preferred to stay undercover and did not relish being in the public eye or revealing the true nature of his work. Nor did he wish to offer detailed analysis of his recent cases against the IRA. Was he also concerned that the Doherty camp might resurrect a current controversial story of his dealings with a senior RUC officer on the streets of New York? Americans did not approve of British policemen working undercover in their cities.

Schulte's history of counter-terrorism was impressive by any standards of success. Between 1981 and 1983 he led an IRA weapons procurement case in which he arrested four IRA men and intercepted 50 weapons, 4500 rounds of ammunition, bomb-making components and military support equipment being shipped from the United States to Ireland. In 1986 he had tracked down Frank Sutcliffe, who was attempting to procure for the IRA sophisticated weapons which included a .50 sniper's rifle, laser range-finding equipment and night-vision sights. He had traced Sutcliffe to sniper and counter-sniper training camps and returned him to Ireland where he was convicted. Three years later he arrested Donal Moyna, an IRA research and development specialist, who was in possession of counterfeit money. In 1990 he foiled a plot by two men to purchase twenty M16 rifles for the IRA. In the same year he was also involved in uncovering an IRA plan to acquire sophisticated technology for remote-controlled detonation of bombs; and another IRA plan in California to purchase surface-to-air missiles. But of all the cases the one which intrigued him, and which remained part of his life, was the continued presence of Joseph Doherty in a detention cell.

It became plain as he rehearsed his testimony that his interest had grown more personal than professional, because he alone had tracked down Doherty in New York, one of his first successes as head of the FBI task force. But he felt repeatedly cheated that the judicial system appeared incapable of resolving the matter and returning Doherty to a prison cell in the United Kingdom. He knew all the ploys used by IRA men fleeing British justice, and how they utilised the assistance of sympathisers in the US. As he left Millman's office I suspected he would leave a lot unsaid in the Doherty case. Whatever happened he did not wish to be compromised as a witness, answering questions about the workings of his secret world.

Later that day the US Attorney Otto Obermaier arrived. He seemed dismissive of Millman, and appeared to foresee no problems arising from the Doherty bail hearing: he would personally conduct a cross-examination which would weaken Doherty's years of testimony. Millman pressed ahead with polite interjections, which Obermaier waved away as irrelevant or wearisome. Obermaier believed he could handle the case without relying on the studious and detailed analysis presented by his subordinate. He directed his comments exclusively to Millman and paid little attention to my presence beyond a short discourse on the history of the IRA and the nature of membership of the organisation. Possibly he deduced that if I was knowledgeable about these matters it was Millman's responsibility to brief him. I wondered whether Obermaier was trying to impress me with his use of authority or was trying to show he was capable of addressing a complex legal case with a casual indifference to its history. Obermaier remarked that the judge scheduled for the hearing, the Honourable Miriam Goldman Cedarbaum, was the ideal person for the role. He revealed, indiscreetly, that he had taken her to dinner that week and they had talked about the Doherty hearing. He treated this piece of information with a degree of amusement and seemed unconcerned about the publicity or political debate surrounding Doherty.

Before he left the office I informed him I could not appear as a witness because I did not, for personal reasons, wish to be drawn into a legal battle which was not a defence of my writings.

The hearing was scheduled to begin at 2.30 pm on 4 September in the US Federal Building. By then I was well acquainted with the intricacies of the history of the proceedings, and was glad I was an observer, determined now to learn more about it with a view to unravelling some of its complexities. An intuitive feeling came to me – that this was an extraordinary story, that somewhere within it was a hidden agenda which determined that not only the United States Government but also the British Government would pursue Doherty to the bitter end.

On Tuesday 4 September, after having lunch with Frank Schulte, I walked to the courthouse. My route took me past Joe Doherty Corner and I paused to look at the street sign, a testimony to an IRA man who was halfway through the 2645th day of his incarceration in the Metropolitan Correction Center. Outside the court building, technicians were assembling television equipment, and inside there was a mass of people blocking my path to the doors of the courtroom. Many were journalists who were unable to gain access: the press gallery was oversubscribed. One of Millman's colleagues in the US Attorney's Office arranged for me to be escorted away from the crowded corridor, and I was taken to a room near the judge's chambers. As advised, I stayed there until the judge had entered the court; then, after being led to the press gallery, I found myself less than twelve feet from Joseph Doherty.

The courtroom was crowded with friends of Joseph Doherty and leading politicians who supported his cause. He sat smiling, without a trace of nervousness, his demeanour that of a confident man: he wore a white cotton shirt, red tie and grey pin-striped suit. In no way did he resemble the photograph which the British tabloid press habitually used, portraying him with a beard and lank hair: this man was well-groomed, clean-shaven.

Half an hour earlier, he had been wearing regulation orange prison overalls in the nearby detention centre, waiting to be led to the return-and-departure area. Doherty looked all around him – and smiled at the large turnout of officers of the US Marshal Service positioned strategically around the courtroom. It must have struck him that the atmosphere was more in keeping with courts in Northern Ireland, where there had long since been greater justification for such tight security. The presence of the marshals reminded me of a remark Millman had made to Obermaier – that a heavy security presence was a necessary ploy. It would publicly reinforce their argument that Doherty represented a threat, a sure flight risk if allowed bail. Although I didn't say so, I considered this an absurd tactic; but they believed Judge Miriam Cedarbaum vulnerable to such a display of force.

Doherty, having established eye contact and acknowledgements with the people in the public gallery, turned to his legal team, Mary Pike and Steve Somerstein. I noticed his eyes were fixed on Mary Pike: I had learned they had fallen in love. Doherty was cautious about expressing his feelings for her publicly, but a member of the staff at the detention centre told me that they often held hands, and just before his court appearances would embrace. He remarked later that he needed the warmth of her embrace and final words of advice and encouragement.

The court session began with the customary opening statements of position: first defence, Steve Somerstein, then Claude Millman. Doherty bore not a sign of stress. His court appearances were a regular – and attractive – feature of his history. Court presented him with a platform to outline his political history; his dedication to the IRA cause; his continued assertion that he posed no threat to the United States; that he was never a bail risk. In keeping with procedures, Doherty was first faced with a direct examination by Steve Somerstein.

*Somerstein:*  Mr Doherty, can you tell us where you currently reside?
*Doherty:*  At 150 Park Row, Joe Doherty Corner.

Muted laughter from the public gallery; behind the prisoner's cool exterior I caught a smugness, betrayed only by a slight smirk. His answer summarised the absurdity of an unfolding story. What bizarre chain of circumstances, I wondered, permitted a convicted killer from Belfast to give his address as a street named in his honour? In honour of his detention – and so named by the very city which had held him in custody for over seven years?

Doherty replied to a series of questions which established the year he joined the IRA, and then the year in which he claimed to have resigned – which he maintained was 1982, prior to his travelling to the United States. Doherty's evidence continued with an outline of his terrorist history: escapes from prison; violent confrontations with police, soldiers and members of the elite

British Special Air Service Regiment, the SAS. He answered questions from Somerstein with crispness and authority: this was a well-rehearsed and, more to the point, experienced witness. There was an innate cleverness about the ways in which he fashioned his testimony. He appeared always courteous and in control, showing no bitterness or acrimony. I felt he understood he was talking to an American audience who knew little of the intricacies of the IRA and its rules of membership. I was also aware of how Doherty entered the US and the back-up services in New York which provided him with a new identity as Henry J. O'Reilly, a work permit, and accommodation. He was an IRA hero in republican circles in Ireland: his capture would have damaged IRA morale, and he had been sent to the United States to evade detection by the British.

His delivery and his occasional use of American vernacular was designed to endear himself to his court audience. Doherty ensured everything he said confirmed his claim that the British regarded him as a prisoner of war, but that he was in truth a friend to the US. He was also patently aware of the presence of leading politicians in the courtroom, and showed himself intent on convincing the judge of their commitment to his claim that he be freed on bail:

If I was to be approached by the IRA on the outside and asked to go back, I could never see the day they would do that. But if I was ever asked, I would not go, because as I said, Your Honour, it is my obligation to the court, and to these people here; and to the financial contribution they are willing to make for my bail bond; and for their reputations. There is so much at stake. Beyond that, there is the Irish-American community, and thousands upon thousands of people across the United States. This includes 132 members of the House of Representatives. This includes the AFL-CIO. This includes seven to eight city councils, and four, five state legislatures. Who have all passed these resolutions that I be released on bail.

I knew the list was long. Everybody who was anybody in American political life, from congressmen and senators to religious leaders, aligned behind Doherty; even George Bush's son telephoned Doherty in his cell, and publicly supported him. Nor was it inconceivable that he was telling the truth when he said he would honour his bail. Doherty was a money-spinner for IRA fundraisers and a propaganda weapon against the British. Why would the IRA jeopardise that by ordering him back to Ireland? Other IRA men were granted bail in cases handled by Schulte, and they honoured their bail. Something told me that Doherty was a special case for the British and American Governments. What was the agenda which determined he should be denied bail, and relentlessly pursued through the courts?

To be truthful. If I was granted bail and I was to go back to face the hangman's noose, I would go back, Your Honour. If I was to lose my case before the Board of Immigration Appeals, I would pay my own ticket and I would gladly go back and graciously get on that plane, without any malice towards the United States. I have been given a fair shake in New York City from the judicial branch of Government, and also from segments of the Justice Department, the Board of Immigration Appeals and the immigration officials that have rendered their decisions in which I have prevailed.

He knew whom to praise because he had been successful in several hearings, even though the decisions in his favour had been overruled by the executive arm of the US Government. Two Attorneys-General, Edwin Meese III under Reagan, and Richard L. Thornburgh under Bush, both intervened to overturn Doherty's judicial successes. The longer I sat in the courtroom, the more I felt an overriding sense that this was a story which did not fit into any pattern in my experience of the politics of conflict. I waited for Obermaier to render Doherty helpless and inadequate but it did not happen: the US Attorney had not fully applied himself to the *minutiae* of Doherty's history in Ireland, or his seven years of testimony in the American courts. He failed to see that he was dealing with a witness well schooled by US lawyers but, more importantly, an IRA man who was trained in anti-interrogation techniques. Doherty was familiar with subtle forms of questioning and with the harsh reality of British army interrogation techniques of the 1970s.

Obermaier began his cross-examination by reminding the court of his personal opinions and how he believed the judge should view the case.

I am intrigued because the issue from my perspective is the same. Whether it is a murderer from a foreign country should be allowed bail, or whether it is someone from the IRA, the Provos, whether from 'Free Cuba' or some other group. The relevancy and the vital issue in this case is whether someone like this petitioner, with his criminal history, can be allowed to be on bail. The point I am trying to make is that Your Honour's consideration should be far broader than merely the IRA.

Judge Cedarbaum said her view was that it would be helpful if there was evidence to show that people such as Doherty were frequently recalled from the US or held under some sort of discipline by the IRA. Obermaier retorted that he failed to see 'the connection' but his case had 'some elements of that'.

Obermaier's cross-examination was at times loose and offered Doherty the chance to extol the virtues of American liberalism.

*Obermaier:* Before you were apprehended in the United States did you file an asylum application other than the one you filed after you were apprehended in 1982?

*Doherty:* I was very vague on the laws. I came to the United States and I knew I was an illegal alien. Other illegal aliens come to the United States not only from Ireland but from other countries. As I said, I was very vague on the political asylum laws and I was twenty-five years of age. I was young and I was very afraid. I was afraid to turn myself in and I always knew from my youth from reading books and by watching television that America was the country that would receive people who are persecuted. I mean, we all know about the Statue of Liberty and stuff. Give me your hungry and oppressed. I knew that as a kid. I knew I would be protected by American laws and I would be relatively safe. I was very vague about the whole mechanism of asylum and how to approach it. I was very innocent of that and when I came here my sort of priority was to get a job, to live as normal a life as possible.

Doherty was clever, always sensitive to the opportunity to exploit his youthfulness, apparent naïvety and Irish-American sympathy for the plight of the 'persecuted'. Here was a man who had left school at fourteen years of age, whose knowledge of history had been learned in prison cells, or in IRA history lectures, and who was now thwarting a leading US Attorney. Doherty was never devoid of a means of replying to the cross-examination, as the following record shows.

*Obermaier:* Is your life in danger in the United Kingdom because of the crimes you committed there?

*Doherty:* I didn't commit any crimes.

*Obermaier:* No crimes?

*Doherty:* No crimes. The British presence in my country is the crime. I was an opponent of that.

*Obermaier:* Were you convicted by an English court of committing crimes?

*Doherty:* I was convicted by a special court, yes.

*Obermaier:* More than once?

*Doherty:* More than once.

*Obermaier:* Did you think it was lawful when you escaped from prison?

*Doherty:* It was a duty.

Doherty was careful not to answer questions but to make statements which accorded with his own political aspirations and those of the people who supported his cause in the United States. His technique was typical of a style which I knew only too well in my years of reporting IRA cases (in the United Kingdom and Ireland). It was a simple technique of keeping replies brief, fitting them to IRA policy rather than the aims of the questioner. His use of the phrase 'special court' was not an admission of guilt but a means of damaging the credibility of his previous convictions by implying that they had not been the result of orthodox court procedure. Doherty was giving a performance which not only delighted his lawyers and supporters but would have endeared him to the IRA. It would not have occurred in a British court where lawyers were more adept at dealing with the strategy used by accused IRA volunteers. Obermaier tried unsuccessfully to force Doherty to admit he was trained to kill, but the witness side-stepped the issue by pointing out that all army manuals, including that of the marines, referred only to tactics and preferred the term 'to inflict casualties'.

Obermaier turned his attention to the judge in an attempt to redress his mishaps. He produced photographs of the SAS captain whom Doherty had been convicted of killing; the photographs showed the body and the wounds sustained. Obermaier intended to offend Cedarbaum's sensibilities and as she glanced at the photos she winced and quickly set them to one side. Millman had told Obermaier at our meeting that he had acquired forensic and morgue records of the dead captain, and Obermaier had said they should be introduced during the hearing, in order to convince Cedarbaum of Doherty's callousness. His decision may well have been a clever move: she seemed to display a sudden antagonism as she looked towards the witness. Judge Cedarbaum displayed an incisive approach to the precise nature of the hearing. It was apparent to me that she hoped Obermaier would concentrate on the relevant issue of whether Doherty was still under IRA control in the US but her expectation did not materialise in the cross-examination.

The hearing was steadily becoming a charade, but one which illustrated several things for me. Doherty was a greater self-publicist and IRA propagandist while he remained in prison and was afforded court appearances. Why not release him on bail? Why continue to provide him with hallowed platforms such as US courtrooms or a prison cell from which he was constantly writing articles for newspapers and newssheets and conducting regular television interviews on the networks? Surely the preferable course of action was to free him until such time as he was deported or allowed to remain in the US. His celebrity status and the amazing degree of support he was able to muster was due to his image as a prisoner of conscience, and to the interference of the executive arm of the US Government in reversing judicial decisions made in his favour. How could this terrorist from Belfast deserve so much attention that the US Government was prepared to impede the course of its own legal process to keep him in custody for a period unparalleled in US legal history, and seek his extradition and deportation at all costs? In the public gallery were leading lawyers from New York City, many of them prepared to post personal sums of $50,000 to $100,000 towards a bail bond. Congressman Gary Ackerman was on file offering $100,000 and a guarantee he would employ Doherty in his legal firm if the court released him. There were others prepared to offer their property as surety and, in all, a total sum of $800,000 was offered as a bond. Unfortunately this was not relevant because the judge ruled that the US Attorney was prepared to seek an additional day to present evidence. For her part, the judge had not correctly ordered her diary and pointed out that the following day did not accord with her schedule. She set a further hearing to resume on 17 September.

Later that day I returned to my hotel for drinks with Frank Schulte to reminisce about the hearing. I expressed my astonishment at the nature of the proceedings but Schulte looked quizzically at me and I assumed my reaction was typical of many people who observed Joe Doherty's court appearances. Our conversation was interrupted by the arrival of two guests of the US Attorney's Office who were staying at my hotel. They joined our table and introduced themselves as Professor Paul Wilkinson and Sherard Cowper Coles. Paul Wilkinson had just arrived from London to learn that the second day of the Doherty hearing was scheduled for

17 September. It soon transpired that he had been flown to New York to undertake the role of expert witness – the role I had declined to fill. He holds the Chair of International Relations at the University of St Andrews in Scotland, and is Director of the Research Institute for the Study of Conflict and Terrorism at St Andrews and at the Institute's office in London. The Institute is registered as a charity and affiliated to St Andrews, and during his time as director Wilkinson authored and co-authored eight books on political violence. His extra-curricular work included a consultancy with CBS News America and my employers, the BBC. I regarded him as an informed and fair commentator, though some of his critics in Ireland believed he was a partisan of British policy there. Such criticism was inevitable in Ireland, where any opposition to the nationalist or republican ethos tends to be construed as prejudice. I knew of no evidence which placed Paul Wilkinson in a partisan role and I accepted his right to be critical of violence. When questioned about the role of the British military or internal policing in Northern Ireland he was equally vociferous in his condemnation of unprovoked violence or savagery by soldiers as by paramilitaries. He was prepared to be forthright in criticising, without equivocation, the killings of innocent civilians by soldiers in tragic episodes such as Bloody Sunday on 30 January 1972. He was also critical of the way in which the English policeman, John Stalker, had been prevented from fully investigating allegations of a police shoot-to-kill policy in Northern Ireland.

Sherard Cowper Coles, a British diplomat, was unknown to me. Why was he in New York? I could only assume – correctly, it transpired – that his presence was also related to the Doherty case. A conversation ensued about the day's hearing, and I was asked for my interpretation of the nature of the proceedings. We discussed my book *The Dirty War*, in particular its study of the IRA. *The Dirty War*'s appendix sets out the IRA's rules, and our conversation focused on whether Doherty lived within those rules, the very point which intrigued Cedarbaum. Two hours later we were still attempting to resolve Obermaier's dilemma; and still there appeared no obvious reason for the presence of the diplomat in our company. Eventually I asked him whether he, like Paul Wilkinson, had just arrived from London. He replied, 'Washington', and duly handed me a business card which read: 'Mr Sherard Cowper Coles, First Secretary (Chancery), British Embassy, Washington DC' – high-powered, but where did he stand in the

Doherty context? The British Government had recently said it was not involved with the Doherty case; but I decided that a relevant question now, at this first meeting, might receive a frosty answer. In any case, his privacy appeared to be of paramount importance to him. He and Paul Wilkinson retired early, and I pressed Frank Schulte for an analysis of the presence and significance of Sherard Cowper Coles. Schulte too was wary of diplomats who said little but were adept at gathering information from the conversations of others. At midnight I went to bed, puzzled about the day's events, but more convinced than ever that I should untangle the Joe Doherty story.

The following morning Claude Millman arrived at the hotel and invited me to Paul Wilkinson's suite, where we were joined by Sherard Cowper Coles. Millman said Wilkinson would be required to return for the 17 September hearing, or on an alternative date. He added that Otto Obermaier wished to meet Paul Wilkinson and Cowper Coles. I was happy to accept an invitation to join them, in order to hear Obermaier's views on his performance and discover why Cowper Coles was with us.

Obermaier's office is sumptuous and elegant, in keeping with his status, his sense of authority and aura of self-importance. I was only an observer and Obermaier to date had shown little interest in my presence or my views. Claude Millman sat near to me as if to indicate a non-participation in the unfolding proceedings. Obermaier relaxed behind a large ornate desk in his shirt sleeves, and Sherard Cowper Coles sat closest to him in a high chair which gave him added authority. Wilkinson was sitting in front of the desk, murmuring concern at the timing of an afternoon flight which awaited him at Kennedy airport.

Obermaier offered a résumé of the previous day's events which did not match my understanding of what had taken place. As always, he was casual in his delivery. It was his office; he was the US Attorney, and we were mere subordinates. However, he quickly realised that the British diplomat with his aristocratic poise was not easily impressed and, furthermore, was capable of bluntness. Looking directly at Obermaier, Cowper Coles said: 'The Prime Minister, Mrs Thatcher, was briefed overnight on this case.'

I was startled by the preciseness of his revelation. We were hearing that Margaret Thatcher took such a keen interest in Joe Doherty that a senior diplomat had travelled to New York and from his hotel room had personally phoned his Prime Minister. Now I realised why he had talked to Schulte and me, and why he was particularly interested in my analysis of the court proceedings: I had spent the afternoon in the courtroom whereas Schulte had been in his office. In effect I had unknowingly briefed the diplomat the previous night. Suddenly I recalled a casual remark made by Schulte when we were having lunch together before the court hearing. He had commented that Obermaier 'had better get this case right', because 'there was heavy political pressure' and failure could end his career. I had almost forgotten those remarks until Cowper Coles mentioned Margaret Thatcher.

Obermaier showed little surprise at the diplomat's reference to Margaret Thatcher, but Cowper Coles pressed home his point: 'The Prime Minister believes you owe us this one. She allowed your Government to use our territory for your F1–11s when they were on their way to bomb Tripoli.'

Coles's statement was an admission of Doherty's significance to the British Government and a rebuke to Obermaier. The diplomat was making it abundantly clear that the US Attorney should recognise the significance of the Doherty hearing. Obermaier, hurt but recalcitrant, replied that he was a lawyer and not a politician. Coles reminded him again of Mrs Thatcher's interest and why she regarded the return of Doherty as a quid pro quo for her support for Reagan's decision to bomb Tripoli.

Suddenly many things made sense. Margaret Thatcher and President Reagan were close allies who saw themselves as creating a new world order against terrorism. Doherty epitomised one of the failures of their efforts. Reagan was no longer in power, but the US Government was still in debt to her. The relentless pursuit of her objectives was being compromised by the highly public presence of an IRA terrorist in New York. Cowper Coles was using political blackmail on her behalf. It was an illustration of the determination of a singleminded woman to ensure that her record on terrorism was not blemished by a failure to defeat Doherty. Her involvement was proof that the British Government's public disavowal of any participation in the Doherty saga was a nonsense.

Cowper Coles left the office with me in tow. It was obvious he had made his point, and Obermaier was anxious to talk to Paul Wilkinson about his future participation in the Doherty case. As I walked from the US Attorney's building I felt admiration for Obermaier in defining his role as a lawyer and refusing to be politically coerced. Equally I respected Cowper Coles for his unabridged revelations.

By this time, I knew I was close to an exciting story which required considerable research, as well as meetings with people who could lead me to an understanding of Doherty, and others who could unlock files containing classified documentation that could unravel the hidden political agenda. I returned to Belfast and wrote to Doherty and his lawyers, but they were unwilling to talk to me. That was not a serious obstacle because others were prepared to help.

In the months that followed I was sent many classified documents, some of them unsolicited. One classified memorandum that I received was an outline of a British Government meeting of July 1983, and one particular paragraph reminded me of the attempt to lure me into the witness box:

It would be prudent for the Northern Ireland Office during the period leading up to the defence's response to our depositions, to give thought to possible witnesses on the general situation in the Province [Northern Ireland] at the time of Doherty's offences. It would be important for any such witness to be dissociated from the British Government, and for him to be able to paint a picture of declining violence and impartial law enforcement and judicial procedures. While such high profile figures as Conor Cruise O'Brien, Lord Fitt or Robert Kee could be difficult to land, the bigger the 'fish' the better.

During the preparation of this book, I never visited Joseph Doherty in his prison cell – an abode otherwise open to the world's media. He never replied to my correspondence. In 1990 he was interviewed by some of my colleagues in the British Broadcasting Corporation. I wrote to his lawyer, Mary Pike, who then told me on the telephone that she was reading one of my books. I subsequently phoned her on several occasions but she did not reply. Neither she nor Doherty was aware of my presence among them in the courtroom in September 1990. I subsequently learned that Doherty was planning to publish an account of his detention in New York entitled 'Standing Proud'.

They knew I was preparing this book, and maybe they perceived a conflict of interest. I was privately informed by a writer who once lived in New York that Doherty 'always talked to Mary and she advised him on whether to undertake interviews'. That information only served to encourage me to conclude either that she did not approve of my previous writings, or that she was worried I might detect flaws in her client's portrayal of his history. I had grown up near Joe Doherty, and knew all his stamping grounds. I retraced my steps throughout that history in the same city, that same society, to seek an understanding of Doherty and to present it accurately. I was left with the inescapable conclusion that he was a young man of limited education, drawn into the conflict because of inherited prejudice, the overpowering emotionalism of the terrible events surrounding him and his association with the cult of the gunman.

His political learning was later imposed on his actions and shaped to accord with them. He was the archetypal republican dedicated to the cause from which he had no desire to escape. He reminded me of many veteran IRA men steeped in the tradition of the movement, schooled in its rhetoric and subservient to its codes. As I watched him in the witness box I knew I was observing an IRA officer who had become a clever student of his own history, and who revelled in his status as a public hero, a defender of the cause for which he had sacrificed so much of his life. He possessed a disarming personality which belied his British tabloid image of a hardened hitman. He didn't bear any resemblance to the man who had pointed to an M60 gun and said: 'That's my baby.' It was easy to ignore the fact that seven years in a detention centre was an intensive education in the revising of his own history, learning the intricacies of the American legal system and discovering how his audience in the US tacitly subscribed to his view of the Irish conflict. He was also a victim of history like so many young men who joined paramilitary organisations on both sides of the religious divide. He was a product of the inevitable, and seemingly endless, violence in Ireland, from which none of the combatants emerges morally unscathed – and the story of Joseph Doherty's legal battle reinforces that assertion.

# 1

# Joseph Doherty:
# The Early Years

He was born Joseph Patrick Doherty on 20 January 1955 in Belfast in a country divided since the Republic of Ireland gained its independence from Britain following a five-year rebellion which began in 1916. The specially constructed state of Northern Ireland, which remained constitutionally bound to Britain, had its own parliament at Stormont on the outskirts of Belfast. Then, and ever since, Northern Ireland's minority Catholic population did not seek to give its allegiance to this new statelet, and harboured a resentment of its government institutions.

Catholic antipathy was equally matched by the intransigence of the majority Protestant population in Northern Ireland, who perceived it as their state, and shaped it to accord with a Protestant ethos. The resultant effect of this singlemindedness was the fashioning of laws and structures which deprived Catholics of civil and religious liberty, and defined their political aspiration of a united Ireland as a subversive ambition.

Joseph Patrick Doherty was born into a society whose local geography clearly evidenced those divisions. Belfast was traditionally a working-class city, created and formed around the mills built by the linen barons of the nineteenth century. Catholics and Protestants alike had poor housing, though fewer Catholics were employed, and Catholic-maintained schools did not receive the government subsidy necessary to provide the type of education offered in state-controlled schools. Catholics experienced discrimination in every sector of life, particularly in job allocation and in housing. The deterioration in living conditions in Catholic ghettos was accelerated by the low proportion of Catholics in employment, and they had little redress. They were denied 'one-man-one-vote', with electoral boundaries artificially created regardless of population distribution, to ensure the success of Protestant/Unionist politicians at every election. The handful of elected Catholic politicians, members of the Nationalist Party, sought to achieve a United Ireland by peaceful means – but the political grouping which many Catholics tacitly or secretly supported was the Irish Republican Army which was committed to the overthrow of British rule in Northern Ireland.

The IRA's roots went deeply into the history of Irish-British conflict; this organisation had led the rebellion in 1916, and for six succeeding years fought a guerrilla war which resulted in twenty-six counties of Ireland gaining independence. The manner in which the achievements of the 1916 rebels were revered and celebrated in the Irish Republic to some degree added impetus to the IRA's continued campaign to 'free' the remainder of Ireland from British rule. That simplification of a complex history is what faced Joseph Doherty and his generation growing up in a Catholic ghetto. As with many young men of his generation, Catholic or Protestant, his heroes were gunmen – the gunmen of the IRA who fought the British in 1916 in Dublin, or the gunmen of the Catholic ghettos of Belfast who defended Catholic neighbourhoods against Protestant mobs during violent communal strife in the 1920s. Protestant heroes were those men who shot Catholics during a terrible few years in Belfast in the 1920s when hundreds were killed, most of them non-combatants. The death toll on both sides was considerable. Protestants defined the majority of Catholics as subversives, with the result that the killing of Catholics was perceived as justifiable in much the same fashion as Catholics supported the IRA killing of policemen, or members of the state's paramilitary police force, the B Specials.

By the time Doherty was born, the cult of the gunman was a significant element in Irish Catholic culture, and in Belfast it was a more acceptable part of common actuality. Catholics felt threatened in the city, and believed they would never receive protection from the forces of law and order – who were predominantly Protestant/Unionist in character, and constituted to defend the state from the very threat which Catholics were deemed to symbolise.

Bigotry and sectarianism were consciously accepted everyday conditions in an overpowering history. Joseph Doherty was the eldest boy born to a Catholic couple in the New Lodge Road area of

North Belfast. In 1955 that part of the city was predominantly Protestant, and much of it contained lower- and middle-class districts. Joseph Doherty's neighbourhood, the New Lodge, was a small Catholic enclave bordered on one side by the Protestant district of Tiger Bay which was staunchly loyal to extreme Unionist values. One of the main access routes to the New Lodge was the Antrim Road, which was to figure prominently in Doherty's life. In such confines, the New Lodge was a tightly knit community with a strong republican tradition. It had experienced communal strife, and its proximity to several Protestant ghettos only served to increase its population's sense of fear, suspicion and isolation. Sam McAughtry, a well-known writer, lived in Tiger Bay at that time and his thoughts in a broadcast mirror the mood of Protestants who lived adjacent to Doherty's home:

In the 1950s the IRA had a border campaign and there were always indications that there was a dormant republican armed movement there, waiting. When I was running the streets my heroes were gunmen. Some of them were, anyway. There was a guy reputed to have been a wonderful gunman. He was fearless. He could walk into Catholic areas. He even chased a Catholic into his own home along North Queen Street [New Lodge area]. When a crowd gathered and the Catholic's mother began screaming about the closeness of her son to death, the gunman joined the crowd and claimed friendship with the Catholic boy he'd been chasing. He then walked up the hall of the boy's home and shot him dead and then walked out of the house and escaped. We told this story among ourselves with awe. We thought this was a somewhat heroic achievement. We were told that the Catholics buried their dead in the back yards of their homes and covered them with tiles so that we would not know the extent of their casualties.

The glamour of the gunman was no less appealing in the Catholic culture of the 1950s. Paddy Devlin, who later became a leading figure in the Catholic Social Democratic and Labour Party, was sufficiently inspired by the cult of the gunman that he joined the IRA in his youth. He later rejected the IRA and republicanism, but Devlin's thoughts on why he was encouraged to join are a means of understanding the environment in which young Joseph Doherty found himself:

Elderly people would tell us stories about various Catholic gunmen who defended the areas against Protestants or Orangemen. When you're only three or four years of age and you've been regaled with these stories, you tend to get under the bed very quickly. Those things do come through . . .

Joseph Doherty's family history encompassed hero worship. Both grandfathers were prominent in the republican struggle against British rule in Ireland. His maternal grandfather, Alexander Darragh, received a War of Independence medal for serving as an IRA volunteer after the 1916 Rising in Dublin, and the medal was a treasured possession in the Doherty household. His fraternal grandfather, James Doherty, was the greatest influence in his formative years. He had been a senior officer in a Belfast battalion of the Irish Citizen Army, which was formed by James Connolly, one of the leaders of the 1916 Rising, subsequently executed by the British. Doherty says his fraternal grandfather would often tell him stories about the Dublin Rising and IRA exploits in Northern Ireland. Their friendship, and the child's acceptance of his grandfather's views, was clearly evidenced by items bequeathed to him by his grandfather. These included a pension book and IRA medals.

When he was five years old Joseph Doherty was sent to a Catholic primary school near his home where he received what he later described as a 'British-orientated' education:

We were taught English instead of our own national language. You take the history classes we went to. It was mostly on the Tudors and royal heads, kings and queens of England. We weren't told nothing about our own country. When we took geography, we were given the map of England, Scotland and Wales, Europe, the United States, but we were never given a map of our own country. So it was resented by a young person at my age that I couldn't learn where the hell am I living. I knew more about Birmingham and Manchester than I knew about my own city and the beautiful countryside that was around it.

Doherty's description of his education may be accurate in respect of the curriculum, but his telling of it indicates a boy with a bitterness and resentment symbolic not merely of life in a ghetto, but of someone schooled in a hatred for the system which controlled his life. He was not untypical of children whose families were steeped in such a culture: it offered them a focus for the discontent they felt towards a state which was denying them as they perceived it an expression of their identity. This gave young minds the impetus for rebellion and sowed the seeds of conflict within them. The family was not the only source of republican thinking; there were the street corner and, most importantly, the school playground. 'In the back of the school,' Doherty said, 'we would talk about James Connolly and the 1916 rebellion and all the different rebellions in County Clare and County Cork. It was also pretty basic to street conversation. It is where I learned it basically.'

At eleven years of age he was ready to transfer to secondary intermediate education and gradually became more aware of events surrounding him. The year was 1966 and the relative quiet of the 1950s and early 1960s in Belfast was about to be shattered. Catholics were becoming more assertive about their demands for civil rights, and young Catholic intellectuals were watching closely the agitation for civil rights in the United States and the political sloganising which was being fashioned among students in Britain and the European continent.

The Protestant Unionist reaction to Catholic agitation was to define it as 'subversive' and to analyse it in relation to IRA ideology, which was entirely designed to overthrow a state whose ethos was Protestant and formulated in the slogan 'For God and Ulster' (Ulster being the Unionist term for Northern Ireland, though historically Ulster encompassed a larger area which after 1920 became part of the Irish Republic).

The gun returned to politics but its introduction was from an unexpected source – the Ulster Volunteer Force, an extreme Protestant organisation dedicated to defending 'God and Ulster'. The UVF was remobilised in 1965–6 by a group of Unionist politicians who sought to engineer acts of violence which could be wrongly attributed to the IRA, and thereby to create sectarian tension so that civil strife would force the IRA into an aggressive posture. The expectation of these politicians and the UVF was that communal violence would be blamed on the IRA, and the state would be forced to act against the Catholic population. This would in turn result in an end to Catholic agitation for political reforms.

Implicit in the re-creation of the UVF was a fear that political reform would result in an erosion of the Protestant ethos, destroying the Protestant domination of the state of Northern Ireland. At this time the IRA was militarily a spent force and had become a part of the social agitation because it decided to remove the gun from politics.

The UVF saw the gun as crucial to their cause, and in one

supreme act of violence they changed the situation utterly. In the early hours of 25 June 1966, a UVF unit led by Gusty Spence shot several young Catholic men, killing one of them. Spence became a hero. Like many of the terrorists on both sides, Spence was a product of inherited prejudice and social conditioning. As a young man his heroes were gunmen and he was, he admits, a bigot. Spence's actions and the bitter, anti-Catholic sermons of the firebrand preacher, Ian Kyle Paisley, served to heighten tension, particularly in the ghettos of Belfast; nevertheless Catholic agitation for reform continued.

Doherty witnessed all these events, and identified with the Catholic support for a developing civil rights movement. He was politically immature and admits he did not understand the mechanism of discrimination or political terms such as 'gerry-mandering'. He simply felt that the Catholics such as his family and friends were second-class citizens. He says that from the age of seven years he knew there was 'something different about himself' and that he was treated differently by the state: 'I noticed that my environment was poor. The others [Protestants], they had bath-rooms. We never had bathrooms, we had outside toilets. They had all the swimming pools, football, the cinemas, in their neighbour-hoods. All we had was a ghetto situation.'

His transition to secondary intermediate school would have been perceived in a normal society as a means of furthering his life and providing him with an opportunity for career advancement, but his parents regarded it as a negative exercise. They told him to ignore academic subjects because Catholics were not eligible for professional jobs. They said that when he was of a legal age to leave school they would find him an apprenticeship as a plumber or carpenter. This bleak view of the world left its mark:

I used to hear my father and mother sitting and talking. My father would be saying 'never mind' the English and arithmetic. Concentrate on the woodwork and metalwork. He would say to my mother that they would send me to Australia, or to his Aunt Pat in Canada. Sort of get me out of the country. They didn't want me to go through the forty years of their struggle as second-class citizens.

His mother was not so keen to lose her son but Doherty senior and an uncle often repeated claims that when they applied for jobs they were asked to reveal their religion, which was a means by which Protestant employers ensured that Catholics were denied jobs. Many of Joseph Doherty's uncles and aunts emigrated because of the situation in Belfast and lived in places as far apart as Canada, Australia and South Africa. This was a typical feature in the history of many other Catholic families in Northern Ireland.

Joseph was barely fifteen years old when he left school and was apprenticed to an uncle as a plumber, or 'engineer' as it is known in the United States. His departure from school coincided with major events on the streets of Northern Ireland. Civil rights marchers were being batoned by police, and the society was sliding into anarchy. The deterioration in the civil order was not initially perceptible to Catholics because they were enveloped in the euphoria surrounding the civil rights campaign which was steadily gaining momentum, as cracks appeared in the Protestant/Unionist edifice. There was a real prospect of change in the air, and this did not go unobserved by the teenage Joseph Doherty.

I noticed with the older generation that there was great enthusiasm among the people in the city. People were saying that there is going to be great changes. I would hear people in the house, I would hear people in the street saying: 'My God, maybe we will get some reforms now, our children won't have to leave, maybe our John could get a job and isn't it great we can live within the state.'

Within the civil rights movement there were also republicans who possessed a different agenda, believing the state was irreformable and should be overthrown. Joseph Doherty was not knowledgeable about the precise character of politics but was wrapped in the elation of the moment.

I felt the enthusiasm which was in the neighbourhood and also because the civil rights movement was non-violent and it was really non-republican. The songs that were sung were 'We Shall Overcome' instead of IRA songs. I noticed that Dr Martin Luther King was marching in the United States and the great steps he was taking and the reforms that was given to him by the Federal Government and that maybe we could do the same thing as Dr Martin Luther King and maybe strive for civil rights within the country and work within the state.

There is little doubt that such enthusiasm existed within the Catholic community, though I suspect Doherty's memories may be embellished with convenient political rhetoric. Republicans never tacitly accepted the notion of working within the state. They saw the civil rights movement as an ideal platform for uniting working-class and middle-class Catholics in opposition to the state. The more astute republicans were men with longer-term objectives, who recognised clearly that civil rights agitation would move politics to a more extreme position where the very existence of the state would be questioned. There were also those within a student movement, the People's Democracy, who held radical views similar to the IRA's that the state was irreformable. Joseph Doherty's later observations about the civil rights struggle may have been framed to eliminate any suggestion that there was any IRA agenda. It could also be argued that his opinion is reflective of a politically naïve teenager viewing a period of history which was changing rapidly, and that he has selected from history what most appealed to him at that time. His parents were certainly enthusiastic about any prospect of change in their circumstances, because by 1969 they had four daughters and their hopes for the future were central to the welfare of their family.

If they had concerns about any of their children, those concerns must have centred on their son, whose teenage years had not passed without blemish. Doherty now says that, like many of the youth of the mid-to-late sixties, he was involved in juvenile crime; but that is a gross misrepresentation of the typical youth of the 1960s in Belfast, even in the ghetto areas. Quite simply, young Doherty was a gang member in the New Lodge Road, involved in petty crime such as burglary and larceny. His offences began when he was twelve years old and the courts put him for a short time in the care of priests who ran a borstal training centre in West Belfast. There may be little significance in his behaviour as a juvenile other than that he was becoming involved in crime at a time when his own society was moving towards a prolonged period of lawlessness. Some of those who grew up alongside him say that he was a fresh-faced youth, small in stature, mischievous and likeable. He did not display a keen intelligence, but was cunning and streetwise. This collective description of him is interesting in the light of later events in his life and the means by which he acquired a political intelligence and an ability to articulate his memories of his boyhood and adult life.

In 1969, when he was fourteen years old, the situation in Northern Ireland, and particularly in Belfast, changed terribly. Widespread communal violence erupted, with hundreds of Catholics forced from their homes and whole streets of their houses razed to the ground. In August 1969, Protestant mobs, some of them led by members of the B Specials and RUC, invaded Catholic neighbourhoods in Belfast: Doherty's New Lodge Road district did not escape unscathed. In Derry, Catholic rioters fought battles with the police in what became known as the 'Battle of the Bogside' (a large Catholic enclave). As the Catholic population lost all confidence in the forces of law and order, the civil rights movement ceased to be the peaceful-protest organisation which existed in 1968. Some of its members anticipated civil disorder in the spring of 1969 and siphoned off funds to be used for the purchase of weapons. The important signs, which should have been perceptible to those concerned that peaceful protest might lead to violence, were not recognised in an event which took place in January 1969.

In that month student radicals, among them republicans and Trotskyists, organised a People's Democracy march from Belfast to Derry. The march was designed to create sectarian strife. The organisers routed it through extreme Protestant areas, provoking the inevitable violent confrontation. At an area known as Burntollet on the outskirts of Derry, the marchers were viciously assaulted by a mob led by members of the B Specials and supporters of the Rev. Ian Paisley. One aspect of that march went unnoticed, but its significance is unquestionably relevant to the history. En route to Burntollet, the marchers camped overnight at the town of Magherafelt, and on that evening armed IRA men protected them as they slept.

By August 1969 the dreams of those civil rights workers who sought peaceful reform were shattered by the sound of bullets, armoured cars and the incessant ranting of extremists, as the Catholic community came under siege. Their political and religious leaders appealed for help to the governments in Dublin and London. British troops arrived and were positioned between the two communities, creating in effect a dividing line between the ghettos. None the less both communities were already setting in place their own defence structures in the form of barricades and defence organisations. Where was the IRA which Joseph Doherty revered as the defender of the nationalist/republican population?

# 2

# The Origin of
# a Terrorist

The IRA was militarily unprepared for the attacks on Catholic areas. Having taken the gun out of Irish politics they sold their weapons to Welsh nationalist groupings in Britain. In Belfast the small number of Catholics who possessed sporting rifles and shotguns offered them for the defence of their areas. The IRA unearthed an old arms dump and discovered a Thompson sub-machine-gun and several hundred rounds of .45 ammunition. The gun was rusted and required major repairs. A .45 revolver and a .22 rifle were also found, and these were used in action. The Thompson was employed in the Lower Falls area to deter Protestant mobs, armed policemen and the B Specials from re-entering the area. The heavy sound of the old 1920s weapon being discharged on semi- and automatic fire was sufficient to encourage the B Specials to think it was a heavy machine-gun. The police (Royal Ulster Constabulary) retaliated by sending armoured cars into the Falls area. The vehicles possessed .300 heavy Browning machine-guns which were not designed for use in an urban environment. The Brownings were fired indiscriminately and one of the casualties was a baby boy lying in bed in a high-rise apartment.

My journalistic career began with the conflict and I vividly remember watching flames engulfing Catholic homes in the Falls area of West Belfast on 14 August 1969. It reminded me of scenes from a hundred war movies: people fleeing with the belongings they could salvage; children screaming; and handcarts brimming over with the tattered remnants of bedding and clothing. On 15 August British troops patrolled Belfast, but they were few in number and were confused by the geography of a divided city. I stood on a street corner while Bombay Street off the Falls Road was set alight by a Protestant bomb. A boy who was attempting to remove elderly people from some of the houses was shot dead. Before the assault on Bombay Street the British army was warned of the danger of such an event. While the houses were ablaze, a colonel of the Prince of Wales Regiment arrived on the scene and was escorted by priests into the nearby Clonard Monastery. The priests took him to a vantage point where he could see the houses alight and they appealed to him to protect the monastery and the streets surrounding it. No soldiers or police were dispatched to the monastery or Bombay Street. Five hours after the beginning of the firebombing I watched two junior members of the IRA, one armed with a .22 rifle and the other a shotgun, exchanging fire with loyalist gunmen who were intent on providing cover for fire-bombers trying to encroach on the rear grounds of the monastery. Soldiers arrived at the scene hours later but by then Bombay Street was gutted and the shooting was over. On 14 and 15 August the only guns the IRA could muster in Belfast were an ageing Thompson, a .303 Lee Enfield bolt-action rifle, four .45 pistols and the two guns used in the defence of Bombay Street. The IRA's unpreparedness cost it dearly in terms of Catholic support.

When all the troops finally arrived, Belfast resembled a city recovering from a World War II blitz. Shops, stores, houses were burning; looting was rampant, and makeshift barricades littered the city, which saw the largest displacement of population since World War II. Thousands of families were homeless, the vast majority Catholics. An exodus of Catholic women and children led to Red Cross camps being set up in the Irish Republic. Fear and naked prejudice pervaded Belfast; from some neighbourhoods, Protestants also fled as Catholic mobs retaliated: in the north of the city a whole street of Protestant families fled, but before leaving they torched their homes to prevent them being occupied by Catholics.

Within the Catholic ghettos there was disillusionment with the IRA. Wall slogans parodied them as 'I Ran Away'. Many people with republican sympathies began to analyse the IRA's reasons for its inaction. It was apparent that instead of defending Catholics the organisation had been too busy moving towards a Marxist philosophy designed to exploit the civil rights protests in the interests of working-class solidarity. The failure of the IRA to change the politics of Ireland by force after the partition of the country in 1920 had led to a re-evaluation of strategy within Catholic radicalism in the 1960s. Now, the IRA was shaping a Marxist ideology of Irish politics, when events on the streets of Belfast and Derry returned society to the sectarian conflict which had always hallmarked Northern Ireland politics. Those republicans who recognised the antipathy towards the IRA in August 1969 joined defence committees – with a view to resurrecting the fortunes of republicanism: the Catholic community was suddenly being protected by the 'old enemy', the British.

Several members of the IRA who observed this development quickly assumed important roles within the defence organisations, seeing them as a means of establishing a new IRA which did not necessarily possess a Marxist philosophy. These men also believed that if the IRA were to survive it should return to its basic policy of physical-force politics. The Catholic Church seemed prepared to offer tacit support to this new breed of republican formed from the romantic nationalist tradition. Both the church and the Southern Irish Government were frightened by the leftward shift in IRA politics in the sixties, and were keen to see this new grouping emerge within the defence organisations.

It is often only a short step from defensive to offensive. The traditionalists used the defence organisations and their committees to acquire weapons from the Dublin Government. By January 1970 they were in a strong position to set up a new IRA which became known as the Provisional IRA. It was led by men who valued the history of armed struggle against the British. They revered the tradition of those who risked their lives for freedom in the Easter 1916 Rising, those leaders summarily executed by the British. The Provisionals assumed the same mantle of romantic nationalism, and its blood-sacrifice tradition. The Marxist IRA were left behind to become transformed into a non-militarised political constitutionalist party known as the Workers' Party. The Provisionals were quickly accepted by Catholics, and thousands of young men joined their ranks. Motivated in most instances by the defence of their community, others were attracted by the power expressed by the 'Provos' who soon controlled all Catholic working-class neighbourhoods. The British army remained in a passive peace-keeping role, and did not yet attempt to remove the barricades or question the authority of the Provisional IRA.

Joseph Doherty's young mind was not immune to the myriad experiences and influences generated by the turmoil. He lived on the fringe of the New Lodge area and his proximity to a staunchly loyalist district heightened his fears.

Along with the Protestant crowds were members of the police and B Specials. I seen this myself. As soon as they started burning on the west of Belfast, they started coming into our district. The house I was living in with my parents was on the fringe of the Catholic ghetto and the Protestant ghetto. Of course the people in the district organised them-selves into the defence committees. They set up barricades to keep the police, the B Specials and the Orange [Protestant] mobs out of the ghetto. I seen that the civilians on the Protestant side had guns and machine-guns and they were standing with the general police. The ghetto came under attack, and of course the barricades went up and defence committees were formed in each street and there was also a central committee which co-ordinated all these committees. There were first-aid centres and food supplies were brought in.

The violence of those days in August 1969, which resulted in huge population displacement, deaths and widespread injury, traumatised large areas of Belfast, and generated a siege mentality. A governing body of the defence groupings, the Central Citizens Defence Committee, assumed total control but not the type of control suited to a democracy. Behind the barricades, the gun became the effective power, and the absence of the norms of a policed society disappeared. Crime and racketeering flourished. Illegal drinking clubs were established in both Catholic and Protestant areas to replace those licensed premises destroyed in the rioting. The clubs came under the authority of the para-militaries, and in Catholic areas provided a source of income to purchase weapons for the newly formed IRA. In a significant sense, violence was becoming institutionalised. The Provisionals paraded, and openly recruited members, as did loyalist organis-ations. On the Protestant side the UVF (Ulster Volunteer Force) found itself competing for recruits with a new paramilitary organisation, the Ulster Defence Association, the UDA. Men in combat gear, their faces obscured by balaclavas, became the vigilantes of the defence committees on both sides, controlling access to all areas. The IRA decided to impose its will on the vigilantes and recruited them into auxiliary IRA units. The members of these units were not fully fledged members of the IRA but that tactic provided a fertile recruiting ground. Most auxiliaries were given weapons training and were content to play a vigilante role rather than become fully committed to IRA policy and discipline.

It was soon noticeable that Catholic attitudes to the presence of British troops were experiencing a gradual transformation. Retrospectively it is easy to recognise that the 'old enemy' and the IRA could not survive amicably in such close proximity, but that was not the empirical situation when the troops first arrived in Belfast in August 1969. At first they were welcomed by all Catholics irrespective of nationalist or republican aspirations, and the historical enmity between the Irish and the British was not evident. In a warm and friendly welcome British soldiers were invited into homes, and were constantly served food and drinks as they stood on duty in the streets and roads of Catholic neighbourhoods.

Joseph Doherty remembers the euphoria surrounding their arrival in his part of the city:

People were afraid, and by seeing the British army with their armour, their khaki jackets, etc., it was far different from the black uniforms of the police. If it had been US Marines or French troops it would also have been all right as long as they were troops. They came in between the two sections of the community and people thought, 'My God, they are calling in peace troops and maybe we will get a break.' They were welcomed with open arms by the people of Belfast. There were sandbags placed at the corner of our house and the British troops would be lying there with machine-guns. My mother would bring them down blankets, cups of tea and cakes. They were very, very friendly and we would take troops into the house and let them use the bathroom. It was a very, very friendly atmosphere between the nationalist population and the British army.

Looking back on that period one is tempted to think that within the Catholic enclaves there must have been a collective amnesia in respect of Irish history. The mythology of Irish history, and the real or imagined hatred of the British, were temporarily suspended. It was not expediency which created what Doherty describes as the 'very, very friendly' relations between troops and civilians, but a genuine appreciation that they, and not the IRA, arrived as the saviours and defenders of a beleaguered Catholic community. The transition from friendliness to outright hatred was gradual and was not lost to the mind of fifteen-year-old Doherty:

The older people inside the ghetto were telling the younger people to be careful of the British army. They would say the army was coming in as a

'Trojan Horse'. They were not coming to protect Catholics but to protect the state and the police. The younger people up from me, who were in their twenties and thirties, were saying, 'This isn't the 1920s, this is 1970. The British army couldn't get away with anything like that.'

Doherty does not define 'the older people' who were engineering suspicion about the role of the troops, but history has determined that they were the republicans with the traditional view of history, the emerging Provisionals. They feared that fraternisation with the troops would lead Catholics to accept the British presence and create a realignment of constitutional nationalism with the political status quo, thus reinforcing British sovereignty and partition. On a subliminal level there was a genuine suspicion of British soldiers and their role but this did not seriously undermine the 'very, very friendly' relations.

However, the attribution of blame for a dramatic change in relations must be fairly divided between the Provisionals and the army authorities. The army began to perceive the Catholics as posing a greater threat to the security of the state, and consequently ignored the blatant paramilitarism in the Protestant areas. Commanders seemed easily intimidated by large displays of Protestant paramilitary strength. Consequently, they supported a blunted British perception of Northern Ireland politics as allied to a Protestant Unionist government; this system defined threat only in respect of Catholics, and soon served to place the troops in a confrontational role with Catholics. An army presence was more apparent in Catholic districts, with the predominantly Protestant RUC accorded responsibility for Protestant communities. Thus the passive, British peace-keeping role was steadily eroded. The police demonstrated that they were partial to loyalist sentiments, and Catholics again began to feel that security measures were directed towards them: British soldiers pointed their guns in one direction and that was enough to convince even Catholics with no republican leanings that the role of the army was being revised.

Joseph Doherty remembers an incident which highlighted this for him:

On one particular night when our district was attacked, the British army was there. This was when I first noticed that the British army was between the crowds. They were in full combat gear with tin hats and had their rifles pointed to the crowd with bayonets fixed. They weren't pointed towards the Protestants. They were pointed towards us and yet it was us who were coming under attack!

Doherty says that arguments developed between members of a Catholic mob, who wanted to know why they were singled out for special attention in a fashion which was decidedly onesided. The Catholics were also incensed at the presence of policemen who were standing watching the Protestants. It appears, says Doherty, that evasive action was only taken against his people, and this led him and others to identify with a republican analysis.

People started to understand that the troops weren't really there to protect the Catholics, and that they had come in to prevent the state from collapsing. As the old people in the district had predicted, the British army did actually come in to protect the state. They were taking orders from the state, and they were coming in and doing arms raids in our ghettos.

Doherty rightly points out that the army began to search for illegal weapons in Catholic areas. This angered him as it did nationalist politicians. Similar searches did not occur on the same scale in Protestant areas. One explanation is that there were almost 100,000 legally held weapons in Protestant hands in Northern Ireland and Protestant paramilitaries did not require illegal arms caches. The Protestants also felt safe in the knowledge that the police, who were also armed, belonged to their community.

On the other hand, Catholics did not have such a source of weapons to permit them to feel safe and initially they acquired guns with the aid of the Dublin Government. Reputable nationalist politicians such as Paddy Devlin appealed for money for weapons to protect Catholics. Devlin was a leading figure in the Central Citizens Defence Committee and was convinced that the police would not protect Catholics. He later resigned his position when the new breed of IRA men, the Provisionals, began taking control of the defence structures. The Provisionals, with their age-old objectives, were not content with procuring weapons merely for defence; they had a hidden agenda which they knew would lead to a renewed conflict with the British, and they were building a new IRA with that ambition uppermost in their minds.

An example of a major arms search occurred in July 1970 in the

Lower Falls area when a joint police/army operation acted on information that a weapons consignment was stored in a house in Balkan Street. Security forces uncovered a Schmeisser sub-machine-gun, fifteen pistols, a rifle, explosives and ammunition. The haul was the property of the older IRA known as the 'Officials'. The Provisionals quickly moved their weaponry out of the area but encouraged large-scale rioting as a diversionary tactic to allow their men to escape unhindered. Grenades were thrown, injuring five soldiers, and the situation worsened with every minute.

When word of the violence reached my news editor he found himself unable to encourage any of his staff to enter the riot area. I was about to go home but decided it was a good story, and volunteered for duty. In the Lower Falls I was confronted by makeshift barricades manned by young men like Joe Doherty. There was no gunfire, and unknown to me that was a temporary lull in the proceedings. Soon, the violence resumed, with stone-throwing from Catholic mobs, and canisters of CS gas fired by soldiers. The whole area of several hundred streets turned into a battleground, with children assembling piles of stones and milk bottles. One thousand canisters of gas were fired into the maze of streets, some of them launched from large army catapults. Old people and children choked in the clouds of gas. Someone handed me a handkerchief which I used to cover my nose but my throat continued to burn. Clouds of gas hung over some of the streets while some rioters appeared immune to it. They were the young men who were constantly in confrontation with soldiers, and they seemed to have developed some kind of physiological resistance to the gas.

I ran to the nearby Royal Victoria Hospital, explained that I was a reporter, and asked for a face mask of the type used by surgeons. With a mask on my face I returned to the riot scene and walked down Raglan Street, where I saw a group of men removing an assortment of rifles, sub-machine-guns and pistols from the boot of a car. I knew it was time for me to leave the area. At 10.00 pm army helicopters broadcast a warning to people to return to their homes or be arrested. The army denied they were imposing a curfew but that is exactly what they did. The inevitable gun-battle took place, costing the lives of five civilians with injuries to a further sixty civilians and fifteen soldiers. When the Official IRA finally retreated, a massive search was undertaken, with looting by soldiers, and wanton damage to homes. The army recovered 107 weapons, 21,000 rounds of ammunition and 300lb of explosives. Catholics were angry about the curfew and the army's behaviour. As they saw it, the weapons belonged to the Official IRA who, until that day, had not been waging war against the soldiers.

This successful recovery of arms by the British military was offset by the overall reaction of the Catholic population, who criticised the massive concentration of troops and complained that such a deployment only occurred in Catholic districts. The Provisionals were pleased because they lost no weapons; the arms supplies of their rivals, the Officials, were seriously depleted; and, in line with Provisional hopes, Catholics were clearly developing a gradual antagonism towards the British.

The views of Doherty about that period are not dissimilar to those of men such as Paddy Devlin, who is no longer a politician; nowadays a broadcaster and writer, he is totally opposed to IRA violence. He wrote a pamphlet in the early 1970s entitled *Tuzo, Whitelaw, and the Terror in Northern Ireland: British Policy in Northern Ireland, Terrorisation of the Catholic Community, Appeasement of Orange Militants*. Tuzo was the General Commanding British Troops in Northern Ireland and Whitelaw was the Secretary of State for Northern Ireland appointed by the British Prime Minister of the day.) Devlin's pamphlet stated:

The British Military, brought into the North in August '69 to provide protection for Catholics whose homes were attacked and burned in the Falls and Ardoyne areas, have a primary responsibility for protecting defenceless Catholic homes in East Belfast and elsewhere. . . .

This they have singularly failed to do. They have refused to come to the assistance of innocent families under attack. Instead they have called in the UDA to protect those who are under attack from this same set of bigots. This horse trading between the military and the UDA has led to chapels, schools and Catholic-owned businesses in East Belfast being destroyed. The military continue their repression of the Catholic ghettos. In spite of merely nominal activity there, in comparison to elsewhere, the military are engaged in intensive screening, beatings and intimidation of residents.

Joseph Doherty says that five months after the arrival of troops, 'old people started to tell us to organise against the British army. People were beginning to see the soldiers as occupying troops.' Certainly, within one year of the arrival of the army, soldiers were using tactics in Catholic areas which clearly indicated their role to be more substantial than that required of a peace-keeping force. They patrolled streets, and regularly stopped young men and questioned them about their neighbourhood. A familiar tactic was for a soldier to ask a civilian to position himself in a search position with both hands against a wall and feet spread. Then questions were asked of the civilian: his name, address, where he worked, where he was going, from where he was travelling and his political affiliations. This procedure was the beginning of a screening process to provide intelligence on the majority of the Catholic population. Joseph Doherty was subject to what was termed the stop-search tactic:

I would be stopped, told to get against the wall. I would spreadeagle against the wall. The soldier would search me, ask for my name, where I come from, where I was going, what was my father's name, etc. My father and myself would be stopped together in this way. The women would be stopped in the street, told to open their coats, shake their coats, put their hands in the air. The kids would be stopped and prams searched. Newborn babies would be searched. It seemed a very large occupational force. You couldn't walk down a street without British soldiers running about, their faces blackened, saying 'Get up against the wall.' The whole thing started to get worse and worse and worse.

The search procedures were condemned by Catholic politicians and clergy. The military methods had the effect of public humiliation, and eighteen-year-old soldiers, ignorant of the complexities of the politics of Northern Ireland, often behaved aggressively towards civilians. They were unable to distinguish between republicans, IRA volunteers and constitutional nationalists. They displayed a blanket acceptance that all Catholics in ghettos were potentially subversive.

Before the end of 1970, Joseph Doherty decided to commit himself to the IRA: 'The army had dawn raids. They would come in and search a block of houses at a time. This was when the shooting level, or the guerrilla war, was very, very low. This was uncalled for. At that particular time, from being a nationalist I became a republican.' Doherty's claim that there was, as yet, no serious guerrilla conflict is correct. While the Provisionals were steadily building their organisation, they studiously avoided major confrontations with British troops. However, they continued to fuel resentment of soldiers, and warned Catholics that they risked punishment if they 'fraternised with the enemy'.

Considerable enmity still prevailed between both wings of the IRA; but the Provisionals emerged the stronger grouping both in manpower and in weaponry. Doherty turned to the Provisionals, who shared his adherence to traditional republican values. They were the 'old people', who were fomenting hatred of the old enemy and promising the reunification of Ireland. The Official IRA were those who had failed to defend Catholics, and were forever 'talking about communism' and 'working-class solidarity', terms which the young Doherty did not understand, and which were anathema to orthodox republicans in Ireland. Doherty was subject not only to the influences of the ghetto but to the pronouncements of Catholic political and religious leaders. In making up his mind about joining the IRA, he was impressed by the solidarity at every level of his community in its criticism of troops, police and the institutions of the state. It was a heady time, when public comment on all sides was inflammatory, if not downright dangerous, and when violence was becoming an accepted way of life. Revenge was central to communal thought, and new ideals were paraded openly on the streets in the guise of combat jackets, balaclavas and guns. The 'cult of the gunman' had returned, and with it the glamour which was attractive to young, impressionable minds and, in particular, Joseph Doherty.

The IRA's status in the Catholic population throughout Northern Ireland's history was that of an organisation inextricably linked to Catholic teaching of history. Partition of the island was taught to be a British wrong and the Protestants who enforced it in Northern Ireland were usurpers. Young men and girls were encouraged to revere nationalism and to learn the poetry of Padraig Pearse, one of the leaders of the 1916 Rising. His language and literary style was rooted in a blood-sacrifice tradition. The arrival of the Provisionals, claiming the image and likeness of Pearse, was a restatement in Pearse's words that 'Ireland unfree would never be at peace'. In the early 1960s a controversial film arrived in a Belfast cinema. It was *Mise Eire*; its theme, the 1916 Rising. Catholic schools organised trips to the cinema for large numbers of pupils from primary level upwards.

The Roman Catholic Church controlled its own schools, where religion and politics were often inseparable. Protestants were portrayed as a godless people, the oppressors, British lackeys who deprived Catholics of basic civil rights. When the 'Provos' took to the political stage, the moral right of such a force merely to be there was already long enshrined in the history of Catholic teaching in Northern Ireland. The concept of armed struggle in defence of Catholics, and to achieve the right to political self-determination, was taught as a morally sustainable doctrine. Teenagers like Joseph Doherty recognised in IRA ideals historical canons which were central to what they learned at home and in school. IRA recruitment was encouraged and offered the opportunity for teenagers and young men to mimic their heroes. In a socially disadvantaged community, young IRA men were afforded self-respect and revered by the older generation who perpetuated the historical myths.

The older generation of republicans who saw the failure of IRA campaigns from the mid-1920s were jubilant with the sudden increase in nationalist fervour. They were not in a position to condemn the Provisionals, who were after all enlivening the tradition which they honoured. The church, compromised by its past, encouraged the growth of the new IRA. Some priests even provided the Provisionals with assistance and transportation. For example, a priest led an IRA bombing team into the tiny village of Claudy in 1972 and planted a 'no- warning bomb' which killed five people, one of them a young girl, Katherine Aiken. The town was predominantly Protestant as were all the victims. The late Cardinal Conway was informed of the identity of the priest by the British, who decided it was preferable not to arrest him for fear all priests would become targets for loyalist hit-squads. The culprit was moved north-west to a remote Catholic establishment over the border in the Republic of Ireland. He later died of a terminal illness in another Catholic institution in Donegal. No one has ever printed this story until now – but it supports the thesis that the unspoken imprimatur of the church at the outset of the conflict in 1969–70 provided a basis for young men to accept a destiny which was morally underpinned by their clergy. Joseph Doherty had been reared in just such a Catholic republican ethos and was the ideal recruit for the IRA.

# 3

# The Junior IRA

In the autumn of 1970, Doherty sought membership of an organisation which would control his life from that moment onwards. He joined what he would later describe as a 'boy-scout' movement, but it was really Na Fianna Eireann, the junior wing of the Provisional Irish Republican Army. The term 'boy scout' derived from the early history of Na Fianna Eireann, which was founded in 1909 by Countess Markievicz (Constance Gore-Booth) with an avowedly republican ethos. Its origins were rooted in a belief that there should be an organisation to counter the 'pernicious influences' of the British Boy Scout movement established by Baden-Powell. Thereafter Na Fianna, or 'the Fianna' as it became commonly known, served as a stepping-stone, a fertile recruiting ground for the IRA. In October 1931 it was outlawed by the Government of the Irish Republic, and by the 1950s and late 1960s there was no trace of any ethos similar to that of Baden-Powell's Boy Scouts.

Na Fianna Eireann provided a secret lifestyle for boys and teenagers. Recruits were taken to IRA training camps in remote parts of the west coast of Ireland and County Donegal in the north of the island. They were taught rudimentary survival skills, the republican analysis of Irish history and the rules of the republican movement. In effect, they were put through an indoctrination process by men with a history of republican politics and armed resistance. They were prepared for the moment when they would be faced with a choice of joining the real IRA. Before the violence of 1969, potential recruits to Na Fianna were screened to ensure they did not have criminal records. It was a security measure to guarantee that prospective candidates were not motivated by a desire to use the threat of the organisation against others, or to exploit it as a cover for criminal activities, or to join simply for the glamour of belonging to a secret organisation. An additional concern on the part of the IRA was that recruits should be 'pure', good-living in a strict Catholic context, and that they should not be vulnerable to inducements from the police or Special Branch, the secret arm of policing which targeted subversives.

In 1969–70 the IRA was too busy with conflict, and with recruiting as many people as possible, to concern itself with the principles or refinements of recruitment. The anger of nationalists or republicans at the failure of the police or army to protect them provided a motive for joining the new Provisionals. Young men and boys in their thousands offered themselves to the IRA, and the massive influx of members negated any attempts at vetting recruits. Inevitably, many criminally minded people joined the organisation to cloak their pursuits; others exploited it to present themselves as heroes to their own community. There were also men and boys who joined the IRA and Na Fianna Eireann to acquire a standing they could never have been afforded in a normal society. The same was true in the Protestant loyalist community: those who were 'outcasts' before the conflict now found a convenient means by which they could assert themselves – by expressing authority through their appearance on the streets in combat fatigues. This led to illegal organisations having those in their ranks who would, in normal times, have been society's rejects. The general abnormality of the situation obscured the particular abnormalities of many individuals who joined paramilitary groupings, and men with psychopathic disorders or aggressive tendencies were suddenly given acceptable personae – and/or the means by which they could vent their anger on others. Criminally minded members were able to operate with impunity in a society where there was a total collapse in the social order. The paramilitaries controlled the lives of everyone who lived behind the barricades which sealed the ghettos from the rest of society – but they were concerned with power rather than social order.

Doherty's borstal record was no obstacle to his membership of the Fianna, and his route to membership was a typical one:

Well, of course Na Fianna Eireann is a semi-secret organisation and, of course, it's illegal. I knew somebody who knew somebody, and what you do is put the word out. I got in contact with a member of Na Fianna

Eireann. I told him I wanted to join. He asked me why I wanted to join. I told him I wanted to learn more about the republican movement, and I wanted to contribute something to the ongoing struggle.

The processing of Doherty's membership was swift and un-complicated. There was no form-filling exercise, merely a conver-sation with a member of the organisation which took place in the back room of a house in the New Lodge district. The recruiter explained the aims and objectives of the Fianna and of the 'republican movement'. The latter is a term which will occur frequently in this book and it is worth defining its use. 'Republican movement' is a euphemism to cloak the illegality of all those proscribed IRA organisations which come under that umbrella term, such as Na Fianna Eireann, the Irish Republican Army and Cumann na mBann (the women's grouping). It is not unlawful to be a republican or to express the republican aspiration that Ireland should be unified. Therefore members of those organisations which are illegal use the term 'republican movement' to mask their true affiliations. When Doherty was informed of the nature and objectives of the IRA, which is the governing body of all those illegal bodies within the republican 'family', he found himself in total agreement with its principles and was granted membership.

It is doubtful that his agreement encompassed much knowledge of the IRA beyond a romanticised and mythologised perception of its history. He was probably drawn towards it by a symbiosis of inherited prejudice or learning, and an emotional reaction to the extraordinary events which were impinging on his life. At that stage he was a teenager with a limited education, and had not displayed either academic ability or promising intelligence. One or two of his schoolfriends say he was 'very average' but 'clever', meaning 'cunning'. At the time he made his commitment to the Fianna he was a school-leaver and was apprenticed as a plumber in the care of an uncle, who was to train him in the trade.

Doherty's IRA recruiter promised that if he proved worthy of his role in Na Fianna Eireann he would be eligible to join the IRA when he reached his seventeenth birthday. Doherty admits this offer was made, confirming the true nature of the 'boy-scout' move-ment: 'He told me that some day, when I got to the age of seventeen, if I wanted I could join the Irish Republican Army – as the British call us, the Junior IRA. We were what you call a stepping-stone to the Irish Republican Army, like army cadets in the United States, scout cadets, whatever you call them.' Doherty's use of the parallels with regular armies such as the United States armed forces is a clever attempt to disguise the precise nature of terrorism. The US armed forces or British armed forces do not use boys or juveniles in the role for which Doherty was being trained.

His understanding of the aims of the Fianna was that 'it went along with the aims and objectives of the republican movement in general, in other words the reunification of a thirty-two county republic and the evacuation of the British of course.' What Doherty chooses to exclude from this thesis is that the IRA was dedicated to the overthrow of a sovereign British state, by force if necessary, by 'armed struggle'. Its undeclared motive was that, in seeking the reunification of Ireland, it might also be obliged to seek the overthrow of a democratic state in Ireland, namely the Republic of Ireland. That objective has always remained a secret, because the IRA is aware that such an aspiration, if publicly voiced, could easily compromise its privileged position within the Irish Republic. At the outset of the conflict in 1969–70, the Fianna Fail Government in Dublin was happy enough to conspire with the emerging Provisionals in the procurement of weapons for use in Northern Ireland. Members of that Government, such as Charles J. Haughey, who became a temporary President of Europe in 1990, were avowed republicans who supported the aspiration to Irish unity.

A valid historical thesis is that the Southern Government was concerned about the pro-communist and radical left-wing shift in IRA politics in the late 1960s, and perceived the IRA as a threat to the Irish state. However, the Provisionals represented a traditional republican orthodoxy; they would keep the violence north of the Irish border and recognise the value of their friendship with the Dublin Government. Within IRA General Orders was a stipulation which the Provisionals enforced, and have done so to this day. This 'order' forbids military operations against the Republic of Ireland, and was first introduced into IRA General Orders in 1956, when an IRA breakaway group threatened to extend IRA military operations to the Irish Republic, in the belief that the Republic required 'reforming' as much as Northern Ireland. This threat was enough for the Dublin Government at that time to consider suppressing the IRA in its territory. The IRA leadership acted quickly and formulated the following addition to General Army Orders, No. 8:

1   Volunteers are strictly forbidden to take any military action against 26
    County forces under any circumstances whatsoever. The importance
    of this order in present circumstances, especially in the border areas,
    cannot be over-emphasised.
2   Minimum arms shall be used in training in the 26 County area. In the
    event of a raid, every effort shall be made to get the arms away safely.
    If this fails, the arms shall be rendered useless and abandoned.
3   Maximum security precautions must be taken when training. Scouts
    must always be posted to warn of emergency. Volunteers arrested
    during the training or in possession of arms will point out that the
    arms were for use against the British forces of occupation only. This
    statement should be repeated at all subsequent court proceedings.
4   At all times Volunteers must make it clear that the policy of the Army
    is to drive the British forces of occupation out of Ireland.

The introduction of General Order No. 8 was cleverly designed
to allay the fears of the Dublin Government, and to pre-empt any
action by them which might prevent the IRA from training and
organising in the Republic or using it as a base for operations
against Northern Ireland. It had the desired effect, until the Irish
Government decided in December 1956 that the IRA was a threat to
the state and the British–Irish relations. Throughout the late 1950s
the IRA waged a campaign of bombing and shooting against police
stations along the border, using the Irish Republic as a haven from
which IRA units struck at Northern Ireland. In the Republic the
IRA were beyond the jurisdiction of the British, and especially the
RUC and B Specials; but the Northern Ireland Government
introduced internment without trial and rounded up leading
republicans, with the result that the IRA campaign of violence
ended in failure, although it continued sporadically until 1960.

The Provisionals recognised the significance and value of this
General Order, though they secretly knew that if they ever
achieved the overthrow of the British in Northern Ireland they
would then be required to overthrow the Government of the Irish
Republic to achieve the aim of a 'New Ireland'.

Joseph Doherty, therefore, joined an organisation which
possessed both a long history and long-term objectives, some of
them hidden from public scrutiny. He was also fulfilling a dream of
following in the footsteps of his grandfathers, whom he much
admired. As a teenager with few prospects in life and insignificant
in his own peer grouping and community, he was about to 'take to
the stage' with romantic Irish nationalism. A historical importance

was guaranteed for him to an extent he could not then have envisaged. The 'boy scout' was trained in camps in remote hillsides in the Irish Republic, and in back rooms in his own city. He acted as a scout for IRA volunteers who were training or operating. He carried verbal messages between IRA units and transported weapons. There was little of Baden-Powell's Boy Scout ethos in his training, as he willingly admits:

Na Fianna Eireann was a cultural group. It was to teach young people like myself, who had no knowledge of history, my language, my culture, Irish sport. It was to come together for Irish classes etc., but of course, during the war period, we took on a different role as well. We were taught guerrilla warfare. We were given arms lectures. We were given the basic tactics of the Irish Republican Army, the organisation of the Irish Republican Army, certain staff decisions, Northern Command GHQ. We were basically getting ready to go into the army.

Doherty was fully instructed in all IRA orders, the nature of its constitution, the rights of volunteers, the penalties for disobeying orders and the rules used at courts martial. These were contained in what is known as the 'Green Book', a secret manual which all volunteers are required to know in detail.

The 'Green Book' has changed only minutely since 1970, and its initial formulation by the Provisionals was shaped according to the rules that had always existed within the traditional IRA. The only perceptible changes related to 'Volunteers' Rights'. The 'Green Book' tends to remain unchanged unless a General Army Convention decides otherwise. Conventions are held every two years and changes are rarely made. My copy was given to me by a member of the IRA Army Council in 1990, and, dated 1988–9, is the most recent available version.

Members of Na Fianna guilty of transgressions are rarely subject to the harsh penalties outlined in the 'Green Book' but the fact that they are instructed in its contents is a sufficient deterrent to keep them under control. The 'Green Book' is strictly for volunteers of the IRA, but the fact that the IRA controls all groupings within its ranks, including Na Fianna Eireann, permits the conclusion that all are bound by it.

Doherty's initial responsibilities within the Fianna were confined to his neighbourhood, and were sufficient to provide him with a training in guerrilla warfare: 'We did the intelligence work.

We would sit on the street corner with a football or hurley stick.' (A hurley stick is similar to an ice-hockey stick and is used in fifteen-a-side games, with a small leather ball. In working-class neighbourhoods boys and girls practised their skill with the stick and ball by pounding the ball against gable walls, or by using the street as their playing area.) 'While playing with the hurley we would keep an eye out for troops and give signals.'

What Doherty described was the inoffensive play of kids to cloak terrorist activities. Soldiers on patrol rarely suspected that laughter and play were designed to deceive them. The IRA tactic was for a member of the Fianna to organise street games and, when soldiers arrived on the scene, to distract them and lull them into a feeling that everything was normal. Fianna volunteers used prearranged signals with others in the Fianna unit to indicate the presence of soldiers, their numbers, their weaponry, and whether their actions suggested a fixed military intent, such as a search operation, or a routine patrolling duty. Those signals quickly found their way to the IRA commander and his units, and the information was put to use in several ways. If the patrol was detailed to find a known republican, advance warning of the soldiers' whereabouts ensured that the wanted man was rushed to hiding, or ferried to safety outside the district. If IRA arms training was taking place, or an operational brief, any advance notice of the military presence was obviously invaluable, enabling arms to be swiftly returned to underground dumps or hiding places in the roof-spaces of houses, or to be temporarily removed from the area by car.

The playful atmosphere of the street often contained a more sinister dimension. Prearranged signals from children informed an IRA active service unit that soldiers for whom they had been waiting had arrived within what the IRA designated an 'ambush zone'. The young Doherty's activities also included the 'reporting of the guerrilla war' by conveying IRA messages from place to place about the success or failure of IRA actions in the streets of the New Lodge area:

Our main responsibility was to be scouts, the intelligence scouts of the IRA. If an IRA man was on the run from the British army or police and wanted to get from A to B we scouted the run in advance of him, and while he was travelling. We would watch out for the British and if we spotted a patrol we would drop a handkerchief to indicate that a patrol was in the vicinity.

Doherty claims that he was also engaged in 'social work', a term intended to suggest that the Fianna possessed a social conscience. He did not assist elderly ladies to negotiate barricades or cross the road, but patrolled the neighbourhood in search of teenagers or young men suspected of drug-taking: therein, he was, for instance, assisted by others in the Fianna to stop and search young people in discos. His power as a member of the organisation was immediately apparent to others of his age group or to teenagers much older than him. He says his role included policing the New Lodge in search of young people who were using alcohol. Suddenly from being a juvenile criminal he was a guardian of the IRA's moral code. The penalties for drug-taking were severe and included 'punishment shooting'. A drug-taker who was a habitual offender or pusher was shot through both kneecaps. Severe beatings were meted out to drug-users as a regular punishment, the victim being taken to a derelict house or alleyway and beaten with hurley sticks. Considerable room existed for abuse of such IRA measures, because they were judge and jury, and their punishment was more excessive than any delivered by the Northern Ireland judiciary. Whatever the merits of combating the use and sale of drugs, checking abuse of alcohol or quelling gang warfare, there was nothing admirable about the range and type of punishment meted out by the Fianna and the IRA.

The lawlessness of the period not unnaturally increased the potential for drug and alcohol abuse among the young, and afforded drug-pushers greater scope for their operations. In the absence of normal policing, and the fact that the security forces were solely concerned with terrorism, the IRA assumed the role of protector and judicial authority in the society it controlled. In such dangerous times, Doherty became a vigilante, almost of the type glamorously portrayed in celluloid: 'You have certain drugs coming into the city, though not as much as New York but you had certain drugs. We had to stop the drugs and make sure that kids didn't drink. We would patrol the dances to make sure that the kids would not get out of hand.'

Control of rioting became an additional responsibility for Fianna members. Doherty says that the Fianna helped to organise riots against British troops, and sometimes encouraged people to take to the streets, either to throw stones and petrol bombs at soldiers, or alternatively put an end to a disturbance: riots were a device used by the IRA to hamper army search operations. As a former member of the Fianna who was active in 1970–1 explained to me:

We would start riots to keep 'the pot boiling'. The troops always reacted badly, and ordinary people were brutalised. This had the effect of maintaining a hatred of the British within the population. Sometimes we would start a riot because the troops came in and damaged homes and batoned ordinary people. There was always a desire for revenge within the population. The soldiers were undisciplined, particularly the Scots regiments. They were traditionally Protestant and loyalist. Many of them came from Protestant families with ties in Northern Ireland. They hated us Catholics. They identified with the Protestant/Unionist cause in Northern Ireland. They were essentially anti-Catholic and anti-Irish. The Orange connection between Scotland and Northern Ireland was clear in the way they shouted offensive slogans at people. The only regiment that exceeded them in brutality was the Parachute Regiment. They were not trained, nor were most British troops, for civil conflict within the UK. The Paras were not only hard and brutal, but they would go on the rampage in an area and wreck people's homes, destroying what few possessions they had. We encouraged people to riot to vent their frustration. Of course we would start a riot if someone was being arrested. We would get the women out. The soldiers found it difficult to deal with screaming women and would sometimes release their man. If troops were coming into the area to search for weapons and explosives, we would engage them with an impromptu riot so that the IRA could get the guns and gelignite out of the district.

We would also be told to get into the crowd and stop a riot in progress or stop one taking place. This was designed for occasions when the IRA was planning an operation in the area and didn't want too much military heat in advance of it happening, or because there were too many guns and men on the run in the district. You see, if our area was holding weapons for other units or providing safe-houses for men wanted elsewhere in the city, the last thing the IRA wanted was a full-scale riot that would provoke or allow the Brits an excuse for sealing off the area, and conducting a full-scale search operation. Everything was tactically planned. Rioting was as much part of the armed struggle as anything else. It brought out excesses by the army which was good for our propaganda. On the other hand the army did not need to be provoked. They shot dead thirteen innocent people during a demonstration in 1972 without provocation. That was the Paras for you.

Membership of Na Fianna was open to serious abuse because it gave teenagers unrivalled power within their peer groupings. It permitted old scores and rivalries to be settled, encouraged a preoccupation with guns and violence, and undermined the authority of teachers in schools in the ghettos. A school friend who taught in a West Belfast secondary school told me of the difficulties he faced when imposing discipline in his classroom:

The atmosphere on the streets in 1970–1 was not conducive to stability and it carried over into the classroom. Kids were more concerned about the most recent riot than about learning. I knew the ones who were in the Fianna because they swaggered around my classrooms as though I didn't exist. Other kids were frightened of them and endeared themselves to them as a means of self-protection. On one occasion I reprimanded a Fianna boy for unruly behaviour, and made him stand outside the classroom. After lessons, I was walking across the playground when I was approached by this boy and two of his classmates who were also members of the organisation. One of them held a revolver inside his jacket with the butt protruding to let me know he was armed. They stopped me and said: 'Listen, sir. We're takin' your car.' These kids were fifteen years of age and there was damn all I could do about it. I knew there was little to be gained by opposing them. They returned the vehicle the following day. God knows what use they made of it. Fianna members also disrupted classes by encouraging the pupils to engage in rioting by stoning troops from the confines of the school playground. Sometimes in the middle of a lesson they would spot an army foot patrol passing the school and without warning climbed out of the ground-floor classroom windows and pelted them with stones. All the kids resented the soldiers because army tactics were not subtle. Some of these kids were witnessing military searches in which homes were wrecked, and mothers and fathers subjected to verbal and sometimes physical abuse.

Paddy Devlin, former SDLP Chief Whip, experienced the elation of boyhood membership of the Fianna and later the IRA. Recalling the factors which drew him to republicanism, his experiences, occurring a decade before the birth of Joseph Doherty, provide a poignant reminder that times were unchanged in the 1970s.

In the republicanism I grew up in I was never conscious of working it out, rationalising it. I was only conscious of living in a ghetto, of drifting along with what was going on in the ghetto. We didn't like the police, and we got a great kick out of them following us. We were kids who joined the Fianna and drilled in Falls Park. We knew the police would be along every Sunday at 10.00 am and we had our scouts out and waited for them. We would let them get closer and closer and then we'd get off side and the police after us. There was a great kick out of this, and we went to school and all the kids in the school looked up to us. We were the great heroes. And the thrill I got out of that may well have been my reason for staying with it. I was interned when I was about seventeen, and that sort of excitement was something I always sought. I didn't know anything about the British Empire, and Patrick Pearse was the only person shot in 1916. It was only when I got into prison that I began to read about it.

In 1970 the excesses of the British army were matched by the IRA, who carried out 150 bombings of what they termed 'economic targets'. The explosions were designed to force the army to withdraw a large number of troops from the ghettos to protect the commercial and industrial life of Northern Ireland. The IRA claimed it was a defensive strategy, and the offensive role against the army only began because of the excessive behaviour of soldiers in the ghettos, and because the role of the army was not peace-keeping but the subjugation of the nationalist population. There was a perceptible change in the role and behaviour of the military in the summer of 1970. Catholic clergy and politicians predicted that if a Conservative Government came to power in Britain the army would be devoid of restraint. This reasoning was based on a recognition that Unionist politics were indivisible from Tory politics and a Tory Government would be partial to a Protestant/Unionist analysis of the conflict. In some respects that was correct, except that the major change which occurred in the army's behaviour derived from frustration rather than deliberate policy considerations. In May 1970 the Conservatives won the general election from a Labour Party which had shown a genuine appreciation of nationalist claims of police brutality and political repression. The Labour Party had disarmed the police for their overzealous use of weapons in 1969 and their identification with loyalist violence, and had also disbanded the B Specials. Suddenly Edward Heath and his Tory Party were in power, with an army which naïvely believed that a military solution was possible, and that it should handle all rioting. Before long Protestant and Catholic rioters bore the brunt of a tough, uncompromising military, to the dismay of church leaders on both sides. A new general was in charge and, alongside him, Brigadier Frank Kitson, an expert in counter-insurgency warfare. The military were faced with a demand from the Unionist Government at Stormont for more severe methods to be used against one side of the community, namely the Catholics. Unionists appeared oblivious to the large, overt paramilitary build-up within their own community, and their ignorance of loyalist paramilitary violence was expedient and bigoted. Loyalist guns were for killing Catholics and not the overthrow of the state, whereas IRA weaponry posed a real threat to the Protestant/Unionist edifice. The acceptance of this thesis by the British army determined their view that the terrorist threat was in the Catholic community. They were prepared to deal with

Protestant rioters in the same way as they would the Catholics, but the burden of their responsibility was to deal with the IRA.

The army's role in respect of the IRA was downright naïve and dangerous. It undermined moderate Catholic nationalists who thought the army was impartial – and it played into the hands of the IRA propagandists. Kitson was convinced that the IRA had to be dealt with immediately, otherwise it would resurface within five to ten years. His solution was a policy of attrition and de-escalation. Attrition was defined by Kitson as arresting the extremists, although he admitted that legal constraints were a deterrent to snatching those leading members of the IRA who were planning and directing the violence. Attrition as a policy developed into much more than arrests, and Unionist Government ministers recognised the army's constraints and demanded internment without trial. As internment loomed, Catholics became disillusioned with the slow pace of change, and with the British Government's failure to encourage Stormont to introduce much-needed reforms.

Violence increased in Catholic areas and rioting was deemed an offence which carried a mandatory sentence of six months' imprisonment. The effect was that many Catholics with no attachment to the IRA were sent to prison. This policy was not only unduly harsh, but it provided the IRA with propaganda and future recruits. Rioting was a feature of daily existence and many innocent people who unwittingly found themselves in the midst of a full-scale battle were arrested, and either sent to prison or given suspended prison terms.

On one occasion I was unable to leave the Ballymurphy area for twelve hours during a riot which began at 6.00 pm and escalated with few lulls in the fighting. The majority of the rioters were not members of the IRA, but became combatants because they detested the brutal tactics of the soldiers. It was the period when the army devised 'snatch squads' within its regiments. The soldiers chosen for these squads were the toughest and most physically powerful men. Their task was to penetrate the ranks of the rioters and snatch the ringleaders from their midst. The tactics of the snatch squads on that evening and night in Ballymurphy were fearsome. Heavily clothed with helmets, visors and batons, they stood facing the rioters, shouting abuse, banging their batons against their hands before rushing into the midst of the rioters. An order was shouted to several snatch squads to find their targets and CS gas was fired to force an untidy withdrawal by the rioters. Ten canisters of gas landed in the midst of the crowd as the snatch squads sprinted towards them, and the rioters withdrew in confusion to regroup. Heavy military boots and expletives from the snatch squads terrified those of us who retreated into doorways. A fair-haired teenager was cornered by five snatch squad soldiers, beaten unmercifully with batons, dragged unceremoniously towards the open doors of an armoured personnel carrier and tossed inside. I watched three other people suffer a similar fate. In turn, this aggravated the determination of the rioters, who injured many soldiers with stones, or ball-bearings fired from small hand-held catapults. The mob never seemed to diminish in numbers, and I was told that there was a type of relay system whereby rioters retired for food or rest, and were replaced by others on standby.

Matters worsened in July 1970 when the army stated that rioters were liable to be shot. The army may have had petrol-bombers in mind but its message was unclear and appeared extreme. Joseph Doherty and other members of the Fianna who were in the midst of the rioting were probably unaware that during riots army photographers took hundreds of snapshots from the safety of armoured personnel carriers. The photos were developed at army headquarters and examined in detail to identify ringleaders. Doherty was fortunate at that stage that as a sixteen-year-old he was unlikely to be judged a ringleader, and equally the army was unaware of IRA structures or the role of Na Fianna Eireann. That knowledge was quickly acquired as violence escalated, and the army began to devote its resources to understanding and categorising the nature of the IRA and its operations.

On 11 August, an army prediction about serious risk to rioters was tragically realised in Doherty's neighbourhood. In the course of a full-scale riot, Daniel O'Hagan was shot in the chest by a soldier and died instantly. O'Hagan's death, far from deterring Joseph Doherty's pursuit of his Fianna role, convinced him instead of the need for an armed struggle against the British. The IRA retaliated by killing two police officers with a booby-trapped car bomb, but even this action did not signal the beginning of an all-out armed confrontation. The Provisionals had been steadily acquiring weapons, ammunition and explosives, and were still biding their time for the moment which they told their followers would be opportune to take on the 'occupying forces'. An arms-smuggling network, based in the United States, provided a constant source of weapons; but the supply was small compared with what the Provisional IRA leadership judged sufficient for the opening of hostilities. The weapons from America were mainly Mark 1 carbines, Garand rifles and Thompson sub-machine-guns. Contacts in the Government of the Irish Republic were busy trying to acquire weapons through European sources, and the Irish army was secretly providing military training in parts of the South. In bomb-making, the IRA developed expertise by using condoms, clothes-pegs and other domestic items to produce booby-trap devices.

The Provisional IRA's reluctance to engage the army was partly based on the premise that only when Catholics fully supported the republican cause would there be sufficient justification to start a war. In order to ensure there was no fraternisation with soldiers, Doherty and other members of the Fianna were told to be the eyes and ears of the IRA, and to report anyone who befriended soldiers or offered them refreshments. Those civilians who foolishly disobeyed IRA instructions were punished, and slogans were painted on the outside walls of homes where soldiers were entertained or given tea or coffee. In the case of young girls seen flirting with soldiers, a warning was issued: if a girl persisted, she was subjected to public humiliation; her head was shaved with a razor; she was tied to a public lamppost; tar was poured over her head and she was covered with a sackful of feathers. A placard indicating the nature of her crime was hung round her neck, and she was left in position until the IRA or Fianna decided enough people had witnessed her punishment. In all these situations there was the irony of Catholic girls marrying soldiers. The sister of leading republican Danny Morrison married a soldier, although they were later divorced. Some girls ran considerable risks to date soldiers, and in rare instances even invited them to visit their homes in off-duty clothing. 'Tarring and feathering' was not only reserved for females but also used for young men found guilty, in IRA parlance, of 'minor misdemeanours'.

In early 1971 the IRA Army Council issued a secret order that Belfast units were free to engage the British troops, because, they calculated, the Catholic population was now sufficiently alienated, and would provide moral or logistical support, such as refuge for men on the run, or vocal political assent to hostilities. Joseph Doherty's apprenticeship in terrorism took place in an atmosphere of bombings and shootings – and the Provisionals did not restrict their attacks to military targets. Some Provos who joined the IRA because they hated Protestants for attacks on Catholic homes in 1969 sought their own revenge, and bombed a Protestant-owned bar injuring several people. Sectarian conflict was always inevitable, though at that stage it was neither a serious concern nor a prolonged risk to human life, compared with the IRA–British military hostilities.

The Commander of Land Forces, General Harry Tuzo, was faced with growing pressure to agree to stronger measures. The Northern Ireland Government had the Special Powers Act which allowed for the immediate introduction of internment without trial. On 10 August 1971 the army swooped on houses across Northern Ireland. The operation, codenamed 'Demetrius', led to the arrest of several hundred males within the Catholic population, half of whom were released within two days. The Provisionals learned from a civil servant of the scope and date of the operation and their leadership went into hiding.

Many of those arrested were men with nationalist or republican sentiments, with no IRA affiliations. The army selected them by using dated police intelligence files which related to the IRA of the 1950s. Other people with radical political views were also seized, and the exercise was a failure. Of those IRA men held in the swoop, the majority were members of the Official IRA, who posed a minor threat to the army. There were also members of the civil rights movement in the haul of suspects, and people whose identity was mistaken – with the result that the Provisional IRA was eventually presented with a massive propaganda victory. Twelve of those detained were selected for what the European Court of Human Rights later described and condemned as 'degrading and inhuman treatment'. They were hooded for seven days, subjected to white noise, prevented from sleeping and constantly interrogated. The remainder of the men held in custody were taken to an old aerodrome near Belfast, which was ringed by barbed wire and machine-gun posts. They were denied recourse to the law, and placed in corrugated huts in compounds inside the perimeter wire. Between the introduction of internment and the end of 1971 the IRA fired nearly 20,000 bullets and threw 1500 bombs at troops.

Joseph Doherty and other members of the Fianna were constantly on standby to support IRA operations, which occurred daily from the New Lodge and other ghettos. Paddy Devlin, by then prominent in the Catholic Social Democratic and Labour Party, publicly described General Tuzo as the 'instigator of barbarities':

To most people he is a name without a physical shape. Although rarely seen, he plies the press constantly with a view of events involving security forces that would take tears from the unfortunate victim's own family, be that victim beaten, tortured, imprisoned or shot dead, by his own military's hands. . . . With the advent of internment General Tuzo's troops brutalised everyone detained in that round-up. . . . The military still carry out their own type of interrogations. These are conducted by their own intelligence officers within the confines of their outposts. Each post has its own 'torture rack apparatus', to which the unfortunate prisoner is submitted.

Torture did take place, but the phrase 'torture rack apparatus' misleadingly suggested a mechanical or wooden structure reminiscent of medieval persecution: it was the language of emotionalism, though some might say understandably so. Devlin and the leaders of the SDLP were opposed to the IRA campaign, but equally they were appalled by the behaviour of the army and the introduction of internment. The IRA and SDLP, as well as the Catholic Church, were united in condemning internment, and the SDLP responded by calling on Catholics to engage in a campaign of civil disobedience, by refusing to pay rent and rates to the state.

Devlin reserved some of his bitterest comments for the way in which the army ignored the loyalist threat:

More than 20,000 troops occupy nationalist areas, against a mere token force in loyalist areas. The peace that General Tuzo spoke so euphemistically about is broken thousands of times daily by loyalists, known as the Ulster Defence Association, in patrol marches and demonstrations of masked, armed men in paramilitary dress answering to military commands. They now have full movement in all areas as a result of an agreement with General Tuzo's security forces (I have tapes confirming this).

Devlin's assertions and those of other nationalist leaders were symptomatic of a period when harsh words were said in harsh and emotional times, but whether they were ultimately helpful is debatable. The IRA was encouraged by the solidarity of Catholic political leaders and their opposition to internment and the army's attempts to achieve military victory.

Joseph Doherty was singularly aware of troops constantly searching homes, arresting suspects, screening them and interning them. Brigadier Frank Kitson believed it necessary to screen the entire Catholic population as a means of gaining further intelligence on the IRA; stop–search procedures were central to his policy, which enabled the army to compile dossiers on every household – the occupation, schools, car registrations and suspected political affiliations of every human being in the Catholic ghettos. Doherty was prominent in street rioting and his family history determined he would be closely scrutinised. Several days before Christmas 1971 he experienced a search operation.

It occurred during what we called 'the dawn raids' by the British army. It was about five o'clock in the morning. They came to our house, which has only two bedrooms. My mother and father slept in one bedroom and my four sisters in the other. I was the odd-man-out and I was sleeping on a floor in a downstairs room. I wakened with the sound of tanks [he is referring to heavy armoured personnel carriers or motorised carriers with a Browning machine-gun fitted to a turret] coming down the street. I jumped up and I tried to get up the stairs to warn my parents but the door was kicked in. I looked round and there must have been fourteen or fifteen soldiers. They had tin helmets, their faces blackened and they carried machine-guns and rifles. They told me to halt, freeze – or they would shoot.

What Doherty described was a typical army raid. It was deliberately carried out at a time when the occupants of a house were sleeping and unprepared for the swift action of soldiers who refrained from the civilised manner in which most people enter another's home. The timing of the raid afforded sparse opportunity for flight or weapons concealment. For many who were undressed or partially clothed, it was a frightening and humiliating experience, and the search was conducted with force and often led to wanton damage of property. Doherty continued:

I put up my hands and went downstairs. The soldiers proceeded to go upstairs and search the bedrooms. I heard them shouting at my mother and father to get out of bed. My father did get out of bed but my mother was half naked and was very, very embarrassed at the six or seven British troops in the very small bedroom with rifles pointing at her, telling her to get out of bed. She said: 'Will you get out of the bedroom while I put my gown on.' A British officer approached her, put a Browning pistol to her head and told her: 'You Irish bitch, get out of bed.'

Doherty says they took his mother from the bed and then entered the room where his sisters were sleeping – girls aged eleven to fifteen years, who were naturally terrified. He heard them crying as they were removed from their beds, taken downstairs and placed in a back room of the house. Every member of the family was eventually placed in the same room. Doherty and his father were ordered to place their hands above their heads while the soldiers went on a 'rampage'.

They pulled out the bread, the only bread we had, and threw it on the floor. Just the normal British army search. They wrecked the house searching for arms. They proceeded to come into the room and told myself and my father that we were being arrested and taken in for questioning. Myself and my father were taken out and put into one of the tanks that was there. In all there were three armoured personnel carriers. The vehicles were called 'pigs'.

In examining Doherty's testimony of events it is important to recognise that his language is that of someone who hates British soldiers. Whether or not that should detract from what he says becomes a matter for one's personal judgement. If there is embellishment, it appears to occur in the way in which he seeks to propagandise events by using such words as 'just the normal British army search'. That generalisation may simply reflect Doherty's own experience, but I believe he seeks (for political advantage) to relate it to all searches. Not all searches were conducted with brutality and carelessness, though it is accurate to say that too many were carried out in the fashion described by the young IRA recruit.

Doherty, with wearisome reiteration, refers in his testimonies to 'tanks', even though he clearly knows the difference between 'armoured personnel carriers' and 'tanks'. Perhaps he prefers to portray the search operation in a context which suggests that massive vehicles more typically deployed on battlefields were being used in his street: it is as if he wishes those untutored in Northern Irish affairs to visualise the Russian tanks that rolled into Prague. His constant use of 'tank' to describe a smaller, less hostile vehicle is politically motivated: all Fianna members and IRA volunteers were familiar with the exactitude required when signalling the types of vehicles entering a neighbourhood.

Me and my father were put in the back of the tank. A British army officer sat facing me with his gun. We were brought into what's called Glenravel Street Police Station to the British military end of the station, as the police had one end of the station and the British the other and they were in control of the ghetto surrounding the station. We were put into a large gymnasium. There seemed to be twenty or thirty other people. These were neighbours, neighbours' sons, and everybody was sitting round in a circle with their hands above their heads. The British army was marching in between us. They took each person in for questioning until they came to myself.

Doherty was taken into a room where he was made to face a table at which several British officers were seated: he judged one of them to be a major. Soldiers with rifles stood positioned in the four corners of the room. The teenager was asked: Was he a republican? Did he know the names of any republicans? Did he know members of the IRA? The identity and political affiliations of his neighbours?

Doherty senior was similarly questioned, but was also asked about his trade union. Were its members republican? Did civil rights people work alongside him? Or political agitators of any kind? Father and son were each subjected to an hour of questioning and released.

During the house search Joseph Doherty may have behaved in a fashion which aroused suspicion because Fianna members were schooled in anti-interrogation techniques, and often betrayed a cleverness which interrogators defined as a sign of terrorist membership. His arrest was probably the result of a photographic file at army HQ illustrating the frequency of his participation in rioting, and his association with known republicans. It was just as likely, however, that an informer in his area brought him to the attention of military intelligence. Within twelve hours of his release, soldiers mounted a second dawn raid on the Doherty home, smashed open the front door and removed the teenager to Glenravel Street army base. 'I was taken through the same procedure as the previous night. The major told me that they knew I was in Na Fianna Eireann.'

Doherty responded with a degree of bravado, or maybe the inexperience of youth, by admitting membership, and claiming that under the Geneva Convention he was not obliged to say anything further. After several hours he was released. He believed that they were obliged to let him go, because by law he was a juvenile and could not be interned. According to his account of the event, they didn't appreciate his refusal to co-operate with their questioning and warned him that they would 'get him', when he reached the age of seventeen. He went into hiding, 'on the run', in IRA parlance, and stayed in the homes of relatives and family friends. He was unable to remain indoors indefinitely, and was constantly moving location to evade detection. On 22 January 1972, twenty-four hours after his seventeenth birthday, they arrested him. He was walking along a street in the New Lodge area when several soldiers jumped over a wall and seized him. He was returned to the Glenravel base, and presented to a military intelligence officer and the same major. From there they transferred him to Girdwood Barracks, a quarter of a mile from his home. This was a large army base which, unlike Glenravel, did not have a formal police presence, but did have in attendance members of Special Branch. On his arrival, Doherty was pulled by his ear and confronted with a calendar and the words 'Happy birthday, Joe.'

He was in a detention centre. Girdwood, Magilligan and Ballykinlar were the three army bases employed for the processing of the large number of men lifted in Operation Demetrius. Each base was under full army control, with no formal police presence except for members of Special Branch.

Student leader Michael Farrell, who was one of those detained on 9 August 1971, gave this account of the treatment of the prisoners:

Almost everyone had been beaten up. Many had been blindfolded and terrified by being thrown out of a moving helicopter which they were told was high in the air, but in fact was only a few inches off the ground. More had been forced to run the gauntlet barefoot between lines of troops with batons and across wire and glass-strewn ground.

When such stories filtered out of the detention centres, and were augmented by the revelation that certain men were being selected for 'special treatment', the propaganda war intensified. Horror stories were created, as well as claims by men such as Paddy Devlin of the SDLP about 'torture rack apparatus'. In the forty-eight hours after internment 104 men were released. The remaining 256 were interrogated, some in-depth, and transferred to the *Maidstone*, a ship converted into an internment centre, to Long Kesh airfield, which had been recently converted to an internment camp, and to Crumlin Road prison in Belfast. Between August 1971 and

Doherty's arrest the detention centres continued the task of processing suspects. Each centre had people skilled in interrogation techniques.

Desmond Hamill, in his book *Pig in the Middle: The Army in Northern Ireland 1969–85*, quotes an army officer's view of the internment procedure:

Naturally one worries – after all, one is inflicting pain and discomfort on other human beings, but the facts are that first, the interrogators were not army but Special Branch officers, and second, that society has got to find a way of protecting itself . . . and it can only do so if it has good information. . . . Now the softies of the world complain, but there is an awful lot of double talk about it. If there is discomfort and horror to be inflicted on a few, is this not preferred to the danger and horror on perhaps a million people? So internment and this very, very small scale interrogation was set in train, and both were eventually talked out – because the world has become a more talkative place than it was when we used these techniques in colonial situations.

That view, typical of an army officer of the period, did not take account of the failure of the process, the fact that most of those initially arrested were innocent, and that degrading and inhuman treatment only served to exacerbate tension and handed propaganda to terrorists. He was correct in asserting that such techniques were previously used in colonial situations, such as Kenya, Aden and Cyprus, but 1971 was, as he accurately commented, a time when the world was a 'more talkative place'. It is worth noting how the officer shifted blame for the interrogations towards Special Branch, who were central to the questioning process. But it was the army who had the colonial experience of special techniques, such as the use of sensory deprivation; and it was the army who deployed those tactics, and trained Special Branch in the skills of interrogation.

Joseph Doherty's account of his treatment at Girdwood during a two-day stay is important in determining his credibility with regard to that aspect of his terrorist career:

Girdwood is a notorious torture centre. I was given what is known as SD [sensory deprivation] treatment; only I didn't get as much as the rest of the people there because I was what they called 'a small fish'. I was insignificant. So I was put in what you could describe as a partition, like a toilet. I was put on a chair and told not to lift my hands off my knees. This was a white wall like a pegboard with holes, and after about an hour you started getting very, very dizzy as holes got bigger and bigger. I wasn't allowed to move and the temperature was kept very high so it was very humid. The police officers of British intelligence were walking behind us. This went on for hours.

After a while I was put into a cell. This was a round cell which was completely white and you can't even notice the door because the door is embedded in the wall, so all you see is holes everywhere. I was told to sit in the middle of the room with my hands on my knees and not even move my head. They told me they were watching and looking in to give me a good punch in the nose, so I complied and kept my head straight. After a while they would take me in for interrogation. This is in one of the interrogation rooms. I think it is 7 and I was put in the one interrogation room. There was Special Branch officers from the RUC police and a British intelligence officer. When I went into the room they stripped me down to my underpants. They told me to stand in a corner and when I would stand in the corner they would put a rag over my eyes so that I could not see. They asked me about the general population. Who did I know? All those sorts of questions, and then started beating me about the back, etc. Then they would pull me underpants down and make fun of me private parts, and at that time they would squeeze them, which is of course, of all the male members. It's pretty sore, y'know. They kept on questioning me, beating me, but they didn't seem to have any time for me, as I could hear the screams from all the other blocks where they had IRA suspects and other political suspects. They came in and said: 'Bring him down to number 2 room and give him the electric shocks.' These were wires coming out of an electric box which they put on to people's testicles. They would give me things like this. Of course I was scared in the main. They put me back in the cell but I wasn't important, they just wanted to bring me in, ask me a few questions, etc. They didn't think Na Fianna was important. They wanted to know other information about the Irish Republican Army and I didn't know because I knew very, very few people that was in the Irish Republican Army.

When I first examined Doherty's testimony of his experience at Girdwood, I decided to compare his allegations with available historical evidence. I was inclined to accept his description of sensory-deprivation treatment, and the humiliation to which he was subjected. His evidence was in keeping with many of the experiences related by internees of that period. However, one claim surprised and puzzled me and that was his description of torture, in particular the use of electric shocks. My own research never yielded any such allegations. The reputable source material written about the internees, and about the twelve men known as the 'Guinea Pigs', who were given 'special treatment', is devoid of such a claim. The 1978 Human Rights Court found that the twelve men were subjected, not to torture, but to 'inhuman and degrading treatment', which included sensory deprivation in many forms such as hooding, white noise, deprivation of sleep, and a diet of bread and water.

The available evidence implies that Doherty embellished his account of his treatment at Girdwood. His motivation was to portray himself as a political prisoner similar to those ill treated in Third World countries, in Chile or Argentina. He delivered his 'torture' testimony in 1984, to the United States District Court, Southern District of New York. Later in this book I will explain in greater detail his reasons for seeking to depict himself in that fashion. Suffice it to say that the veracity of his evidence about that particular detail of his life is at least open to question.

As to his claim that he knew 'very, very few people in the IRA' – he was operating alongside IRA men, many of whom were well known in their own ghettos; he was in a better position to know the identities of many IRA men because he was assisting them. His assertion that he was 'a small fish' also proved incorrect. He was released from interrogation after forty-eight hours, and taken to the front gate of the base. There he was handed over to soldiers, who handcuffed him, placed a pillow-case over his head and transferred him to an armoured personnel carrier in the custody of armed guards. The 'small fish' was about to be given special treatment.

# 4

# Incarceration

The armoured personnel carrier rumbled through the streets of Belfast and delivered him to troops guarding the *Maidstone* prison ship:

They took the hood off my head, and all I seen was this big ship sitting at the shore at the dock. They told me to get up, so they brought me up the gangplank. When I got to the top of the ship they opened up the hatches and told me to get down the stairs. I was pushed down the stairs. When I got to the bottom I was handed over to the prisoners.

Conditions on the *Maidstone* were deplorable. Over 200 men were kept in the hold of the vessel. Half of them were members of the IRA, and the rest comprised men awaiting trial for terrorist offences or men with radical political views. The poor intelligence used for the initial internment swoop ensured that Doherty was in the company of a wide range of people, some of whom by his own account were 'trades unionists and civil rights activists'. Doherty discovered that one man represented all the prisoners and conveyed their demands to the authorities. The IRA, which had its own command structure, debriefed Doherty about his stay at Girdwood and informed him that 'as a member of the Junior IRA you will be taking orders from us'. They told him they would 'look after him', and asked whether he needed cigarettes or any other luxuries.

The IRA also had an escape committee, which constantly planned ways of breaching the security of the vessel. Two weeks before Doherty's arrival seven IRA men sawed through porthole bars, covered themselves in butter and oil, and swam across Belfast Lough. The coating on their bodies protected them from the icy sea and they reached safety in the Markets area, where they were met by IRA units who spirited them to safe-houses in Belfast and across the border in the Irish Republic. On his arrival Doherty assisted the escape committee by keeping a constant watch through portholes to assess the level of security outside the ship. There were cultural and games committees, and many of the internees used wooden panelling and stair rails to carve harps and items which represented Irish cultural symbols. Wood was also shaped into guns for use in arms lectures. The IRA made sure that all its men were constantly aware of their affiliation, the ideals of the organisation and the means and tactics of guerrilla warfare.

Doherty was the youngest person on board and, whatever his commitment to republicanism, his association with older, ex-perienced IRA men hardened his resolve to play a significant part in the ensuing guerrilla war. The IRA had a television set which informed them of events in the world outside and Doherty says one event shocked them all, and brought a great change in his attitude. On 30 January 1972 members of the Parachute Regiment shot dead thirteen unarmed civilians after a civil rights protest march in Londonderry. The BBC television news that evening depicted the horror of the event; all on the ship felt angry. People around him wept, shouting their anger at the televised scenes. Doherty vowed that if he was released he would join the IRA and 'fight for his country'. If there was ever any hope that the Doherty of those days would eventually reject violence, it ended on the *Maidstone*. Maybe the deaths of those people on what became known as 'Bloody Sunday' was the final catalyst, but his presence on the ship in the company of experienced IRA men was probably sufficient to condition his thinking and stiffen his commitment.

Twenty years on, it is difficult to come to terms with the presence of young men such as Joe Doherty in prison camps. He was not alone in finding himself interned at such a formative age. Gusty Spence, who was commander of the Ulster Volunteer Force in Long Kesh in the early 1970s, told me: 'In my compound I had a boy who was still in his school blazer. That lad had shot two people in the head. He was a quiet, inoffensive schoolboy and that's what he was – a schoolboy.' Gusty Spence, a loyalist hero to a whole generation, became the longest-serving prisoner in Northern Ireland. Jailed in 1967, he served eighteen years, during which time he epitomised the cult of the gunman within his own community. He later rejected violence, and I turned to him for an understanding of how young men such as he and later Joseph Doherty were drawn into paramilitarism. 'Paramilitarism was a way of life,' he said. 'People turned to the paramilitaries for protection. And it's difficult for parents because if you cosset a boy too much you will probably drive him into the organisations. The young lads frightened me to some degree because it was gun, gun, gun all the time.'

Internment provided the means for Doherty to gain an education in the politics of conflict – which many of his contemporaries on the streets did not possess. As with Paddy Devlin, decades earlier, prison gave the IRA an opportunity to educate their members about the history of republicanism. Doherty was not the only member of his family to experience internment. One year later his sister, Anne, was held in the women's prison at Armagh, and at a subsequent date the husbands of three of his sisters and several cousins were also interned.

At the beginning of February 1972 Doherty was taken with other prisoners to the British officer commanding the *Maidstone*, and informed he was being transferred to Long Kesh; he was ferried by helicopter to the site of the old airfield which resembled a World War II concentration camp. His departure was part of a process of divesting the ship of its inhabitants, because the escape of the seven IRA men who had swum ashore illustrated the insecure nature of the vessel, and in any case Long Kesh was the major internment centre. On leaving the ship he was presented with a formal internment order and suddenly the 'small fish' was swimming in bigger waters.

As the helicopter hovered over Long Kesh, Doherty saw barbed wire, 'tin huts' arranged in compounds, searchlights, watchtowers and guards patrolling with dogs. Long Kesh was an intimidating reminder of war, straight from the cinema's images of Colditz; Doherty compared it with 'Treblinka, or Belsen', a parallel again illustrative of a propaganda technique to depict the worst scenario – although as a teenager his first experience of an internment camp was undoubtedly a terrifying one.

Most of the internees were republican, though Doherty claims that the majority were 'innocent people belonging to the political parties that existed in Northern Ireland'. A small percentage had no affiliations with the republican movement, but most of those interned were in fact republicans, innocent in that they were not charged with offences, or permitted the due process of law, and at least half of those were members of the Provisional or Official IRA. Doherty's stretching of the historical evidence is evident in his claim that most of the prisoners were people 'belonging to the political parties in Northern Ireland': he is referring to nationalist or republican politics; and there was no evidence to indicate significant numbers of SDLP or Nationalist Party members in the camp. Yet internment was indiscriminate, particularly at the outset of its introduction, and people who subscribed to a republican or nationalist view of Irish history were deemed a threat to the state; all Catholics in the ghettos were potential subversives. This eventually led to an exaggerated view of the numbers of innocent people arrested, and it was to this interpretation that Joseph Doherty later applied his analysis. It is true that those in Long Kesh in February 1972 included student radicals, and others who believed the state was irreformable but none the less did not agree with the IRA's campaign of violence.

Doherty says that the camp was divided into compounds, with a chairman democratically elected to represent the views of the men. Within this structure the IRA had its own command mechanisms for its volunteers, but he remained a member of Na Fianna Eireann under IRA control. Internees wore their own clothes and the IRA in each compound drilled their men in the open air every day. Committees with responsibility for games, history lectures and escape plans were responsible for the day-to-day life of Long Kesh. Doherty and IRA volunteers were given weapons training and lectures on the tactics of urban guerrilla warfare.

Doherty was kept in Long Kesh for four months, a short stay compared with the experience of most internees. His youthfulness may have militated against a longer term of imprisonment, although there was also a policy of 'negotiation' between the British Government and the IRA which took place in June 1972 and resulted in the release of a large number of internees.

In June 1972 the British Government flew IRA leaders to London to discuss the basis of a ceasefire; those talks followed the abolition of the Unionist Government at Stormont, removing the last edifice of Protestant/Unionist domination of Northern Ireland. Those two crucial developments incensed Protestants, and led to the murder of scores of innocent Catholics at the hands of loyalist killer squads. The IRA ceasefire collapsed after a brief respite in IRA–British army violence. When Joseph Doherty was released he returned to the streets of Belfast and found himself in a very dangerous city. From

June until the end of the year several hundred civilians were killed, the majority of them Catholics, and loyalist gangs carried out some of the most grisly crimes in the history of the conflict. Ironically it was not until February 1973, six months after the first internment swoop, that the British Government decided to apply the policy to loyalists. In that month, two loyalists were served with interim custody orders, and by April of that year the number had increased to twenty, compared with the hundreds from Catholic areas.

Joseph Doherty lost no time in travelling from Long Kesh to his home to inform his parents of his good fortune. As he walked along the New Lodge Road he was apprehended by paratroopers who told him he was under arrest. He had been free for a mere two and a half hours. Women from the neighbourhood recognised him and rushed from their homes to prevent his detention.

All the women came into the street. My God, there must have been seventy to ninety women. They surrounded the tank and forced the British army to release me. They weren't abusive to the soldiers. They persuaded them that 'Christ, the lad's just out of jail, give him a break.' The army released me but told me 'we will get you tomorrow night'.

It was not unusual for a released man to be returned to custody to be screened for several days. If Doherty had been taken into custody he would probably have been removed to Girdwood army base where interrogators would have sought to establish whether he was politically reformed, or whether he could be 'turned', that is pressurised into acting as an agent for Special Branch or military intelligence.

His first task as a free man was to fulfil his long ambition to join the IRA, a task made easy by the fact that IRA officers in Long Kesh had vetted him, and provided him with the name of an IRA contact in the New Lodge district – the IRA's recruiting officer for its 3rd Battalion, based in the north of the city. He questioned Doherty about his history in the Fianna, his arrests and his motivation for joining the IRA.

I told him that at a very young age I wanted to fight for my country. I thought the British shouldn't be here. I thought the best way to bring peace was for the British to withdraw and the best way to get the British out of the country was the traditional armed conflict. He began to explain the aims and objects of the republican movement, the constitution. He showed me the constitution of the movement. He showed me the army regulations and orders. This is the standards of regulations that's in the Irish Republican Army, you know, breach of security, breach of orders, etc.

When the recruiting officer had satisfied himself that Doherty knew the precise terms of his contract, he swore him into the IRA. The officer produced a Bible, a .45 revolver and an Irish tricolour, the national flag of the Irish Republic, and proceeded with an age-old ceremony. As Doherty placed his right hand on the three items stacked one on the other, he swore an oath: 'I Joseph Doherty swear to give allegiance to the Irish Republic and to the consti-tution of 1918 . . .' Doherty was told he was a volunteer in the IRA, and a soldier of the Irish Republic. For the next three weeks he was lectured in the history of the IRA, the use of weapons and guerrilla tactics. He learned how to handle the typical IRA guns, such as the Thompson and the carbine; how to keep them in working order; how to break them down and reassemble them while wearing a blindfold. He was told he was 'a volunteer in C Company, 3rd Battalion'. Belfast was divided into three battalion areas under the overall command of the Belfast Brigade. In each battalion the companies were subdivided into units. Each company accorded in hierarchical structure with the battalion and brigade. There was an officer commanding, an adjutant, intelligence officer, quarter-master, and so on. The quartermaster was responsible for the procurement, concealment and distribution of guns and explo-sives to the individual units or sections within the company structure. Doherty was placed in D section, and told that he was 'an infantryman with the role of confronting the British army'.

He says his job also included defence of the ghetto, intelligence gathering, and policing duties or what he humorously calls the 'cat-up-the-tree policy': 'There was also social work or what we call the cat-up-the-tree policy where a woman would come round to the Irish Republican Army and say her cat was up a tree. The officer in command would send two volunteers to get it. We weren't just an army, we were a service to the general public inside the ghetto.' In my experience there were not too many IRA men clambering up trees to rescue stranded cats – nor were there many trees in the narrow drab streets of the Catholic enclaves in Belfast. If the IRA were compassionate, there was little enough evidence of it, though at a later stage the development of the political arm of the IRA strategy, namely Sinn Fein, led to an upsurge in social work and the setting up of advice centres in republican neighbourhoods. Doherty's 'cat-up-the-tree policy' bears small relation to a period when an armed conflict was taking place in earnest and when stray cats or social work were not on the IRA agenda.

Doherty and his fellow volunteers were constantly on standby. In the Ardoyne area, for instance, volunteers under the command of Martin Meehan were ordered to be ready at 'a moment's notice' to engage soldiers, a policy which resulted in the deaths of eight soldiers from one regiment in a short period. Each section in the Ardoyne and New Lodge areas had access to three or four weapons which could be used in short, sharp encounters. Local company commanders did not always follow proper procedures before sanctioning an operation. There was a degree of ill-discipline in the rush for company volunteers to blood themselves.

Eamonn Mallie and Patrick Bishop in their book *The Provisional IRA* offer a vivid example of how IRA actions were ordered in the Ardoyne:

Meehan [company commander] wanted action, action, action. He couldn't get enough operations his way. The daily routine for Company members was to turn up at a call house, pick up a weapon from the tiny armoury of two armalites and a sub-machine-gun allotted to each Company, then set off in pairs, usually by car, to cruise the narrow streets in search of a target. Meehan's instructions were vague. Little planning went into the operations. They were simply under orders to engage any troops entering the district. The encounters between soldiers and Provisionals were brief.

The tactics in the New Lodge were no different. Volunteers quickly engaged foot or motorised patrols and after a short exchange retreated into the narrow streets of the ghetto. The New Lodge was on the edge of the commercial life of Belfast and it also became a base for conveying bombs to targets in the city centre. Doherty seeks to depict IRA operations as firmly controlled and sanctioned but that was not always so. The required procedure was that the battalion staff gave directions to company commanders, who in turn relayed them to section leaders and volunteers – but officers like Meehan who was company commander in Ardoyne did not wait for battalion approval.

Doherty is correct in saying that as a volunteer he was not permitted to make personal decisions relating to IRA military actions, and was not allowed to lift a weapon and use it against troops. After every operation, volunteers were required to attend a debriefing with the company intelligence officer at which all details of an actual shooting or bombing were analysed. As a volunteer, Doherty was part of the violence emanating from his company, though he is not forthcoming about any acts of violence which were perpetrated, or whether he was personally responsible for any killings or bombings at that time. He was, however, found guilty, not of a criminal offence, but of a misdemeanour which led him to an IRA court of inquiry. He says he 'got carried away' at a dance after having a 'few drinks', and his behaviour was witnessed by an IRA officer who preferred charges against him. As a result he was suspended from operations for one week. The reason for the reprimand was probably the security risk a drunk volunteer posed to the organisation, particularly if he was an active volunteer. Concern was probably expressed that his behaviour could have led to his arrest by soldiers or that he was showing traits which the IRA did not wish publicly displaced. Doherty relies on the IRA's concern with his image as the motive for his suspension:

The IRA take into account that we must show to the general public republicans in a very high light. You know, culture, in Belfast. If somebody is very, very good, you would say he is a good republican. Republicans are seen as the highest stage in Irish society, and of course, myself walking about drinking and whatnot, that brings the IRA into disrepute, so that at that particular time I was charged, but I have had a clean record all the way through.

During the early 1970s, and following Doherty's release, IRA bombings became a way of life. Civilians suffered terribly, but Doherty explains the loss of life by arguing that all wars have civilian casualties. In court he uses the examples of Vietnam, World War II and the American Revolution. His view of death is epitomised by his comment: 'such is the sad fact of war'. He points out that the IRA always apologises when innocent life is lost, and sets up an internal inquiry to establish whether the fault was that of its own volunteers. He ignores the statistics for the period and conveniently forgets 'Bloody Friday' in 1972 when IRA units from across Belfast planted bombs at numerous business premises in the city. I was a reporter and saw the carnage. Many civilians, mostly shoppers, were killed and scores of people maimed. Doherty says IRA bomb warnings were ignored. The fact is that so many bombs were planted that the security forces and emergency services did not have sufficient warning from the IRA to clear civilians from the large number of targets. I remember sitting in a newspaper office listening to an increasing number of bomb alerts on the police radio frequency. When the first few bombs exploded, pandemonium broke out across the city. Doherty says twenty-five or twenty-six IRA units were involved in the operation but that some of the bomb warnings given to the police were ignored. 'It was a very, very sad day for everybody,' he says, 'including IRA volunteers.' Was his own unit involved? He has never said.

The events of that day will be for ever etched on my mind – the devastation, the senseless waste of innocent life, and the IRA's cynical explanation that their bomb warnings had been deliberately ignored. The police radio communications called announcements of bomb warnings by the score. The first bomb exploded in Donegal Street and it shattered windows in our building. This was one of twenty-two bombs planted within a one-mile radius of Belfast city centre during a busy shopping day. As other bombs went off, people panicked and, in their haste to leave the city, caused traffic chaos. The security, fire and ambulance authorities had no means of clearing such a large area, or reaching the injured swiftly. At Oxford Street a bomb exploded beside a bus station. Two soldiers arriving on the scene were killed; four people in the terminus waiting-room were blown to pieces. Debris and parts of bodies littered the scene; the injured lay bleeding in the wrecked bus station. In all, nine people died in Belfast, some of them teenagers, and scores were injured. The majority of the bombs were planted by members of the 3rd Battalion in North Belfast, which included units from the Ardoyne and New Lodge areas.

That evening I drove through Belfast. Along Oxford Street and through the virtually deserted city centre hung the silence of cemeteries, as if Belfast had become one large burial ground. It was difficult to come to terms with driving along a street where several hours earlier six human lives had been destroyed. I often felt like that in the city; as the years passed, there were so many streets, roads, alleyways where human life was lost to the savagery of the conflict, and sometimes I would suddenly look at a street name and see it in terms of the image of a tortured corpse. To use Doherty's language, there were many very, very sad days for everybody.

In court Doherty has described the happy days – such as St Patrick's Day 1973, when the commander of 7 Company suspended active service operations to mark a day of celebration in the area. According to Doherty this was also a practice on other special occasions such as Christmas Day. Volunteers were only required to be on 'standby', which entailed patrolling the neighbourhood to prevent rioting or drunken brawls, and to ensure that cars carrying loyalist murder squads did not penetrate the district.

Doherty and two volunteers were patrolling a street when they were stopped by an army patrol. Doherty was found to be in possession of a starting pistol, hardly a lethal weapon, but sufficient to contravene firearms legislation in Northern Ireland. His reason for having it was unclear and I can only conclude that it was to be used to frighten boisterous drunks, or impress the uninitiated. He was taken to the place of his first arrest, Glenravel Street base, and questioned.

I was taken to the army section of the police station where I was brought to the cellar and given the routine torture. I will not go into it because it only repeats itself. They were looking for information. I told them that as a volunteer and under the Geneva Convention I am not saying anything. They went about torturing me.

In court, his use of language has always tended towards the extreme, and his willingness to admit to membership of the IRA implied naïvety – or bravado. He was charged with possession of the starting pistol, and sentenced to a one-year prison term. At the age of eighteen he was facing imprisonment for a second term – or third, if one includes his period in borstal. He entered Long Kesh once again as a political prisoner, declared his IRA affiliation before the Prison Governor, and was placed in an IRA compound.

He rightly says that all IRA prisoners, convicted or interned, were accorded political status by the prison authorities. Permitted to wear their choice of clothes which included combat fatigues, they drilled and organised themselves in accordance with paramilitary rules. The IRA command structure as well as the loyalist leadership in the camp, though in separate compounds, were officially recognised, to the extent that the Governor and his staff dealt directly with the opposing terrorist leaders. Doherty was encouraged to undergo education in politics and military strategy, designed to prepare him for the rank of officer. His date for release was set for Christmas 1973, in accordance with three months' remission for good behaviour.

Six weeks prior to the release date he was taken aside by the IRA officer commanding his compound and informed that the remainder of his imprisonment would be spent on an intensive training course: 'I was taken, myself and ten or twelve other prisoners who were getting out. We were given what you would call a West Point or Sandhurst training. We would do drill, command jumps, unarmed combat, how to be an officer, how to give orders, how to use directives and weapons training.' The training was standard practice for volunteers anxious to return to active service, and was testimony to the IRA's interest in those committed to armed conflict. Not all prisoners were put through this type of training, because some decided to leave the IRA while in Long Kesh and return to their families and freedom. Doherty was part of a hard core who made it plain to the IRA in Long Kesh that they wished reinstatement in active service. Such was the secret communication between the IRA in the camp and their colleagues outside that Doherty's commitment and availability were relayed to the IRA commander in the New Lodge.

On the day of his release the officer in charge of his compound, which the IRA designated Cage 13, F Company, told him he had twenty-four hours to report for active service. On his return to Belfast he met his parents – and a prearranged IRA contact, who informed him that he was entitled to two weeks' leave of absence. Doherty insisted that one week was sufficient; he wished to return to active service as soon as possible. On his return to duty he accepted a staff-officer commission in C Company, 3rd Battalion. He undertook the role of quartermaster, and was responsible for the security of arms dumps, the concealment, cleaning and distribution of weapons. When his company needed ammunition he requisitioned supplies from the battalion quartermaster. He was also part of the decision-making process in C Company, which included the choice of targets, and the deployment of men and resources. His life became a hectic round of furtive meetings, while he constantly evaded the watchful eyes of patrolling soldiers. Aware that if he was seen in the company of known activists or in suspicious circumstances his criminal record would lead to his being reinterned, he was unable to visit his parents: the security forces had the family home under surveillance because of Doherty's involvement. The IRA told him to vary continuously his living location, and he remained 'on the run', staying in a different house as often as possible, sometimes with friends or relatives.

On 1 February 1974 he received a directive from the quarter-master of the Belfast Brigade requisitioning explosives for the 1st Battalion. Doherty removed 80lb of gelignite from one of his supply dumps and placed it in a car. He decided personally to transport the explosives across Belfast to the 3rd Battalion area of operations situated in the west of the city. As a staff officer he had no obligation to risk a journey across a city where military roadblocks were a constant feature of daily life. Perhaps he was motivated by the explosives request coming from a high-ranking officer whom he wished to impress, or the brigade staff who were his ultimate superiors. He was delivering what was in effect an unprimed bomb, but his journey was short. As he left the New Lodge he was forced to halt at a military roadblock, the car was searched and he was arrested. His court appearance provided him with a public platform which he exploited to announce his membership of the IRA, and, in keeping with IRA policy at that juncture, he refused to recognise the jurisdiction of a 'foreign court'. A volunteer's non-recognition of the courts was not a personal decision. It was a traditional republican tactic, until the Provisional IRA subtly altered the rules. Joseph Doherty had sought advice on whether to recognise the court and received a communication through his IRA superiors that he was to refuse to accept its jurisdiction. He was in a vulnerable position legally, because the evidence against him for possession of explosives was unambiguous – caught in the act. If there had been any opportunity for him to dispute the charge the IRA might have advised him to contest it, in the expectation that he would return to the streets and active service.

The IRA, in principle, does not recognise British courts, and at the outset of the conflict its members were told to obey that rule. Internment, and the use of special powers of arrest, reduced the numbers of trained men available for active service, and the IRA decided that one means of offsetting that difficulty was to bend IRA rules by advising non-recognition only in cases where a legal defence against conviction was unlikely to achieve results. That decision exemplified how the IRA could react to events, and prove willing to engage in deception to achieve its ends, and it also illustrated how the Provisionals refused to be bound by the doctrinaire tactics of republicans of the past. The IRA argued that if every volunteer were to be arrested, and were then to refuse to recognise the court, the security forces could exploit such intransigence by preferring trumped-up charges against large numbers of republicans. In permitting the use of the non-recognition principle in those cases which were beyond redemption, the Provisionals publicly kept alive their principle of branding the courts as 'foreign'.

For the third time in his eighteen years, Joseph Doherty was once again behind bars. He says that as soon as he entered Crumlin Road prison his first thoughts turned to escape, getting back to the war. He began scheming, assisted by another prisoner. When he finalised a draft plan he presented it for approval to the IRA escape committee in the jail.

You don't walk to the escape committee and say, 'I want to go over the wall.' You must go with plans, how much rope you need, how many blades and how long it will take you to get out, etc. Me and this other fellow volunteer went to the committee officer. He looked at the plans. He said it was pretty good. He says: 'I'll sent out word to the Brigade.'

Doherty's request was one of many. All IRA prisoners were under orders to devise a means of escape. Doherty says prisoners were digging holes, hiding food and constantly storing items which could prove useful. His plan was basic and permission was granted. On a prearranged day at 4.00 am he and a companion, dressed in combat gear, sawed through the bars of their cell and lowered themselves to the prison yard. As they made their way to the perimeter wall with ropes and a grappling hook, they were caught in searchlight beams and apprehended. Doherty was returned to court and sentenced to an additional eighteen months' imprisonment.

His attempted escape from the seemingly impregnable walls of Crumlin Road prison was very much in keeping with the history of Irish republicanism and endeared him to his fellow volunteers. Every imprisoned IRA man was obliged to have escape uppermost in his thoughts. The IRA believed that escape confirmed its status as an army at war: it helped to depict its men as prisoners of war held by a foreign power which had no right of jurisdiction in Ireland. The history of republicanism contained many famous episodes of leading IRA men escaping from jails in Britain and Ireland. Their escapades were central to the myth-making process, and associated the IRA with the heroic celluloid images of *The Great Escape* in which British and Americans outwitted the Germans, or

*Colditz*, the film which portrayed the ingenuity of British service-men who escaped from a heavily guarded fortress.

Planning escapes was a means by which the IRA instilled hope for freedom in its men and, in practical terms, provided a distraction from the boredom and isolation of prison life. It brought the men closer together, gave them a common goal and inculcated in them the belief that as prisoners of war they remained part of the struggle. The POW image ideally suited the men in Long Kesh with its Nissen huts, barbed wire, searchlights and inmates dressed in civilian clothing. However, Crumlin Road had always been the Northern Ireland state symbol of an escape-proof establishment – a factor which further encouraged Doherty to view escape from there as a major propaganda coup. Within the Catholic population there was high regard for anyone who tried to escape but the IRA always knew that a major prison break would enhance its standing as an army capable of outwitting the enemy.

A veteran IRA man who had been a prisoner in Crumlin Road and Long Kesh told me he spent much of his time 'scheming' and 'dreaming' of escaping:

It was always in your thoughts. In a way it was a natural thing to see yourself as a prisoner of war with a duty to escape. Without it there would have been an acceptance that we were criminals, who agreed with our incarceration. There was glamour in it, because we all had visions of how guys escaped from the Germans. You know all those American films about guys building tunnels under the wire. They were heroes, and our people needed similar heroes. We all knew about IRA escapes in history, and I suppose we all wanted to make our own history. Crumlin Road prison was a tough one, because only one or two people had ever escaped from it before the seventies, but that didn't stop us planning. We would debate all kinds of methods like the use of hacksaws, we would make ropes from bedding, build files on every warder and his movements and work at ways of smuggling things like hacksaws into the prison. We made imitation pistols, carved from wood and painted with polish, to resemble the real thing. In Crumlin Road there was no way of tunnelling. It was a heavily secure place with individual cells, courtyards, high walls, sentries, and was easily controlled by the prison staff. The Kesh offered slightly more freedom and it was on an old airfield. It was better for tunnelling but no easy ride. The Brits knew all about escaping. After all, they perfected it.

The authorities reckoned that Doherty was more secure in Long

Kesh and transferred him there. He discovered that little had changed in the camp, except for the IRA command structure. There were two battalions in the IRA section of the prison, with each battalion controlling its own compounds and Nissen huts, while the other part of the camp held ordinary criminals. Irrespective of the geographical division between IRA battalions in the camp, all prisoners were given political status by the camp authorities. In each compound there were approximately 100 men housed in corrugated tin huts. The compounds, approximately twenty-five of them, were ringed with barbed wire – which led to the IRA description of them as 'cages'. Each battalion had a quartermaster, who was able to provide ropes, wire cutters, shovels and light bulbs for tunnelling, and every cage had its escape committee. Doherty was placed in C Company.

Ordinary criminals were billeted in a corner of the camp and designated cooking and laundry duties. Doherty says the authorities did not permit political prisoners to undertake such duties, because they would have used cooking utensils and other equipment for tunnelling.

The British Government recognised that the image of an internment camp was internationally damaging, and proceeded to build a modern prison alongside the camp. At the outset of construction, they established a procedure by which all communication about Long Kesh referred to the camp as the Maze Prison. All press information was designed to ensure that 'Maze Prison' became common currency in newspaper stories about the camp: as a title, 'Maze' had been dictated by the fact that the camp was situated in a townland known as the Maze. The building of a new and modern prison reflected a realisation that terrorism was a long-term problem, and that the IRA was gaining politically from the existence of a concentration camp.

The arrival of large numbers of convicted terrorists created a new dimension. They were achieving political status in keeping with Government policy following internment. The Government wished to phase out internment and to criminalise the IRA by building a new prison for convicted terrorists and in so doing erase the political status which conveyed the image of prisoners of war. The new prison was built in blocks in the shape of the letter H and became known to Catholics as 'the H-Blocks' rather than the Maze Prison. However, in 1974 political status had not been abolished, and Doherty undertook his role as a volunteer prisoner of war. His description of life in Long Kesh is an accurate and vivid portrayal of a prison system which the British Government of today would consider unthinkable, best consigned to history.

I held several staff positions from section leader to company staff to an officer's position. I was a company quartermaster, training officer, drill sergeant. I was in charge of the men in the yard and military formation. My God, I was everything. I was a company finance officer and the highest rank I ever held was adjutant. I was second-in-command of a company of seventy-eight men.

On IRA anniversaries such as Easter, when the 1916 Rising was celebrated, Doherty paraded his volunteers in front of other staff officers. They dressed in the equivalent of combat gear and marched behind flags which were made in the camp. Volunteers paraded round the confines of the 'cage' and fell in line in front of the officers to hear the reading of statements from the IRA leadership in Ireland, from the camp leadership, and messages of solidarity from the other IRA companies within Long Kesh. Two minutes' silence was requested in memory of IRA dead, and bagpipes were played while the flags were lowered. In each 'cage' this ceremony was re-enacted, and if the barbed wire had not been present the scene would have resembled a military parade ground. The loyalist paramilitaries in the camp celebrated their own anniversaries; their special day was 12 July, to mark the 1690 defeat of James II of England by Williamite forces, and they also paraded in full colours on Christmas Day. The British soldiers and prison warders made no attempt to disrupt these displays of para-militarism. Doherty recalls that soldiers showed respect by keeping their guns out of sight and remaining quiet. The warders 'kept well away' from the proceedings, he says.

In 1975 Doherty received written citations from IRA commanders in the camp in recognition of his aptitude for learning and his work in helping other volunteers. In all he received sixteen citations, including one in 1976 which stated:

*Competition*
*Long Kesh 1976*
*Fourth Battalion, Belfast Brigade*
IRISH REPUBLICAN ARMY

This citation is bestowed on Joseph Doherty who won first place in the prize for reciting poetry, for Irish dancing and singing, being the director of an Irish play, a qualified Irish teacher and acting in a play.

The use of the term 'Fourth Battalion' seems odd in relation to the known structure of the IRA, which at that time had three battalions within the Belfast Brigade. The decision to credit the prisons of Long Kesh and Crumlin Road as the 4th Battalion was a sign of the IRA's determination to ensure that prisoners continued to view themselves as active volunteers. It indicated that the IRA was concerned that prison life would mentally detach volunteers from the ongoing conflict. In creating a 4th Battalion within the prisons the IRA was defining prisoners as an integral part of the Irish Republican Army.

Doherty's citations were indicative of the importance given by the IRA to the education of volunteers in prison. His formal education was augmented with a knowledge of Irish history, albeit a prejudiced one, the acquiring of another language, Gaelic, and a developing talent as a public speaker, actor and director. Some of those talents and extrovert qualities would eventually prove useful to Doherty in court battles in the United States many years later. The IRA sought to educate all of its prison volunteers, and some of them read serious books for the first time in their lives, acted in plays and compensated for their lack of formal education. This proved a significant factor when the IRA began to develop a strategy for its political wing, Sinn Fein, and provided articulate speakers for a future campaign of armed struggle and politics, known as the armalite and ballot-box strategy. Many young men like Joseph Doherty, who joined the organisation because of emotional reaction to events, found themselves in prison learning about conflict and acquiring the ideological commitment which provided them with argued motivation.

Several days before Christmas 1979 Doherty was released, and in typical fashion he reported to the IRA within twenty-four hours to request a one-week vacation, which was granted. On his return to duties he discovered that the IRA structures of 1972 had been refined. The IRA was steadily learning that the heady days of conflict were ill-disciplined, and the Ardoyne 'action, action' tactics of Martin Meehan were no longer acceptable. The IRA was preparing for a long war. Membership was no longer accorded to large numbers of teenagers and young men. Vetting was strictly applied, and internal security was of paramount importance. Battalion structures were narrowed to define the role and expertise of volunteers, unlike the 1972 arrangements which were unwieldy. The concept of the company with individual sections was now considered inefficient, and incapable of realising the potential of individuals. It was also easily penetrated by agents of military intelligence and Special Branch. The organisation, like a commercial business, had been through a rationalisation of its structures and role, and the changes did not go unnoticed to a veteran campaigner like Doherty:

It was basically the same IRA but for a structural difference. The responsibilities of a volunteer in the 1972 period was offensive, defensive, social work, police work, intelligence work. In 1978–80, when I got out, the army was broken up – base intelligence units, engineering units, internal security units and, of course, the units to which I reported, the active service units, the infantry.

In what was fundamentally a cell system, engineering and intelligence cells operated independently and provided means which enabled active service units. The intelligence cell supplied the information required to choose, assess and evaluate targets. The engineering cell made the bombs; internal security unmasked informers within the cells, protected the cells from penetration, and adjudicated on matters of IRA indiscipline or treachery. It was a reversal of 1972, when too many people knew about particular operations, too much authority resided within company sections and the result was a lack of co-ordination in operational planning and policy.

The active service unit, the ASU, was designed as a close-knit grouping of volunteers who operated together without contact with others. They were the cutting edge of the conflict. Every battalion area had several active service units, each briefed separately before operations. Doherty was placed in an ASU with young men who were keen for action. Among those with whom he would soon operate were Angelo Fusco, Robert Joseph Campbell and Paul Patrick Magee. Some of the volunteers came from the west of the city, an interesting indication that in putting together such a grouping, the IRA was less concerned about battalion areas, and more intent on shaping a group of experienced terrorists who could operate anywhere in the city. One factor which influenced the IRA decision was the procurement of six M60 machine-guns of the type used in the 'Rambo' movies. The M60, a heavy-calibre weapon, proved devastating if used in an urban environment. The six machine-guns were stolen in a raid on a National Guard armoury in Danvers, Massachusetts, and smuggled to Northern Ireland. Doherty and his fellow volunteers in the unit were trained in the use of those weapons in January 1980, in training camps in the west of Ireland. He denies that he ever handled one, although he admits that active service personnel were keen to see the M60s in training. An IRA source confirmed for me that Doherty and other active service teams were instructed in the M60s before they were made available for Belfast operations. This was an IRA prerequisite to the appearance of any new weapon. Volunteers with access to it were to know its specifications; how to break it down for concealment; how to clean it; and, more crucially, how to employ its firepower in short or long bursts, and what to do if the gun jammed during an operation.

Doherty's claim that he was not trained in its use is a ploy to detach him from the purpose for which it was used. The arrival of the M60 was a deciding factor in Doherty's life. Ironically, the man with responsibility for investigating the theft of the M60s was FBI Special Agent Frank Schulte, who later tracked Doherty in New York.

# 5

# The Active
# Service Unit

Doherty is not forthcoming about his active service role in the first five months of 1980, but the activities of other volunteers with whom he operated at that time lead to the crucial events in which he is known to have been involved. The active service unit was equipped with an M60 and an assortment of other weapons which included two rifles, one of them a Heckler and Koch automatic and several handguns. The role of the unit was to kill policemen and soldiers with a prestige weapon, namely the M60.

On the periphery of the gang (several of whom cannot be named) was James Kennedy, a young man whose peculiar employment history had brought him into close contact with the IRA, and subsequently the active service unit. When he left school, Kennedy joined the Government Civil Service as a clerk, but his employment was terminated because he was absent from work for a six-month period owing to nervous depression. On his recovery, he illegally claimed state unemployment benefits while working as a taxi driver. He enjoyed the freedom of the job and the tax-dodged money. He worked for several taxi companies, driving his own car for 'Downtown Taxis'. According to Kennedy, Downtown Taxis had close links with the IRA, and permitted the IRA to borrow cabs, later pretending they were hijacked. He says that a number of girls in the company's employ served prison sentences, and Downtown employed nobody without IRA approval.

Kennedy got his job because his car was used several times by the IRA, and on one occasion, in September 1979, by an IRA hit-team who killed a prison governor. The police interviewed Kennedy but, in keeping with IRA instructions, he said he could not identify the 'hijackers', and repeated the lie at an inquest into the governor's murder. He approved of the political aims of the IRA, but says he disapproved of violence. Whatever his ideological commitment, he was a minor player in the armed struggle, whether from conviction or fear.

Kennedy knew Angelo Fusco to be an active member of the IRA, who was 'on the run' from the security forces, and who owned a flat in the Turf Lodge area, a short distance from his parents' shop. Angelo rarely stayed in the flat, fearing detection, and spent most nights in his sister's house in Horn Drive in the Lenadoon district on the outskirts of West Belfast. Kennedy was frequently given the task of conveying Angelo to Horn Drive under cover of darkness, and collecting him the following morning for the return journey to his flat in Turf Lodge. Kennedy undertook these journeys without levying a charge, and they became a regular feature of his life after January 1980. On some occasions he also transported other members of the IRA in Angelo's presence. Before long he was introduced to Robert Joseph Campbell, Paul 'Dingus' Magee, Michael 'Beaky' McKee, Anthony Gerard Sloan and his brother Gerard Michael Sloan. He did not meet Joseph Doherty.

But Kennedy had a secret life – of which his IRA associates were unaware. While driving his taxi, he had come under police scrutiny, was arrested and informed he could be charged with several motoring offences, and dishonestly receiving state benefits. His arrest was a familiar police tactic of selecting someone criminally employed, then putting pressure on them to assist the security forces in return for police inaction; a form of 'amnesty'. Kennedy established contact with a police constable and, in the light of later events, may have begun work as a police agent at that time.

Unknown to Kennedy, three members of the active service unit planned an operation for 20 February 1980. The leader of the group was Gerard Michael Sloan and the two volunteers he chose to assist him were Angelo Fusco and Michael 'Beaky' McKee. They forcibly took possession of an apartment, 38F Monagh Road, in the Turf Lodge area, early on the morning of 22 February, armed with an M60, its ammunition belt, a .223 rifle equipped with telescopic sights and a pistol. Outside the premises they parked a car to use in their escape.

Their target was any British army patrol which passed their location. Close to their position an army post ran in an irregular line, roughly in a north–south direction. It consisted of a fence with an entrance into the post towards its southern end; to the west of the fence was a patch of waste ground. From the window of the second-storey maisonette, Sloan and his companions had a view in a northerly direction along the line of the army post. The distance from 38F Monagh Road to the southern end of the fence was approximately 900 feet. Sloan set up the M60 on a window ledge and fed the belt of bullets into the weapon. McKee held the belt to ensure it would feed smoothly into the barrel when the gun was fired. Fusco knelt on one knee and sighted his rifle to check that he had a direct line of fire. At 11.38, a four-man foot patrol of the Royal Scots Regiment moved down the side of the army-post fence. Their objective was to hug the side of the fence, constantly on the lookout for snipers, and to enter the post through what appeared to be a gap in the fencing, but was, in fact, the entrance to their base.

In the lead was Corporal Cochrane, who kept his self-loading rifle pointed towards the rows upon rows of apartments and houses in the Turf Lodge. In keeping with military procedures, each man moved slowly, guarding front, rear – and the area to their right where the gunmen were hiding. As the soldiers neared the base entrance, Sloan and Fusco opened fire. The M60 delivered an automatic burst of eight rounds and the rifle five rounds in single fire. Bullets struck the ground in front of Sergeant Macfayden, and the four soldiers dived for cover. As quickly as the action began, it ended with no injuries. The three terrorists hurried to their car with their weapons and left the area.

Several hours after the shooting Kennedy was repairing his car when he received a telephone call from Angelo Fusco. Fusco said his wife was in a house in Arizona Street in the Falls district and he would be grateful if Kennedy would drive her to their home in Turf Lodge. Kennedy complied. In Arizona Street, he knocked on the front door, and was greeted by Angelo, who, Kennedy noticed, was tense and appeared to be 'under a great deal of pressure'. Angelo asked to borrow the taxi; Kennedy replied that he had been repairing it and that Angelo would be unable to drive it because the gear stick was faulty. As their conversation developed, a man whom I shall call 'Mr A' appeared from an adjoining room. Simultaneously, the front door knocker sounded, and Mr A reached to open the door. Angelo produced an Astra 9mm pistol, quickly pulled back the carriage of the gun, releasing a round from the magazine into the barrel, and levelled the weapon at the door.

Mr A opened the door and a member of the IRA, not yet known to Kennedy, entered; Kennedy, frightened by this episode, handed over his car keys. Angelo told him to sit in the adjoining room and 'make himself comfortable'. In the room were Gerard Sloan and 'Beaky' McKee, with a radio tuned to the local police frequency, listening for news of their morning's attack. Kennedy sat and watched them, unaware of their earlier activities – until his curiosity was aroused by Sloan, who remarked to McKee, 'We missed the bastards.' It soon became apparent to Kennedy that they were referring to an attack on an army patrol.

From where he sat, Kennedy could see the street outside; the venetian blinds did not completely obscure the view. Next, Angelo left the house, clambered into the taxi and reversed it down Arizona Street. The newly arrived IRA man reappeared, carrying a large green canvas bag of a type used by combat troops for storing their gear. When dropped on the floor, the bag thudded metallically. It was removed from the room, placed in the hallway and minutes later another car drew up to the house: bag and vehicle were driven away. Kennedy remained in the room for another fifteen minutes, observing the two gunmen still engrossed in the police radio transmissions. Angelo returned and handed Kennedy his car keys with a warning that there should be no mention of Arizona Street, and what he had witnessed. Fusco sarcastically thanked him for the loan of the car.

One week later Kennedy found himself again in Angelo's company, and the conversation turned to the events of their previous meeting. Angelo talked about the attack on the foot patrol, and Kennedy remarked that, if the M60 was such a good weapon, why did it not deliver casualties? Angelo explained that the angle of fire was 'much too sharp – too acute'. He revealed that Kennedy's car had been used after the attack to transport the weapons from Arizona Street to their 'ultimate destination'.

On 7 April Kennedy decided to go to Dublin with Emmanuel Fusco. The trip was intended as a weekend vacation, with Kennedy driving. On the evening of the second day in Dublin, a friend of the Fusco family informed Emmanuel that there was a telephone call for him from Belfast, and a number he should ring. Emmanuel made his call from the friend's home, and immediately said it was imperative that he return to Belfast. Kennedy reminded Emmanuel that the purpose of the trip was to relax and spend several days in Dublin; Emmanuel replied angrily that he would steal a car, and do his own driving. Kennedy was then persuaded to drive Emmanuel. They left immediately.

In Belfast Emmanuel got out of the car and walked across the road to a house. He returned and politely asked Kennedy to drive Angelo to his home in Turf Lodge. Kennedy agreed; Angelo appeared from the house and quickly jumped into the car. At Angelo's house, Kennedy informed him he was tired, and was heading home for 'a good night's sleep'. Kennedy says Angelo was not happy with this arrangement, became annoyed and aggressive. Kennedy relented, and entered the house, where they drank tea. Then Kennedy rose to leave but Angelo insisted he stay. Kennedy agreed to sleep on a couch. Why Angelo insisted that Kennedy remained there is uncertain. Maybe he did not trust him but was unwilling to act on his suspicions.

While Kennedy slept, the active service unit went into action. Their plan, to ambush a security force patrol, had been formulated while Kennedy was in Dublin. As he was driving back to Belfast on 8 April, several events were slotting into place as part of the planning, and one of them was the return of Emmanuel Fusco to the city. His expertise as a burglar was essential to the scheme.

First a car was needed by the gang and this was acquired in typical IRA fashion. At 10.00 pm Henry Rosbottom, a resident of West Belfast, was driving his Mazda car into his home on the Springfield Road when he was impeded by three men wearing hooded anoraks. They told him they were members of the IRA and were taking his car. They took the keys, and warned him not to report the vehicle missing until lunchtime the following day. Mr Rosbottom was ordered to stay in his home, while the car was driven away. By the time he reported the incident, tragic events had taken place.

At 11.30 pm Catherine Maguire and her brother and father were asleep in bed at their home at 4 Doon Road in the Stewartstown area of West Belfast. Their mother, an auxiliary nurse, was in hospital on night duty. At 11.32 pm the telephone rang in the Maguire home and Catherine wakened, went downstairs and answered it. She only had time to repeat her telephone number when the call was abandoned. She returned to bed but minutes later was disturbed by a knocking at the front door. She went to the door, opened it and was confronted by two men, one of whom jammed his foot against the door to prevent her closing it. The men announced they were members of the Provisional IRA and they were 'taking over the house'. They removed the family to a downstairs room and warned them not to escape.

Emmanuel Fusco's return to Belfast was followed quickly by his minor part in the operation. He was instructed to enter a library building in the Stewartstown Day Centre directly opposite the Maguire home. While an accomplice remained outside to provide a warning in the event of a police or army patrol approaching the scene, Emmanuel planned a forced entry of the library. He scrutinised the building and its alarm system, and gained entry through smashing the glass panelling of a side door. His objective was to get into the building without setting off alarms and make it look like an ordinary burglary. Once inside he ransacked the library before making his escape.

By 6.00 am four members of the active service unit were in the Maguire home – Anthony Sloan, 'Beaky' McKee, Angelo Fusco and 'Dingus' Magee. They were armed with two of the weapons used in the attack on the foot patrol, the FAL self-loading rifle equipped with telescopic sight and the M60 machine-gun, as well as a Garand 30.06 self-loading rifle. By any standards they were extremely well armed, with the awesome capabilities of the M60 representing an overabundance of firepower. Sloan was the motivating force of this group, and he told them he would use the M60. He was overwhelmed with the size of the weapon and was determined to compensate for his lack of accuracy in the previous engagement.

Every part of the plan was beginning to slot into place and as dawn broke three of the gunmen were positioned in the two upstairs bedrooms of the house. One remained to guard the family and to be ready to facilitate an escape route from the house to a Mazda car parked at the rear. At 8.25, as the IRA hitmen scrutinised their target zone, their plan was partly realised with the arrival of Mrs Ann Patterson, the librarian at the day centre. She noticed the damage to the side door and entered the library. Within ten minutes of inspecting the destruction, she phoned the police at the nearby Woodburn station. A constable on duty received her call, and phoned her back to verify that her call was genuine. He notified a mobile patrol and furnished them with details of the break-in.

The patrol decided to investigate, oblivious that they were driving into an IRA trap. In the front of the police Landrover was the driver, Constable Fitzpatrick, and alongside him Constable

Magill. In the rear was Woman Constable Hall and Constable Browning. The Landrover arrived and parked outside the library at 9.00 am. As its crew dismounted they came under heavy fire. Forty-three rounds were discharged from the M60 from one bedroom as well as sixteen rounds from the FAL self-loading rifle. Eight shots were fired from the other bedroom by a gunman with the Garand 30.06. Constable Magill was struck by five bullets, one of which killed him instantly as it entered his chest and exited through his abdomen. The other rounds struck him in the legs. The woman constable was wounded in both hands and Constable Fitzpatrick was seriously wounded in the left elbow. The fourth member of the police unit, Constable Browning, received bullet wounds to the right leg and lower back. The three constables later recovered from their injuries.

By the time Kennedy woke up in Fusco's house the killing was over, and Angelo was seated on the floor listening to the police radio frequency. He told Kennedy that there had been a shooting attack on policemen. Kennedy, who had slept soundly and been unaware of Fusco's absence from the house or participation in the gun attack, excused himself and drove to the Downtown Taxis depot.

At 11.00 am he was standing in the premises when Anthony Sloan and Mr A drove into the depot car park. Kennedy says:

Sloan was usually very particular about his appearance and was always well groomed, but on this occasion he was unshaven, his hair was a mess and he looked as though he hadn't been to bed. He was wearing a black anorak, a rally-car type of jacket with hoops or stripes on the upper arm; the stripes were yellow and red or blue with an emblem or crest between them. A pair of gloves were sticking out of one of the pockets with the finger parts protruding. He was wearing denim jeans. His jacket was lying open and he had a bulge at the waistband of his pants. Both Sloan and Mr A seemed very anxious and uptight. They came in and left a couple of minutes later. They drove off alongside the Andersontown Road in a red Fiat car.

Ten minutes later Kennedy answered the phone in the depot, and on the line was Anthony Sloan complaining that the Fiat had broken down. He gave Kennedy his location and the number of a house at Dalewood Avenue close to Arizona Street where Kennedy had first seen the M60. Kennedy told a fellow taxi driver that he was going to tow Sloan's car, and the driver (whom I will call 'Mr B') agreed to accompany him. They drove to Dalewood Avenue, but there was no sign of the red Fiat. Kennedy pulled his car alongside the house mentioned by Sloan. What he did not realise was that Sloan had deliberately given him a house number not connected with the IRA. Kennedy asked the householder if she had seen a red Fiat or a person of Sloan's description repairing such a car. As the householder made to reply, Sloan appeared from a house opposite, a semi-detached bungalow, and signalled to Kennedy and Mr B to join him. Sloan's precaution in sending Kennedy to the wrong address suggested he was suspicious of the young taxi driver. He was ensuring that if Kennedy betrayed him he would not be at the appointed place. Sloan was undoubtedly anticipating an army or police raid to snatch him. Kennedy left Mr B in his car and entered the bungalow with Sloan.

Sloan said he wished for a favour, but Kennedy indicated that he would be unable to help him because of the presence of Mr B. Sloan said that this was not a problem, and ordered him to bring Mr B to the house. Kennedy did as requested and as he re-entered the house he saw Mr A in the hallway. Kennedy was aware that Sloan was anxious and 'concerned'. He told Kennedy he required him to move 'some gear', by which Kennedy understood explosives or guns. Kennedy retorted that such an undertaking was foolhardy because the killing of the police constable had resulted in the police and army 'saturating the area with personnel and roadblocks'. In a moment of bravado, he asked Sloan why he could 'not do it himself'. Sloan replied that he only had the Mazda which was used in the getaway at Stewartstown, and the police radio transmissions confirmed that the security forces knew the type and registration number of the vehicle. The car was garaged in the house they were in. Kennedy saw the risk increasing and refused to help. Sloan reacted by physically taking hold of Kennedy and threatening to shoot him. Kennedy says he was frightened for his life, and was aware of the risk of antagonising Sloan and Mr A. Sloan directed his threatening attitude to Mr B, while Mr A led Kennedy to the kitchen, where he saw a hand-grenade on a table.

It was the type seen in British war movies. It was oval with lumps over the side and a handle coming from the top of it. Also on the table was a pistol which looked like the gun which Angelo Fusco had in the house in Arizona Street. Next to the table, two rifles were propped against a wall and a machine-gun was on a stand at the wall. One weapon looked like the type British soldiers carried in Belfast, with a telescopic sight on it. On the rifle, the little bump on the flashguard was reversed. The second rifle looked older and longer than anything I'd seen before. A metal box seemed to be attached to the machine-gun and on the box was brown masking tape. There was also a belt attached to the machine-gun with bullets in it.

Kennedy was looking at the weapons used in the killing of Constable Magill and he was terrified. Sloan entered the kitchen and said the weapons were being moved to Mr B's house – an obvious sign that Kennedy's companion had succumbed to pressure to help the IRA. Kennedy enquired if the weapons were to be moved in their present form, as they would be difficult to conceal. Sloan assured him that each weapon would be dismantled. Kennedy was told to sit in the front room and await instructions. The room was a familiar scene with seven men grouped round a portable radio listening to police messages. Kennedy recognised 'Beaky' McKee and 'Dingus' Magee. Minutes passed; then Sloan told Kennedy to reverse his car into the driveway and open the boot. Sloan and Mr A appeared with a green canvas bag identical to the one used at Arizona Street. They loaded it into the car boot and Sloan climbed into the front passenger seat with Mr A in the rear. Kennedy began driving towards Mr B's home at River Close, aware that Sloan was armed with a 9mm pistol and Mr A was seated with a grenade between the palms of his hands. They left Kennedy in no doubt that if stopped at a roadblock they were ready for action, and were not going to give up the M60 and the rifles. When they arrived at River Close, Kennedy reversed the car off the main road and into the driveway. Mr B was there to meet them and the green bag was left in his house.

A few days later Kennedy was listening to a news broadcast which announced the murder of a retired Catholic civil servant from Horn Drive, a neighbourhood frequented by Angelo Fusco. Kennedy says that as a direct result of this tragedy he contacted Anthony Sloan and expressed his concern about the escalation in violence. Sloan replied that the civil servant had informed police at Woodburn station of the presence of the Mazda in his street and had given them a full description of it. 'That's why he was shot,' said Sloan. Kennedy says that he further pressed Sloan for information about the killing of Constable Magill, because he needed to know what he was being 'dragged into'. Sloan gave him a description of the takeover of the house, the fake burglary designed to entrap the police and the actual shooting. Sloan revealed that when he began firing the M60 he was 'so into his actions' that he lost control and was dragged from the window by his accomplices.

Kennedy was given an additional insight into the killing when, two weeks later, he was ferrying Angelo and Emmanuel to their sister's home. Angelo asked him if it had retrospectively occurred to him that his journey from Dublin had been crucial to the operation. Without waiting for Kennedy to reply, Angelo thanked him for moving the guns. Kennedy then manoeuvred the conversation to Emmanuel's role and Angelo replied to the effect that if one needed joinery work one hired a joiner, and if one was planning a burglary one hired a burglar.

A short time after this conversation Anthony Sloan contacted Kennedy and, when Kennedy arrived at a prearranged meeting place, Sloan's demeanour suggested a seriousness by now uncomfortably familiar to Kennedy. Sloan said that a Downtown taxi driver had been arrested and held for questioning by RUC detectives for seven days. He mentioned the man's name, which Kennedy recognised as that of a person whom he had seen in Sloan's company weeks earlier. Sloan added that this person had been questioned about the murder of Constable Magill, and about Mr A, Mr B and the house in Dalebrook Avenue where they had stored the weapons. While it was understandable, said Sloan, that Mr A's name would be raised during interrogation, it was strange that Mr B and the house should be known to police. Sloan regarded police reference to the latter as evidence of an informer in their midst. The questioning of Kennedy was inconclusive, and Sloan left him with a warning that anyone passing information to police would be executed.

If Kennedy hoped that his ordeal was over, or that Sloan believed his denials of betrayal, he was wrong. Several days later, Kennedy received a message from Sloan asking him to go to a house in the Twinbrook estate near Horn Drive where 'someone wished to talk to him'. Kennedy was suspicious and did not comply with the instruction. Six days later, he received a further communication from Sloan asking him to be at a drinking club on the Whiterock Road in West Belfast. Kennedy says he reckoned he would be safe in a club, and that a second refusal to meet Sloan would have cast added suspicion on him. As he pulled his car alongside the pavement at the club entrance, he was met by Sloan, who assured him that he should not worry. He should go into the club, have a drink, and someone would contact him there and provide him with an address where another person would talk to him. As these instructions were being spoken, Kennedy noticed two suspicious-looking men approaching his car. Instinctively, he surmised he was being lured into a trap by an unusually pleasant Sloan.

He reversed his car at speed and drove across Belfast to the east of the city, a predominantly Protestant area where the IRA would be unlikely to trace him. After seeking advice, he decided to drive to Dublin, because he believed his only protection was to plead his case to a senior IRA contact there, and to seek his advice about 'what was in store for him from the IRA in Belfast'. He was advised to return to Belfast even though he was worried that Sloan might shoot him. He drove back to Belfast the following morning and immediately phoned Anthony Sloan, who was in the Downtown taxi depot. Sloan seemed calmer, more sympathetic and rational than on other occasions, and offered to meet him at any time and any place Kennedy preferred.

'During our conversation he said that I had brought suspicion on myself by running off to Dublin, and he had the authority to have me shot. He said he knew I was across town and he had made an arrangement for IRA personnel to cross town if I would agree. He said I was messing them about by running away.'

Sloan's reference to 'IRA personnel' was shorthand for members of the organisation's internal security apparatus. Their task was to seek out informers and take them into custody for interrogation. They were also responsible for the grisly task of hooding and executing IRA staff who seriously transgressed, and for killing informers or agents who penetrated IRA ranks. Kennedy knew the import of Sloan's words and, remembering the advice he was given in Dublin, agreed to return to work the next day and meet Sloan after working hours. He went to Downtown Taxis as planned and worked normally until 6.00 pm. There was no sign of Sloan, and he accompanied another driver to the Lake Glen Hotel for drinks. The hotel was opposite the depot and he left a message at the depot to indicate his whereabouts in the event of Sloan's arrival. Within an hour Sloan walked into the Lake Glen with a man whom Kennedy did not know. The man was 5ft 8ins in height, stockily built, his hair uncombed, and Kennedy judged him to be in his late thirties or early forties. Sloan told Kennedy to finish drinking and go with the stranger. Kennedy says he looked at the man and the menace in his eyes was enough to convince him he had to obey the instructions.

The mystery figure, 'Mr C', was an officer in IRA internal security. He was assigned by the Belfast Brigade to find an informer in the M60 gang. The brigade was already aware that the gang's operations had been compromised following a report of the police interrogation of the Downtown taxi driver. The importance of the gang and its prestige weapon, the M60, was illustrated by the swift action of the brigade staff in ordering an inquiry. Anyone interrogated by police was immediately debriefed by IRA personnel, with the purpose of analysing the substance of police questioning in order to determine what the police knew. When it became apparent that police questions had indicated a knowledge of Mr B and the house in Dalebrook Avenue, IRA internal security contacted the gang and asked its members to confirm the seriousness of the situation. Sloan, acting as his unit's spokesman, said the police could not have known about Mr B because he was not an activist, and had been coerced into hiding the arms cache. The Dalebrook Avenue safe-house had been carefully chosen as a secure place and police could only have learned about it from an informer. The name of Mr A had been raised in the police interrogation, but Sloan did not consider that unusual, because Mr A was 'on the run' and all suspects in custody were routinely asked if they knew the whereabouts of wanted IRA men. Sloan said that, if an informer existed, the suspicion centred on Kennedy and Mr B, since they had both assisted in the weapons concealment, and both had been in the Dalebrook Avenue house.

Sloan was not prepared categorically to state that Kennedy was the more likely informer than Mr B, or vice versa. He pointed out the possibility that a householder in Dalebrook Avenue might have seen the weapons being moved and told the police. Kennedy's closeness to the Fusco brothers was, at that stage, his only form of protection, because his behaviour was tantamount to that of a man with something to fear. Sloan had explained to internal security that Kennedy was easily frightened and his behaviour was not necessarily proof of his guilt. At the hotel, Kennedy finished his drink and left with Sloan and Mr C. They travelled by car to the Ballymurphy housing estate, an area in West Belfast where the Provisionals were deeply rooted in the community. Kennedy said:

'Sloan took me to his sister's house. She handed him the key to her home and left. I went in followed by Mr C. As I walked into the front room, Mr C pushed me into a chair and Sloan closed the front door.'

Mr C began by asking about the Dublin trip several days earlier, and Kennedy explained he had gone to Dublin because he was frightened by Sloan's behaviour. Sloan intervened and admitted that he 'may have been too aggressive' to Kennedy the previous week, but that he needed to convince him of the seriousness of the situation in the expectation of getting the truth from him. Mr C warned his captive that his position had been made precarious by 'running off to Dublin'. He asked what part he had played in the murder of Constable Magill. Kennedy replied that Sloan had telephoned him and as a consequence he had assisted in the moving of the guns to Mr B's house.

'Have you spoken to anyone about that matter?' asked Mr C. Kennedy hesitated and said he had not spoken to anyone. Then, realising the seriousness of his predicament, he admitted he had spoken to Mr B. In fact Kennedy and Mr B had had a private conversation following the discharge of a pistol in Mr B's home. The incident occurred after the weapons had been moved to Mr B's home and was witnessed by Mr B's young son. 'Beaky' McKee was playing with a pistol, but, even though the magazine had been removed, unknown to him a round remained in the chamber. A display of bravado led to McKee pulling the trigger, and a bullet hit the wall. A day later Mr B expressed his annoyance that the incident could have led to the death of his son or himself.

As Kennedy proceeded to relate this story, Mr C turned angrily to Sloan and rebuked him for not telling him about the matter. He added that Kennedy 'knew too much', and that he should not have known McKee's identity. As the interrogation continued it became apparent that Mr C was perturbed by Kennedy's knowledge of the active service unit, and his closeness to some of its members, particularly Angelo Fusco, and the unit's leader Anthony Sloan and his brother Gerard. 'Mr C suddenly turned to me and said there were basically three options – to put me out of the country, to shoot me dead or to get a bulldozer and run it over my car with me in it. He said there was also a choice of kneecapping me.'

The interrogation halted for a short time when Sloan said there were two possibilities in respect of the leaking of information. Kennedy, he added, was one, and the other was Mr B. The best way to proceed was to question both of them in each other's presence. Sloan's argument was accepted by Mr C, who said that could only happen after Mr B returned from a trip to Canada. When the questioning resumed, Mr C returned to the central issue of how the police could possibly know of Mr B's part in the transportation of weapons or the house in Dalebrook Avenue. He said Kennedy must have told them. Kennedy protested his innocence. He says he knew that if he had relented Mr C would have ordered his execution. At one stage Mr C threatened he had 'two big gorillas from up the country who would beat a confession' out of Kennedy. This was an oblique reference to IRA internal security personnel from South Armagh close to the Irish border. In respect of most of the informers shot in Northern Ireland, interrogations were carried out by a special unit which operated within the rugged countryside of South Armagh and across the Irish border in the townland of Dundalk. It was IRA procedure to lure suspected informers to South Armagh by sending them to meetings in the area, where they were then apprehended and held in remote farmhouses well away from prying eyes. A member of the IRA told me the procedure:

If an informer/agent is discovered it is difficult to hold him for a long period of interrogation in Belfast or Derry. His military intelligence or Special Branch handlers will have a coded means of communicating with him, which ensures that if he does not contact them within given periods that he has been snatched by us. They will then swamp areas with troops to find him. That can be uncomfortable for us and can lead to the seizure of weapons or the abandoning of operations. We circumvent that by sending the informer/agent to a prearranged meeting outside Belfast where we snatch him and send him to our people up the country in South Armagh. When he's there, nobody will find him. If he's executed, our people know every hedge and ditch and it's easy to get rid of the body or to dump it by a roadside. Our internal security people down there are experienced. They've been doing it for years. They know all the ploys. On one occasion we suspected one of our people and we sent him by car on a prearranged route to a political rally in Dublin. Along the route in South Armagh we had a patrol standing by to snatch him. They were dressed in British uniform. They stopped his car and threatened to shoot him, because he was an IRA volunteer. He panicked and gave them a codeword and said, if they checked with their base, military intelligence would confirm he was an agent. That was his death warrant. We did the same by setting up a British-army-type roadblock in Antrim and got a guy who was placing bugging devices in weapons, so that, once they were removed from a dump for an operation, the Brits knew and sent in the SAS to wipe out an IRA active service team. That guy was one of our volunteers, but we got him. The interrogation of informers/agents is important. It establishes a knowledge of the damage we have suffered and it equips us with a knowledge of how these traitors are handled.

Kennedy was lucky he was not being sent to South Armagh, where the interrogators were brutal. His situation was alleviated by the fact that suspicion also centred on Mr B. At one point Mr C warned him that there were armed men outside the house with orders to shoot him if he tried to escape. The interrogation ended after three hours, when Mr C commented that he was 'happy to let things rest for the moment'. He stressed that Kennedy should not discuss the interrogation or any other matter with Mr B on the latter's return from Canada, where he was visiting a sick relative. Kennedy was unable to deduce whether Mr B had gone to Canada out of fear or was genuinely on a family visit. Mr C left the house with the warning that he would resolve the matter of the 'leak' and act accordingly. Kennedy was obliged to drive him from the Ballymurphy housing estate, across Belfast to the Short Strand district, a small Catholic enclave on the perimeter of East Belfast.

That night Kennedy went home a terrified man, with a deadly secret. Unknown to his IRA interrogators, he was the informer, and his police handlers were using him in a dangerous game to penetrate the M60 gang and to trap an experienced terrorist, Joseph Doherty, whom Kennedy had never met. Kennedy's recruitment as a police agent, and his role as an informer on the periphery of one of the IRA's most ruthless active service units, was crucial to Joseph Doherty's fate. It is important not only to examine the sequence of events which I have outlined, but also to establish the way in which his role led to Doherty.

Kennedy was a minor player in the espionage game when he first came into close contact with the IRA. He had been cajoled by his police 'handler' into divulging scraps of information in return for immunity from prosecution for driving offences and social security fraud. Police, Special Branch and military intelligence recruit informers in a variety of ways. They use coercion, blackmail or immunity from prosecution. These are all judged a defensible means to the end of defeating terrorism, but some of the methods are at least morally questionable in a democracy. The culturing or nurturing of informers is a painstaking task. In Kennedy's case immunity was used simply as a way of establishing communication with him, and making him indebted to his police contact. I have no doubt that he passed information gleaned from his daily trips through West Belfast. He was ideally positioned as a taxi driver to perform a surveillance role in areas where members of the security forces could not openly spy on terrorists. However, he was aware of the risk to himself, and did not divulge the type of information which could personally compromise him and jeopardise his life. He did not know that, once he was immersed in this dangerous web of deceit, his spy-masters' stranglehold on him would tighten, drawing him deeper and deeper into the secret intelligence war which had become central to the defeat of terrorism. Kennedy's personality was such that he was ideal for playing the deceitful role which informers were required to develop. He was already leading a double life when he began working as a taxi driver at the Downtown depot – claiming unemployment benefit while earning a living as a driver, and so inadequate that he developed the false persona of a 'university graduate'. A vulnerable and a practised liar, he even told his police contact about his 'student years' at Queen's University.

But he possessed undoubted intelligence and cunning. In September 1979, Mr A took Kennedy's car for use in the murder of Prison Governor Jones, and Kennedy says he was told that if he identified Mr A to the police he would be shot, so he told them he could not identify the man who 'hijacked' his car. I am not inclined to believe him because he was a man with an acute sense of self-preservation. On the other hand, it is possible that he did inform his contact of Mr A's identity, and that it was decided by his handlers that if they acted on the information they would expose him as an informer. In other instances, where an agent/informer provided information about serious incidents which was not acted on, the agent's role within the IRA was so important to intelligence-gathering that he or she had to be protected. In some instances, agent/informers were even permitted to engage in IRA operations as a means of reinforcing their status and commitment to the IRA. What often appeared far-fetched in that theatre of the war was just as often real.

It may be that Kennedy's natural self-protectiveness and cunning persuaded him to maintain a low-level intelligence role, until circumstances dictated that he was being drawn too close to very dangerous people, and the threat of death. His police contact knew where he was working, but was content to have a low-profile relationship with him, probably in the expectation it would develop into a significant role. Secrecy on both sides, and deceit, were essential to the 'intelligence game', which included all the elements of probability and possibility.

Kennedy's informer role seems to have taken a dramatic turn when he realised the IRA was getting too close to him. That moment occurred as a result of Sloan's increasing aggression. As we know, Kennedy went to Dublin and was told that he was likely to be shot, but should return to Belfast to protest his innocence. We may reasonably conclude that he had already divulged information. Everything points to the fact that he compromised the IRA after being forced to remove the guns from Dalebrook Avenue, and that police interrogators left him exposed by using his information in a questioning session with a Downtown taxi driver. An informer has no means of determining the ways in which his information is used.

According to Kennedy, he only told his police contact about these matters before the second 'runaway' Dublin trip. They encouraged him to go there. He says that on his return from Dublin he returned to East Belfast, and telephoned his police contact. What he failed to reveal was that East Belfast housed police HQ, and the Castlereagh Interrogation Centre used by Special Branch and military intelligence. He had also been hiding in East Belfast before going to Dublin – he was not staying with a 'relative' in the east of the city but with his spy-masters, being briefed and debriefed. When it became obvious that Kennedy had come close to the M60 gang, his regular police contact, a mere constable, was obliged to transfer control to Special Branch, military intelligence and the British security service, MI5. Those three organisations had representatives on a security grouping known as the Task Co-ordinating Committee – the most powerful and secretive mechanism within the operating structure of the security forces. Agent/informer information from Special Branch and other intelligence bodies was discussed at that level and used to determine courses of action. Kennedy was very important: he was close to an active service unit which was in possession of a weapon, the M60, which the police and army wanted out of circulation.

Kennedy says that he used to meet his police contact, Constable Hogg, in a bar in East Belfast. Hogg was based in the Andersonstown station in the west of the city, but was the security forces' point of contact with Kennedy. His task was constantly to reassure his informer, and to 'run' him as an agent: others could act on the information. It is likely that Kennedy's fear that he was close to being wiped out by the IRA encouraged Hogg to act quickly, and persuade the intelligence handlers to move with speed before they lost their agent. Kennedy admits that he stayed in East Belfast for several days before returning to work on the day he met Sloan and Mr A in the Lake Glen Hotel. During those days of absence from work, he was in police custody, giving details about the gang, and being briefed about how to behave when he met Sloan. He agrees that he had several meetings with police in East Belfast, but is not forthcoming about the location. His use of 'police' is, I believe, shorthand for Special Branch and military intelligence. His role was so important to police and army strategy that they were prepared to send him back to West Belfast even though he could be shot. They were taking a calculated risk with his life, but the stakes were so high that they believed it was worthwhile.

Before he returned to the taxi depot, the security forces knew everything they needed to know about Sloan and his fellow activists. Why did the police and army not act to arrest them? Kennedy admits that by then he was guaranteed immunity from prosecution for his peripheral part in the murder of the prison governor, and the killings of Constable Magill and the civil servant. His handlers also guaranteed they would spirit him out of the country to a new life in return for his giving evidence against the gang. He was, in effect, a 'supergrass', super-agent, and he put the police in a position to seize the IRA unit.

I believe the Task Co-ordinating Committee were not interested in simply arresting them, and proceeding with a lengthy, expensive trial, since the use of a supergrass's uncorroborated evidence was a high-risk legal exercise which could fail. They preferred to trap them while they were planning an operation and use highly classified troops from the elite, covert, Special Air Services Regiment to wipe them out. If the gang were killed in such circumstances, their deaths would be an understandable statistic and would have public approval. The SAS frequently ambushed IRA active service units and rarely took prisoners. The shooting of unarmed IRA bombers in Gibraltar was such an exercise, and a complete IRA active service unit was wiped out at Loughgall in Northern Ireland. Since Kennedy was not aware of the precise location of the M60 and the other guns, his handlers needed to know more and they sent him to find out. He says 'police' gave him an insight into how the IRA operated and he decided it was 'desirable that they be taken off the streets'. Events moved quickly and, fortunately for Kennedy, his interrogation by Mr C was inconclusive.

For its part, the IRA was convinced that its active service unit had been compromised, but it did not know the extent of the penetration. The Belfast Brigade concluded that the area of operations should be moved out of West Belfast to the north of the city, and that the most experienced operatives in the unit, Angelo Fusco and 'Dingus' Magee, should team up with other experienced volunteers, one of them from the 3rd Battalion, and form another M60 gang. Kennedy was able to tell his handlers about the change in IRA tactics because he remained a confidant of Angelo Fusco after surviving the interrogation. He knew everyone's whereabouts – but his informer work was complete, and he was quietly removed to a police protection programme. Things were about to happen quickly.

Surveillance was placed on Fusco. An unknown informer in North Belfast was swiftly activated to play the role formerly undertaken by Kennedy. Two teams of SAS specialists were put under the command of Captain Herbert Richard Westmacott, an experienced SAS operative. He was told to have his men ready to go into action and to be on constant standby.

In North Belfast, twenty-four-year-old Angelo Fusco teamed up with Joseph Doherty (now twenty-five), Paul Patrick Magee, aged thirty-two, and twenty-seven-year-old Robert Joseph Campbell. All but Doherty came from West Belfast. He was the only one from the 3rd Battalion area where they were about to operate, and who therefore possessed an intimate knowledge of the geography of the district. Although Magee was older, he did not have Doherty's experience or history of IRA activities. There was now a new active service unit which in the IRA's view was positioned far from the scrutiny of an informer. The IRA did not recognise that Fusco and Magee's presence in the unit was the means by which this new grouping was already vulnerable.

# 6

# 'That's My Baby'

The new active service unit brought together young men who represented considerable IRA experience and ruthlessness. Angelo Fusco and 'Dingus' Magee knew how the M60 behaved in a killing situation and how its power was best exploited. Robert Campbell and Joseph Doherty were trained snipers and each had used the M60 in training. Doherty was central to the unit because he knew potential targets in his own neighbourhood, and how to provide the means by which intelligence on those targets was acquired, and the logistical support the unit would need in getting to an operational zone and escaping from it. He was not senior by age, but the other three volunteers were operating on his patch and he was, of necessity and through operational experience, in control.

Doherty's knowledge of his surroundings immediately focused his mind on Girdwood Army Barracks, where he had been twice interrogated. Military vehicles from the base made daily trips countrywards along the Antrim Road, past the New Lodge and through a four-road junction. The junction was situated a quarter of a mile from Doherty's house, and had switching lights to control the flow of traffic across the Antrim Road and the Cavehill and Limestone Roads which traversed it. From another army base, military vehicles proceeded towards the city, along the Antrim Road to Girdwood. The traffic lights made all vehicles slow down or halt, and this provided the site for an ideal ambush of stationary army mobile patrols, or military trucks transporting provisions and men into and out of the city.

One problem which Doherty did not take into account was a children's playground on the edge of the junction, a heavy flow of buses, civilian cars and shoppers on foot. The fact that he was unable to know precisely when a military patrol would pass was indicative of the ruthlessness with which he viewed his purpose. The Antrim Road area was also the siting for several large Protestant and Catholic secondary schools, with a total pupil population of several thousand. Between 8.30 am and 4.30 pm many of these pupils travelled on buses, in cars or walked across that junction. Any firing at that position represented a danger to civilians, especially from the M60 with its indiscriminate fire-power. Those were not considerations in Doherty's mind, and yet he lived in the neighbourhood and knew every aspect of its character and daily life. Doherty may argue that there would have been no firing in the event of civilians being in the vicinity, but there were *always* civilians and children in the vicinity, and his choice of the location is a prima-facie argument for alleging that he was prepared to risk civilian casualties to achieve his objective. If he regarded the risk to civilians as incompatible with his role as an IRA 'soldier', he would not have selected that junction as his ambush point. The day he chose for an attack was Friday 2 May 1980, a weekday, when the Antrim Road was sure to be a busy thoroughfare.

At the countrywards corner of the junction were several terraced houses, numbers 363, 365, 367, 369, whose ground floors had been converted into shops: the absence of gardens served to increase the pavement space in front of them. Number 363 stood at right angles to the junction. Alongside it ran a narrow street, Camberwell Terrace. The conversion of number 369 into a shop resulted in a peculiar structure with two doorways, one for the shop, and a late Victorian entrance which remained intact. Someone not familiar with the terrace could easily have assumed that the Victorian entrance was really the entrance to number 371. In fact, 371 had its own entrance, and its garden stretched to within several feet of the Antrim Road. The whole terrace from the junction connected houses numbered from 363 to 381. At 381 was a street, Jubilee Terrace, which joined Castleton Gardens. The whole terrace represented a square block. Those converted dwellings 363 to 369 were all two-storey, each with an attic. Numbers 371 to 381 were three-storey dwellings. The first floor of number 371, the house in the middle of the block, had two windows which provided a direct line of fire along the Antrim Road. It was an ideal position for an ambush, offering a clear view of Cassidy's shop on the ground floor of 369, and the wide pavement which fronted the four converted buildings. Cassidy's shop, a typical newsagent-grocery business, also sold sweets, and was therefore a favourite haunt of children. The second doorway led to the floor above Cassidy's: the old entrance had been retained because of its aesthetic value, and to allow the first floor of 369 to be used as a dwelling.

Doherty chose 371 Antrim Road because of the line of fire it offered. An alley behind the terrace afforded clear access to Castleton Gardens, and from there the gang could travel to the Antrim Road and proceed towards the country, or to the Shore Road from where they could reach the New Lodge area in five minutes. Doherty knew the route, but surveyed it again to examine the attendant risks in an escape. He arranged for the transportation of the M60 and weapons used by Fusco's unit – with one exception: he had an automatic Heckler & Koch rifle of the type used by the SAS, which he preferred to the antiquated Garand 30.06 employed in the two previous actions I have described. The weapons, therefore, were the M60, the Heckler and the FAL self-loading rifle equipped with a telescopic sight.

The procedure would be the same as the one used in the Magill murder – the M60 to be fired from one room, and the rifles from the other. The M60 required a single window, because of its dimensions and the space required for the ejection of spent cartridges. A family who lived in the house were to be held hostage, and a vehicle was to be hijacked the evening before the ambush. Doherty personally planned the operation, and finally briefed the others on Thursday 1 May. Fusco, Magee and Campbell travelled from West Belfast to the planning meeting – under constant surveillance from members of the British army's covert intelligence teams from another secret grouping, 14th Intelligence Company. Members of that organisation were trained in intelligence-gathering but also in the tactics of speed, firepower and aggression, the hallmarks of the SAS, as demonstrated to the world in their storming of the Iranian Embassy in London in July 1980. Teams from 14th Int. were involved in controversial killings in Northern Ireland, but were not thought to be as efficient in their killing methods as their counterparts in the SAS. At their base in England, the SAS had what they called a 'killing house', where they practised and trained in the art of assassination and siege techniques. Their training was exactly designed to deal with a terrorist cell in an ambush position such as number 371.

As information reached the Task Co-ordinating Committee that the Doherty unit was preparing an ambush at the Antrim Road on 2 May, all 14th Int. operatives were ordered to detach themselves from surveillance in the area for fear their presence be discovered, and the trap for the terrorists compromised. As in all instances where the SAS is tasked, secrecy is stringently imposed and complete authority for the execution of the operation is devolved to them and only them. Use of the SAS habitually signals an order to 'terminate with extreme prejudice' and is rarely an arrest operation. They requested that all army and police activity in the area cease from early morning on 2 May.

Military intelligence concluded that, if the M60 was to be used, IRA tactics would be familiar and there would be a house takeover, but they did not know which one the IRA would choose. They identified the terrace at 363–381 Antrim Road as the likely vantage point, and number 371 as the probable venue because of its line of fire. Captain Westmacott chose seven SAS men for the operation. For reasons of security, they were referred to as soldiers A, B, C, D, G, H and S. His plan was to allow the terrorists to enter the building and then slowly halt the normal flow of traffic along the Antrim Road in order not to alert the IRA unit. He would use two motor cars with soldiers S, G and H in one and the rest of the squad in the other. Soldiers S, G and H would enter the rear of the building and he would lead the others through the front door. They would each wear a red armband so that once they entered the building they would be easily distinguished from the terrorists. It was an additional measure to ensure that, if a gun-battle began before they gained access to the house, troops or police arriving on the scene would know from an advance briefing that armbands identified the SAS troops as security forces personnel. Westmacott was concerned that, if reinforcements were needed, his men might be mistaken for terrorists and shot. His fear was heightened by the fact that he and his men would be in civilian clothes, and would not resemble soldiers. Civilian dress had been chosen to give him and his team an approach to the ambush point without attracting attention. He knew the IRA might have someone positioned with a two-way radio somewhere in the vicinity of the junction, with instructions to warn the Doherty unit of approaching troops or police. Having examined maps of the area, he said, in briefing his men, that the only way to get to the IRA position was for one car to draw up on the wide pavement at speed, whereupon four SAS men would rush to the outside wall of the terrace.

He knew he needed luck, and hoped the civilian dress of his men would create a momentary lack of suspicion in the minds of the IRA unit – sufficient to allow his team to reach the exterior walls, and thence, within seconds, the entrance to 371. The second team would enter from the rear, by proceeding from a countrywards direction into Castleton Gardens, and into the alley adjoining it and Camberwell Terrace. If his team were spotted at the front of the terrace, they would create a diversion with firepower to engage the gang while his second team entered the building from the rear. Westmacott knew his options were limited but he had to 'go for it'.

At 9.30 pm on 1 May, Doherty ordered two local volunteers to take possession of a van belonging to nineteen-year-old Henry O'Neill. The van, a blue Ford Transit, was parked in Spamount Street near the Doherty family home. Its owner was a plasterer who was repairing a house in the street. Almost twenty-four hours after the van was taken, O'Neill gave police the following statement:

I had just locked my van and entered the house on which I was working when two hooded men came in and asked for the keys. I refused, and these men said they were Irish Republican Army and if I didn't hand over the keys I would be dealt with then and there. When they got the keys they told me not to report the van missing or leave the house. After this myself and five other workmen in the house were taken to a bedroom, and these two hooded men remained downstairs. A short time later I heard the van being driven away. We remained in the bedroom until 4.30 pm when the hooded men returned to tell me my van was up the road. I searched the general area but I was unable to locate it. The person who took the keys from me was 5ft 7ins in height. He was wearing a blue parka jacked zipped up, denim jeans and black shoes. The other hooded man was similarly dressed but taller.

That was what O'Neill told police two days after Doherty and his unit used the van for their operation. The truth was to be found in a later statement by O'Neill:

I'm sorry for telling lies about what happened. I should have told the truth at first. On Friday I collected the workers who are employed by my father and drove them from Lurgan to Belfast. We were going to work in Spamount Street where we were plastering houses under repair. A man came into the house and said, 'We want the keys of your van.' I could see another man standing at the door with his back to me. I shook my head and said, 'No, no.' This man then said, 'Right, outside.' I walked into the hall, and the man with his back to me turned and said, 'We are the IRA and we want the fuckin' van.' I tried to explain that the van was watched by police and army but he said, 'Give me the keys now or you'll be dealt with.' I noticed he had his hand up his sleeve and thought he had a gun.

Neither terrorist was wearing a hood, although they were not personally known by O'Neill. One told him to drive him to a location several streets away, and finally ordered him to return:

I was told to go back to the house and, as I was walking down the street, I met a man called Rodgers who collects weekly subscriptions to the Green Cross [a republican front organisation which claims to collect money for the welfare of IRA prisoners' dependants]. I asked Rodgers what was going on but he did not answer. I went into the house and the other IRA man was there. He told me the van was being used for security reasons and would be returned at midnight. I knew it was going to be used for something. This man told me to bring the rest of the workmen into an upstairs bedroom. He told us not to identify him, and we decided to tell police they were wearing masks. It was also decided that I should not mention driving the van for them. The workers who were present when this was discussed and agreed on were: Billy O'Neill, Mel Haughey, Paul McAreavey, Stephen McConvill, Eamon Gilvary, Noel Lavery, Adrien Hull and Joe Thomas. We stayed in the house until 3.30 pm and I went down and asked the man about the van.

I am sorry I lied about the description of those men. I will never help them again but at the time I was afraid.

The Doherty unit was not alone in the planning of their ambush. Aside from the men who hijacked the van there were others with individual tasks to ensure the smooth running of events leading to the entry of the active service team into number 371. Doherty's later account of events leading up to the morning of 2 May is one which tends to minimise his participation and suggests that he was a minor player. He dismisses with unconvincing rhetoric the decision to use number 371, and the attendant risk to civilians. First he maintains that prior to May he was at a training camp being drilled and briefed in how to combat the SAS and similar army groupings. He claims he only received instructions about the 2 May ambush forty-eight hours beforehand. Campbell, he alleges, was selected as operations officer; at one specific meeting an IRA intelligence officer informed him of the target area and who would be with him. Doherty describes it as follows:

Well, of course the target area itself, there were traffic lights. Everybody knows where you have traffic lights, you have a better chance of slowing down or stopping at these traffic lights. It was discussed that – what is normal – that civilians are not the target and we were to make sure that the military vehicle was severed from any civilian vehicle that was about, because usually in Belfast, if there is a military vehicle in front, they stay well back and, if there is a vehicle behind you, you push on. I think it is not just the civilians that think this, the army themselves so that they can get away quick. They don't want to be caught in a traffic jam. Usually when military convoys come down they are on their own. Of course this brings risk to civilians but we were told on this particular occasion, watch for your target, aim at your target and watch for the surrounding vicinity of the target.

What Doherty says is a lie. The Antrim Road was a two-way traffic system with the probability of additional traffic where the Cavehill Road and Limestone Road met. His reference to the behaviour of army vehicles is not accurate. I have sat behind the wheel of my car only feet away from army vehicles on numerous occasions when signal lights have halted the traffic or there has been a traffic jam.

Before midnight on 1 May, O'Neill's Ford Transit was driven to the rear of number 371 to be used as the getaway vehicle. The weapons were in the hands of the battalion quartermaster, broken down so that they could be easily and safely conveyed to number 371 early next morning. At 8.30 am on 2 May, Doherty, Fusco, 'Dingus' Magee and 'Fats' Campbell met in a house in the New Lodge for a final briefing. The battalion quartermaster and an intelligence officer were also present. Magee was told he would be the driver throughout the operation, the other three, the shooters. They were warned that in making their escape they should ensure they did not use all their ammunition in the ambush, because they might have to shoot their way out of the area. Two of them – Doherty says he was not included – were told to take the Astra 9mm pistol and gain entry to 371, where Magee would hold the occupants hostage in a downstairs room throughout the operation. Doherty and one of the four would walk to the building not later than 10.35. By that time the quartermaster would have transported the guns to the house. Thirty to forty minutes would be needed to assemble them. From that moment they would be free to select their target.

At 10.30 am nineteen-year-old Rosemary Comerford and her

two-year-old son Gerard were in number 371 preparing for what she believed was a normal day. Her husband was at work.

My flat is on the ground floor. We occupy the whole floor. Above there is a bedsit and a fella lived in it on his own but I didn't know him. At 10.30 a knock came to the door and I opened it. Two men were standing there and one of them said they were Irish Republican Army. The man who spoke had a handgun pointing at me. This man said they were going to take over the house and they were going to hold me and my son as hostages. He then took us into the bedroom at the rear of the house. The other man who did not speak remained in the bedroom with us. I could hear the other man moving about the flat. I think the man who stayed in the bedroom with us brought the handgun with him. At about 12.30 pm my sister, Theresa, called with her three-month-old baby. The man who was in the bedroom with me told me to go and see who was at the door. When I told him it was my sister, he told me to let her in. I did so and he told her she would have to stay with us in the bedroom. At 1.00 pm my husband, Gerard, came home and the same happened.

Doherty says he went to the second floor to 'secure' the building and another member of the unit checked the top floor. The occupant of the second-floor apartment was, fortunately for him, not there. Doherty, Campbell and Fusco began assembling the weapons while Magee guarded the hostages.

It took almost forty minutes to put the individual parts of the weapons into a working shape. From that moment they were ready for action. According to Doherty, Campbell gave them a short briefing:

As before every operation, the officer-in-command would sit there and brief us again that we are going to hit this certain target coming down. Watch where you aim. Keep at least five rounds in the magazine. I only got one and we hadn't any spare magazines. Watch what you are firing at. Take aim at the target. Don't over-access the firepower. In other words, don't go crazy with the gun. This is a normal procedure we go through on all operations.

Doherty implies a discipline which was absent when the Fusco gang ambushed the soldiers and killed Constable Magill. Doherty was an IRA officer of considerable experience who, by his own admission, had just completed a tough training course at the request of the Belfast Brigade. Even if one accepts that, for convenience, Campbell was elected to be in charge of the unit on that day, I do not believe a person of Doherty's tenure in the IRA required such basic advice. My contention is that this statement made at a later date was designed to convey a disciplined soldierly exercise.

He also argued at a later date that the IRA did not take hostages. The Maguire family, held during the Magill murder, and the Comerfords may scarcely be called willing captives. O'Neill and his workmen did not travel to Belfast to be treated to a hijacking – which later landed O'Neill in court.

At noon on 2 May, Doherty, Campbell and Fusco began the waiting game, but in a two-hour period no target presented itself. The SAS team were in Girdwood base checking their weapons. They knew from an SAS colleague hidden near 371 that the IRA unit was in position. Unknown to the IRA unit, another member of the SAS was concealed nearby and walked past the terrace. He scrutinised each building and detected unusual behaviour in 371. He radioed Westmacott.

Doherty says 'nothing came by'. It did not occur to him that there was little traffic on what was normally a busy road. The IRA had not taken the precaution of placing scouts in the area or establishing two-way radio communication with the men in number 371. They, like the SAS, were keeping a low profile for what they expected to be a devastating operation. Doherty says 'what looked like a one-man patrol jeep' was driven by the house. He did not see a man in a short dark jacket pass the house on several occasions on foot.

I think at one point what looked like a communications vehicle passed. I think that went by but I was sitting in the room and it was one of the other volunteers. This is a one-man patrol jeep, you know, with the radios, stuff and supplies. We took turns, maybe one half-hour each to watch at the window for army vehicles. Sight burners we call them.

At 2.00 pm Captain Westmacott ordered his two teams of men into their vehicles. One vehicle containing three soldiers was detailed as the lead car. It was to proceed into Camberwell Terrace at number 363, from there to Castleton Gardens and then the rear of 371. The second vehicle was to stop at the wide pavement in front of Cassidy's shop. Speed was essential, and their training in aggression and covering tactics was vital to their survival. There were several flaws in the plan. A frontal assault was tantamount to bravado and an underestimation of the abilities of the IRA unit. The fatal mistake was that, though number 371 was designated as the target, the Victorian doorway of 369 was marked on their maps as the entrance to 371 and, unknown to them, that factor would determine the life of one of them. At 2.07 pm the first SAS team of three men passed the junction and turned at Camberwell Terrace, and into Castleton Gardens. At the same time Westmacott and four men drew alongside the pavement outside Cassidy's: soldier C was driving, and alongside him sat soldier D. In the rear Westmacott was seated between soldiers A and B; soldier B had a sledgehammer in his hand. All five alighted from the car with speed and precision. Soldiers C and B, who were closest to the house, sped towards Cassidy's shop. Soldier B hit the Victorian door of 369 with the sledgehammer and it burst open. Soldier C ran in, his weapon aimed at the staircase facing him.

As they went through the door, soldier D moved to the front of the car to give them covering fire, his sub-machine-gun aimed at the upstairs window of 369. Westmacott and soldier A moved to the rear of the car and took up a similar position. Soldier A, who was alongside Westmacott, offers the following description of what happened:

I began running towards the doorway of 369 and I noticed a muzzle flash and breaking glass coming from the first-floor window of what I later knew to be number 371. I felt a number of rounds passing close, one of which burned my right cheek. I could see Captain Westmacott behind me and to my right. I was suddenly aware that he was stopped. I ran to the front door. I was aware of more than one weapon firing from 371, but I could not establish the other firing points. B and C went upstairs to clear the rooms and I stayed downstairs as cover man. Soldier D came in and informed me his communications were out of order. We both went to the landing on the first floor. D and B went to the top of the house to check it out.

Meanwhile Westmacott was lying six feet from the door of the house, mortally wounded.

Soldier C remembers a burst of automatic fire directed at him as he ran with B to enter 369. Even at breakneck speed he returned thirteen rounds of semi-automatic fire at the first-floor windows of 371. He recalls 'clearing the house' in typical SAS fashion to 'secure it'. At that stage, with the pace of events quickening, they were following orders to take what was the wrong house even though the firing was coming from 371. Their behaviour was indicative of a singlemindedness which did not allow for flexibility beyond providing covering fire for each other, as in the account of soldier C who fired thirteen rounds at 371 as he entered the wrong building.

Soldier C says that he was on the second landing of 369 when he was told that Westmacott 'was down'. He says he told his colleagues there was no one in the building and the terrorists were probably next door. Nevertheless soldier C and the others searched the cellar of 369 before meeting in the hallway to discuss ways of forcing an entry to the house next door. Soldier B went out first and ran into the garden of 371; C took up position alongside the door. As he did so, a burst of machine-gun fire riddled the door from inside, and C concluded that to attempt to get in would be suicidal. C fired a sustained burst at the door, at a height which he estimated would kill anyone behind it. His bullets made a perfect circle, illustrating the accuracy of SAS marksmanship.

That fatal error in map reading almost claimed the lives of more than Westmacott. The fact that the firing was coming from 371 did not deter the SAS soldiers from entering what they assumed to be the correct entrance to the building. Their training was such that their minds were focused only on one objective, and nothing was going to deter them from attacking what they believed was their target. No one noticed that Westmacott was lying on the pavement with his orders scrawled on the palm of his left hand. Those orders contained the fatal error pointing to the entrance of his target as the doorway adjacent to the shop entrance. Those orders did not indicate that 369 had two entrances. He assumed that the Victorian entrance was the door of 371. An indication of the way in which SAS soldiers operate is to be found in an account of the Iranian Embassy siege in London which happened two months after the Antrim Road assault. Frank Collins, one of the troops ordered to take the embassy from a terrorist unit, told the *Daily Mirror* newspaper that it was 'chaotic'. His description of how he and others behaved under fire provides an explanation for the singlemindedness of Westmacott and his team: 'We were told "Go, Go, Go." I felt excitement and fear but was in autodrive, moving like clockwork. You can't stop, can't lose momentum, just fight through.'

Westmacott's other, three-man team had driven into Camberwell Terrace before the lead car reached the pavement at 369. They proceeded into Castleton Gardens, parked their vehicle, quickly alighted and ran to the alley behind the terrace. Soldier H was in the lead and his description of what happened is fascinating:

We took up position in the alleyway. The first thing I saw was a blue Ford

Transit van, facing on to the road. The driver's door was open. From my position I could see the upstairs rear of three houses. At the same time I saw a man running from the entrance of 371 towards the driver's side of the van. While this was happening we came under fire from the upstairs rear window, first floor of 371. I heard a bullet whistle past my head and strike brickwork above me. I moved out of the line of fire, and at the same time challenged the man who at this time was attempting to get into the vehicle.

That man was 'Dingus' Magee, the terrorist driver who was about to prepare for the IRA unit's escape from the house. He was not armed and soldier H was not certain he was a terrorist, otherwise he would have shot him dead. SAS soldiers do not miss targets at that range, although the covering fire given to Magee by his IRA colleagues may also have temporarily unsighted the three-man SAS team. Soldier H's command to what appeared to be a fleeing civilian was to halt and put his hands up. Magee complied with the instruction. 'I further shouted to him, to lie down in the alleyway, and he did this. I then moved past this man to the rear of 371. Once I was there I told one of my colleagues who were covering me to come forward and bring this man with him. We then ordered this man to lie face down. We handcuffed him, hands behind his back.'

Soldier H took this action even though he did not know the identity of the stranger. It was procedure to 'neutralise' anyone within the fire zone who posed a threat. They were working quickly and did not have time to question their prisoner to establish whether he was a terrorist. While two of them were securing him, the third member of the team was alert, ready to give cover fire. Soldier H waved the third soldier into the alley.

I shouted at him to cover me while I gained access to the garden of 371. I approached the rear of this house along the garden path, looked through the ground-floor windows and saw nothing. I could hear, above me, my colleagues shouting at each other and I made contact with them. They shouted to me that the terrorists were next door. I went back again to the rear gate of the garden and moved down to 373. The gate of this house was locked and we forced it open. I ran down the garden path to the rear of this house.

Soldier H was experiencing the same problems as his colleagues at the front of the building. There were no markings on the garden gates to indicate house numbers. The firing from the upstairs windows of what he later discovered was 371 did not assist him in the search for a correct entry into the building. The pre-planning was proving disastrous. As he ran down the garden of 373 he fired three rounds at the windows of that building before forcing the back door. His colleagues followed and the three of them searched the ground floor. It suddenly occurred to them that they had entered the wrong house. They returned to the alley and approached the gate to 371. He says they decided it was 'too dangerous' to proceed any further. 'We covered the back of these houses and carried out a search of the van. We found a carrier bag containing a pistol and a loaded rifle magazine. Soldier G took possession of these.'

The three-man team grabbed Magee and drove him in the van to Castleton Gardens. They rightly surmised that they had one of the terrorists in their grasp and that he possessed information about the nature of the threat in 371. They placed Magee face down on the ground and soldier G began questioning him. Magee revealed his name, that three guns were in the house, and with a movement of his head indicated that number 371 was their position.

Meanwhile, in the front garden of 371, a stand-off had arisen. The SAS team knew it was suicidal to attempt to rush the terrorists. Soldier C was left in no doubt that the IRA gang were armed with rifles and the deadly M60. He shouted to the gunmen to surrender and throw their weapons into the gardens. A voice replied that they were 'armed with an M60'. A spent M60 cartridge was thrown into the garden as proof of the existence of the weapon, and of the intent of Doherty, Campbell and Fusco.

Josephy Doherty and his fellow hitmen understood the critical nature of their predicament from the moment Captain Westmacott and his team alighted from the car. Each terrorist was knowledge-able about the precise character of British military operations. Doherty, in particular, had recently completed an IRA training course designed to acquaint him with the methods and tactics of the SAS and other military undercover groupings. The instant the car drew up, Doherty knew that the men emerging from it were not ordinary soldiers or members of an elite police body such as the Special Patrol Group. Their speed, demeanour and armbands convinced him they were SAS. He knew how to react and exactly what to expect in such a volatile situation.

He gingerly admits that the IRA hit-squad was perturbed by the non-appearance of military convoys. 'It was very, very strange,' he says, and claims that their suspicion that 'something was wrong' convinced them they were 'being set up'. They considered 'pulling out of their position'. For fifteen minutes they debated whether their operation was compromised and if it was judicious to abandon it, but events dictated otherwise.

Fusco was first to notice the apparent absence of traffic and his perception was augmented by Doherty's local knowledge that the Antrim Road was normally a very busy thoroughfare. While they recognised the significance of these observations, Westmacott's car drew up outside 369. Fusco may well have been the terrorist who first spotted the car, but Doherty paid particular attention to it: 'I seen the car pull to a stop outside. I didn't see exactly where it came from. We were looking down. When the car stopped it came to a very sudden stop and five men got out of it.'

The detail which left Doherty in no doubt that they were SAS soldiers was their dress, the type of weaponry they carried and the swiftness of their movements. They were in civilian dress, each of them sported an armband, and they carried weapons not normally used by the established military police: 'They were each carrying an Uzi machine-gun, an Israeli assault weapon not easily concealed. One of them was carrying a sledgehammer. We knew straight away that they were members of the Special Air Service or Military Reaction Force.'

The latter grouping was a counter-insurgency organisation established by British military intelligence in the early 1970s, and it had been involved in controversial shootings. It was structured in a cell formation and made use of members of the IRA and loyalist organisations who were coerced into acting as double agents. Its activities were often of a dubious character and it is my belief that it acted collectively as an *agent provocateur*. There is evidence to suggest that it had an assassination role and that its members were involved in the killing of innocent people. It was a body not properly controlled, and permitted too much secrecy and freedom – and was eventually abandoned in favour of the Special Air Services and 14th Intelligence. Although the use of elite troops such as these may have been regarded as politically and militarily more effective, the controversial nature of their tactics none the less created suspicion and doubt about their methods in a similar fashion to their predecessor, the Military Reaction Force. British army spokesmen referred to the MRF as the 'Military Reconnaissance Force', a choice of language which was designed to obscure the nature of its *raison d'être*. By 1982 the history of the MRF was well known to the IRA but by then it was the elite troops of the SAS and 14th Intelligence which were engaged in undercover work. When the target was an IRA active service unit, the police and army turned for specialist assistance to the SAS, which was specifically trained for siege and ambush situations, and for eliminating armed terrorists.

The wearing of armbands by SAS troops in a combat operation such as the one I have been describing was a factor which convinced Doherty that he was suddenly facing the most efficient killing machine in the British army: 'Through our intelligence we discovered how the SAS operate and that when they operate they wear civilian clothes and orange armbands. This is to identify themselves to regular troops. If regular troops come on the scene and see all these civilians running about they will know the ones with armbands are friends.' Doherty says he learned this detail three months before the Antrim Road gun-battle. He adds that this piece of intelligence was acquired during another IRA operation, although he does not confirm whether he participated in the earlier encounter with the SAS. He qualifies this assertion by alleging that the IRA may have gained the 'armband' knowledge by placing surveillance on the British army. I am more inclined to the view that a previous IRA operation resulted in their learning about SAS methods. As with all IRA intelligence of that kind, it was passed along the chain of command to active service units and individuals such as Doherty, Fusco and Campbell: according to Doherty, he received a briefing every month on British army tactics and weaponry. I have no reason to doubt this and it confirms my suspicion that he was in active service capacity prior to the Antrim Road incident. He is not forthcoming about those months after his release from prison and one must conclude that he did not spend the time polishing his nails.

As to the Westmacott operation, Doherty says that the SAS underestimated him and his fellow hitmen, and the firepower they possessed. He was in no doubt, however, that the SAS had come on a 'kill mission'.

They weren't exactly coming in to give us a subpoena. They were coming in on a kill mission. The tactics of the SAS go back to World War II. It's a behind-the-lines force. It's the cream of the cream of the British army. They go behind enemy lines, destroy railroads and oil refineries. They are more extreme than commandos. To the American forces they would be the Seals or Green Berets. They don't exactly take prisoners. They parachute behind lines and after the war they fought in the colonial wars in Palestine, Malaya, Kenya, Cyprus, and as such they were used as counter-insurgency troops. Especially in Malaya, they were used as jungle troops like the Green Berets, and in the urban wars such as Cyprus they were used as assassination teams. They are what we call the Dirty Tricks Department of the British Armed Forces.

When Doherty saw the speed with which Westmacott and his team left their car, and watched their crouching, darting movements, he knew he was in serious trouble. The question which he fails to answer satisfactorily relates to who fired the first shots? One would naturally assume that if he believed the SAS troops were on a 'kill mission' he would have swiftly retaliated. He says he was armed with the Heckler & Koch automatic rifle prior to the arrival of the soldiers, but he does not confirm who was in possession of the M60 or the other rifle at the moment of the SAS assault on number 369.

Soldier C recalls firing a burst at the windows of 371 Antrim Road as he ran under fire towards 369. Doherty appears unsure about who fired first and it is interesting to examine his testimony when he was later questioned by a US attorney about this matter:

Q:   Who fired first?
A:   I'm afraid I don't know.
Q:   You don't know, do you?
A:   The shooting just started and I fired.
Q:   What did you fire at?
A:   I fired when I saw the SAS men and the car.
Q:   You shot at the men, not the car. Is that right?
A:   I shot at the men and the car. The car and the men came together. They were in the same vicinity. They were in the target area.
Q:   Your purpose in shooting at them was what?
A:   To inflict as many casualties as possible.
Q:   You are not even sure that it was they who fired first? You weren't going to wait for the first shot to be fired, isn't that so?
A:   The actual getting out of the car, the approach to the house, the type of machine-guns they had, coming towards the house, we knew we were under attack. I am talking about a split-second decision when they were getting out of the car. They met us and gave a short burst from one of their small-calibre machine-guns and we returned fire. I returned fire.

*Q:* Did that happen? Did the men getting out of the car open fire before you fired?

*A:* It took them maybe two or three seconds to get out of the car. They came towards the house and coming towards the house, all commandos or elite troops set up a burst. This is another tactic of the SAS. It's what's called 'cover by fire'. When you fire, the person is going to put his head down so that you can move with your cover area. They shot a burst as they were getting out of the car and as soon as they were getting out of the car we were up straightaway and fired within a second, if not less.

Doherty's description of the SAS tactic of using a burst of fire such as soldier C described is accurate, although the SAS team claimed the IRA men fired first. What is important to establish is that Doherty saw Westmacott's car stop, and the SAS soldiers emerge from it. Doherty's IRA training was sufficient to convince him instantly of the identity of the troops and their intentions. Would he have waited or asked for permission to open fire? His own testimony about IRA procedure in such circumstances reflects his ability to react instantaneously.

Of course you act independently. I haven't the time to turn round to Volunteer Campbell and ask for permission to shoot. Of course we are soldiers. The armed services are told to use their own discretion on immediate crisis which is about to appear. You don't keep asking your subordinate: 'Can I pop me rifle over me shoulder or can I do something else?'

During the initial firing Doherty was operating from the window closest to 369 and Westmacott was hit by M60 bullets fired from that position. Doherty says that in the period prior to the shooting he was sitting in a chair with the automatic Heckler on his knees. As in all IRA operations, no one volunteer takes responsibility for 'a kill' or admits who used the murder weapon. He saw Westmacott fall and knew the other soldiers had reached the outer walls of the terrace. None of the IRA men was aware at that moment that the SAS team had chosen the wrong doorway.

Campbell, Fusco and Doherty made their way to the stairs. Their thoughts were centred on their escape plan and Magee was ordered to run to the van parked in the alleyway and to start the engine in preparation for a quick getaway. Campbell shouted: 'Let's get the hell outa here!'

As they made their way towards the rear of the house, Doherty says he noticed another SAS team in the alleyway. Campbell, Fusco and Doherty retreated to the first-floor landing and quickly decided to make a stand. Doherty was assigned a room overlooking the alleyway with Campbell positioned in a room overlooking the Antrim Road and Fusco on the stairs to guard the front door. Doherty's position suggests that he was the person who almost killed soldier H – above whose head a bullet struck the brickwork. If that were so, Doherty was firing the Heckler. This tends to support an assertion that he never used the M60. It is not conclusive proof: in violent situations IRA volunteers share weapons because they are not the exclusive property of any one individual.

The three IRA volunteers were suddenly faced with a classic dilemma outlined to them many times in IRA briefings. Doherty, as a result of recent training, believed he knew what to expect. He says the three IRA men waited for grenades of the stun type or tear gas to be fired at them as a preliminary to an SAS assault on the building but the SAS 'did not seem to want to come back'.

An M60 burst was fired through the front door to frighten two SAS soldiers in the front garden of 371. The SAS teams had lost the initiative and were out-gunned. When they departed the scene, Doherty became aware of the arrival of a convoy of regular troops. He says he heard 'tanks', by which he means armoured personnel carriers.

The presence of soldiers of the regular army was also a turning point in the way in which Doherty and his colleagues assessed their situation. They realised that the threat of an SAS assault and certain death could be avoided. Their minds were now focused on terms for a surrender. Doherty says surrender was considered an honourable option because he and his colleagues were 'more valuable in a prison cell than in a cemetery'.

The decision to surrender had a proviso, and that was the presence of a priest to ensure their safe passage from the building. Even at that point, Doherty and his companions were uncertain regarding their fate, and reckoned that a witness was required to ensure that their departure from the building was not marred by trigger-happy soldiers who had just lost a colleague. Outside 371, the situation was under the control of a Lieutenant-Colonel Millar, who shouted to the IRA men to lay down their weapons and walk from the house. Campbell replied in a derisory fashion that they had no intention of trusting the British military. Lieutenant-

Colonel Millar argued that the IRA weapons should be thrown into the front garden as a precursor to further negotiation. Campbell retorted that they would only talk further with the Lieutenant-Colonel if a priest was summoned. Campbell's diction confused the English officer, who mistook 'priest' for 'police' and abruptly summoned the RUC at North Queen Street station in Belfast city centre.

Constable Joseph Clarke Bryson and Detective Sergeant Norris were sitting at their desks in the station when they received a communication about the shooting. They travelled quickly to the scene to find it cordoned off by military personnel. The body of Westmacott lay covered in a blanket on the forecourt of 369. The policemen were informed of the gunmen's intention to surrender, and decided to seek the assistance and advice of a high-ranking police officer. Constable Bryson telephoned the RUC's Belfast Regional Control, apprised them of the facts and requested them to contact his superintendent at North Queen Street station.

At 2.50 pm, almost an hour after the shooting, Superintendent Charles Morrison arrived on the scene to begin negotiations with the gunmen. He noticed a window almost knocked out on the first floor of 371 and the absence of a top panel in the door at 369. Beneath the blanket covering Westmacott's body, a two-way radio was still carrying SAS communications elsewhere in the city. Lieutenant-Colonel Millar asked soldiers to provide cover while one trooper ran, crouching, to the body and switched off the radio. Superintendent Morrison stood within the shelter of the terraced wall and with a loudhailer began addressing the gunmen. In the events which followed his initial introduction to the gunmen, he bravely proceeded to negotiate, at times placing himself at considerable risk. He says that initially he could not discern the comments coming from the first floor of 371 or see the person delivering them.

I asked this person to move closer to the window to speak with me as I could not hear him clearly and I was then asked by this person to move out to the edge of the footpath beside the red SAS car so that I could be seen. At this stage I was standing close into the shop convenient to 369 and I moved slowly towards the edge of the footpath, speaking all the time to the person in the room and asking him if he could see me now. I moved out on to the road behind the red car, spoke up to the window and asked the person speaking to come forward to the window unarmed and with his hands in front of him. I told this person I would ensure his safety.

In order to reinforce the superintendent's assurance, Lieutenant-Colonel Millar ordered his men positioned opposite 371 to lower their rifles.

Campbell responded by appearing at the window as requested, and was told by the police officer that he and his fellow volunteers would be taken into police, rather than army, custody, and their safety guaranteed. Campbell replied that he would prefer to talk to a priest before agreeing to total surrender. Superintendent Morrison confirmed that a local priest would shortly arrive, and his communication with Campbell broke off at that point. Minutes later a priest appeared and was briefed by the police officer: 'I explained the position to Father Hutton and asked him if he would accompany me to the edge of the footpath so that he could be seen with me. He agreed and we both walked to the red car. I used the loudhailer and informed the gunmen of Father Hutton's presence. Campbell appeared again and I asked him to come down and I would meet with him.'

Campbell rejected the offer and insisted that the police officer enter 371 and meet the IRA unit on the first-floor landing. Superintendent Morrison regarded such a venture as too risky, since he felt the situation was unstable and he might be used as a hostage to guarantee not safety but freedom for the gunmen: 'I declined and asked them again to come down and I would take custody of them at the front door. Campbell asked if the door was open, and I replied that I thought it was but if not I would soon open it. I told him to leave the weapons in the room and come down unarmed.'

Campbell responded to the plea by placing a rifle with a white handkerchief attached to the barrel on the window-ledge. He turned, was handed another rifle and repeated the gesture. Finally he lifted the M60 complete with ammunition belt, put it through the window-frame and placed it on an adjoining ledge. As he laid it down, he patted the barrel of the big gun and remarked: 'Take good care of it.'

Superintendent Morrison then made an error which was becoming only too familiar. He told the gunmen to walk to the front door of 371 where he and Father Hutton would meet them. He walked to the doorway of 369 and waited. No one appeared, and when he shouted to the gunmen they told him he was at the wrong door. Moving to the entrance of 371, he found the door riddled with bullets and slightly ajar. He pushed it open and saw the three gunmen casually walking down the stairs. They requested Father Hutton to walk towards them alone, sought his confirmation that they would be safe, and he allayed their fears. Superintendent Morrison was joined by Constable Bryson and Detective Sergeant Norris, and they ushered the gunmen from the house. Doherty stood on the front steps of the premises, defiantly raised a clenched fist and shouted: 'Up the Provos!' Each gunman was wearing black gloves to ensure there were no individual fingerprints on the murder weapons, to protect their hands from the heat of the gun barrels and to cushion the impact of each gun as it was fired. Superintendent Morrison asked Campbell if there were any other terrorists in the building and he replied: 'There was another fella out the back. Have you got him?'

As the police officers accompanied their prisoners along the pathway to the Antrim Road, Doherty turned his head towards the window of 371 where the M60 was prominently displayed and remarked: 'That's my baby.'

The three IRA men were held in custody in an army Landrover until two police vehicles arrived. They were handed over to men from the RUC Special Patrol Group and escorted to police premises at Castlereagh in East Belfast. That was the site of the RUC's interrogation network and housed some of the most experienced police interrogators.

Meanwhile the body of Captain Westmacott was removed to the surgery of the state pathologist. The autopsy findings illustrated the speed with which death reached the SAS captain:

The man was of good build, measuring six feet in height. He was healthy; there was no natural disease to cause or accelerate death, or to cause collapse. Death was a result of gunshot wounds, the deceased having been struck by two bullets. One bullet entered the left side of the forehead at the hairline and passed from left to right, downwards at about 45° to the horizontal plane and backwards at 35° to the coronal plane. It had passed through the skull, causing extensive fractures and gross laceration of the brain and had left by the right side of the head and neck. The bullet or part thereof had then re-entered the base of the neck still following the same direction. It had damaged the right shoulder blade and then left the body on the back of the right shoulder. This wound alone could have caused death. Another bullet had entered the left side of the neck and it too passed from left to right, downwards and backwards, on much the same trajectory as the other bullet. It had lacerated the windpipe and the oesophagus, and virtually destroyed the upper two thoracic vertebrae, severing the enclosed spinal cord and fracturing the posterior ends of many of the adjacent ribs on each side. The bullet and bone fragments had also damaged both lungs, lacerating the right. Many fragments of this bullet were removed from within the chest. Had the deceased not died so rapidly from the effects of the head injury, the damage caused by this bullet was almost certain to have proved fatal.

I have included the autopsy report, even though many people may view it as gruesome, for the reason that it illustrates the powerful and lethal nature of the M60 machine-gun and the stark reality of violence.

At Castlereagh interrogation centre, jackets and gloves were removed from all the members of the IRA unit and sent for forensic examination. The task of the forensic scientists was to establish whether particles from the discharge components of bullets had their origins in the clothing of the four men. Large amounts of particles were discovered on Fusco's clothing. Items of clothing removed from Doherty and Campbell showed that all three had been exposed to a very large source of firearms residue. Swabs were also taken from the face, hands and hair of the four men. Magee was found to have been 'exposed to a relatively large source of firearms residue'. The forensic samples showed that Magee had faced less exposure but, in the view of forensic scientist James McQuillan, there were enough particles to provide 'one of the best positive cases of exposure to firearms residue that he had encountered in nine years of specialising in that field'. Doherty has always insisted that Magee remained downstairs guarding the hostages. The forensic evidence indicates contrary conclusions. Magee must have been involved in the use of weapons before he left the building to prepare for the proposed escape. That implies that Doherty's claim that only himself, Fusco and Campbell were firing guns is inaccurate. Did he give the Heckler to Magee at some stage and operate the M60? Doherty's 'That's my baby' comment emphasised how he saw his relationship with the gun.

In Castlereagh, Doherty was in familiar surroundings, having spent so much time in custody under interrogation. For the first time, a record would be kept of his performance under questioning. Unlike those early days of the conflict, when according to him military questioners brutalised him, strict guidelines now existed in respect of police interrogation procedures. The question which faced RUC detectives was – which of the IRA unit would collapse under pressure?

# 7

# The Interrogation

Before midnight on 2 May, Superintendent Morrison visited the four gunmen in their individual cells in Castlereagh police station. He stood at the door of Campbell's cell and said: 'You should know me, boy.' Campbell lay on his stomach, glared at the police officer but did not talk. 'I'm the man you spoke to from the upstairs window today,' added Superintendent Morrison. Campbell ignored the remark. Doherty, Fusco and Magee also treated with disdain attempts by the policeman to engage them in conversation. The interrogation of the four did not begin in earnest until the following day and by law continued for a further six days. Morrison's visit was a preliminary excursion of little relevance, and, for their part, the four IRA volunteers knew what to expect because anti-interrogation techniques were a central feature of IRA training. Both sides were aware of the significance of interrogation, the ploys, the subtleties and the cleverness with which questions were framed.

Doherty's first impression of his cell was that it was 'all white and the lights were on twenty-four hours each day'. He was told the interrogation would begin the following day and take place three times each day – morning, afternoon and evening – and each session would last for one to four hours. Doherty argues that he was interrogated by Special Branch, but the fact is that his questioners were detectives from police HQ Crime Squad, which had been set up specifically for handling terrorists. Either he is lying as part of a ploy to portray himself as a political prisoner, or he is unaware of the facts. Interrogation carried out in preparation for court proceedings was conducted by detectives from the CID (Criminal Investigation Department) – but assigned to specific tasks such as those undertaken by Crime Squad HQ. Doherty may indeed prefer to attribute his interrogation to Special Branch because of its tarnished reputation, and its involvement in the in-depth interrogation of political prisoners in the early 1970s, later condemned by the Court of Human Rights. There were many subsequent instances in which Special Branch interrogated suspects in the pursuit of recruiting them as double agents, coercing or blackmailing them into divulging information, or seeking to pressure them into making a statement about crimes. In 1982 police interrogation procedures had somewhat changed with the creation of the Crime Squad and other teams of detectives, skilled in the art of questioning. Police interrogators had been found to have acted excessively, but by 1982 the scope for torture or physical brutality was severely limited. Doherty told a New York court in 1984 that Special Branch had been his interrogators, but the documented evidence in my possession disputes that. Either he was ill informed about police procedures – or was simply lying. In Doherty's portrayal of himself to the American public as a political prisoner of conscience, an important element in his assertion was the involvement of the 'political police', Special Branch, whose task was to deal secretly with political subversion, and, as proven in numerous courtrooms, often in a fashion contradictory to the principles of democracy and justice.

At 11.40 am on 3 May, Doherty was removed to an interrogation room where he was introduced to Detective Constable Hugh Hall and Detective Sergeant Flaherty. Flaherty told him that they were inquiring into the shooting of Captain Westmacott and the takeover of number 371 and he believed Doherty could assist him. Doherty replied: 'I won't be saying anything about it.' He did, however, offer the detectives an insight into his political thoughts. He told them he 'wasn't really a nationalist' but a 'socialist in the wider sense'. He was not concerned about Orange and Green, Catholic or Protestant, and his actions of the previous day were an attempt to change 'the society we live in'. He added that he was anti-establishment, was opposed to money, power and the middle and upper classes. The statement was unambiguous, and re-presented a Marxist philosophy more akin to IRA thinking of the 1960s than the policies of the organisation to which he belonged, namely the Provisional IRA.

Flaherty pursued a line of questioning to establish whether bombing or shooting was a justifiable means of changing Irish society. Doherty replied: 'There are people who claim to be good-living and religious working in munitions factories making napalm bombs and this sort of thing, and they are just as guilty as terrorists or so-called terrorists.' This was a familiar Doherty response to a question which would later become a central feature of his approach to cross-examination in American courts. He has always preferred to sidestep those direct questions designed to elicit his personal views on the moral use of violence by condemning someone else, as though by spreading the guilt, or broadening the issue, he protected himself from having to give a forthright answer. His approach to Flaherty's quest for a reply was to augment his previous comments by alleging that 'people in authority always see themselves as right and those who choose to do things differently are put in the wrong'.

Without being prompted, Doherty talked about how he would change society in the Republic of Ireland and expounded his views on the conflict in Iran, the history of the Shah, how America was wrong in its political stance against Iran, and British policy in Northern Ireland. He reserved much of his vehemence for increasing unemployment in Northern Ireland and Britain, and said the root cause of the particular problem was the oppression of the working class in the slums by the middle and upper classes.

Flaherty tried to steer Doherty away from his political rhetoric by pointing out that, regardless of his political thesis, he was in custody because he had been found in possession of guns following a fatal shooting. Doherty responded that the detective was right in what he alleged but it was a matter which he 'would not go into'. He added that he was prepared to talk about 'anything else' but not about the events of the previous day. Flaherty said it was all very well discussing politics; they could talk indefinitely about world conflicts, but that would hardly change the reality of Doherty's situation.

The verbal fencing between the two continued until Flaherty raised the issue of remorse, and whether Doherty felt guilty about depriving Westmacott's wife of her husband. Doherty responded quickly: 'I'm not sorry, no, not really. It's just the way you look at it. He's a British soldier. They shouldn't be here. It wouldn't have happened if the British weren't here.'

Flaherty asked whether he was concerned that he might have been shot by the SAS during the operation. Doherty retorted that this was a matter which would not cause him loss of sleep, and he was also unconcerned about facing thirty years in prison. Flaherty then took a softer line of questioning, in the expectation that Doherty might well be the type of person unwilling to face life imprisonment: the detective was not wholly convinced by the prisoner's display of bravado. He suggested that it was a terrible thing to see any young man consigned to life behind bars: Flaherty hoped Doherty might become a super-informer against the IRA in return for immunity from prosecution, or a reduction in prison sentence. Doherty remained unrepentant and unimpressed by the line of questioning. Flaherty proceeded to remind his prisoner that he was under oath and asked him a total of twenty-six questions regarding the IRA operation at Antrim Road. Doherty, without flinching, replied, 'I refuse to say', in response to every question.

The interrogation ended, and Doherty was returned to his cell for lunch. After lunch, Detective Constable Hall remained to observe the questioning, but Flaherty was replaced by Detective Chief Inspector Cairns. It was a typical interrogation technique to remove one officer, and allow another to resume the interview. The detectives worked in teams, moving from Doherty to Fusco and the others, constantly changing their line of questioning and briefing each other as they handed over the interrogation of a particular suspect. For Doherty and his co-accused it was a disorientating process. Once he began to feel secure in responding to the questions of one interrogator, he was faced with another who would casually begin the same process, often examining the same issues.

Cairns began by reminding Doherty of the serious nature of the allegations against him and pointed out that twenty-four hours earlier 'a soldier, a human being, was alive and well, walking about this earth, and at 2.00 pm he was dead leaving a wife and child.'

'Are you not concerned that you are alleged to have taken part in this soldier's death?' asked the chief inspector.

Doherty paused, then replied: 'I know your line of thought, your line of thinking. You're barking up the wrong fucking tree.'

The police officer was repeating the procedure adopted by the previous interrogator in an attempt to seek out Doherty's emotions in respect of the killing. In trying to appeal to Doherty to exhibit remorse, he failed utterly. Doherty knew exactly what was going on.

The chief inspector asked if Doherty believed it was the duty of the police to prove the case against him, or whether he would volunteer a confession. Doherty replied sarcastically that he did not care, and the police were free to release him if they so 'liked'.

Detective Sergeant Flaherty returned to the room and joined in the interrogation. He moved his questions towards Doherty's failure to admit that he knew he could have been shot by the SAS. He put it to him that he should consider himself lucky to be alive. Doherty said that did not concern him. Flaherty made the point that it must surely have concerned Doherty, Fusco and Campbell, because they refused to surrender to the military, and instead sought police protection. Flaherty was probing the bravado, expecting to prise open Doherty's tendency to react to any suggestion that he might not be heroic, but it was a futile effort to persuade Doherty to say anything meaningful about the shooting. He replied to the detective in a familiar style with the statement 'I refuse to say'.

Detective Chief Inspector Cairns was not convinced by Doherty's steeliness, and returned to the risk posed to the IRA team by the SAS. The detective's persistence won through, if only temporarily.

'I suppose we or I was afraid that the Brits might shoot. It wouldn't be the first time. Who was shot? Was he SAS or what regiment?'

Cairns replied that it surely didn't matter but was Doherty concerned that the dead man was in fact a member of the SAS?

'I don't give a fuck,' retorted Doherty angrily. 'I'm fed up saying "I refuse to say".'

Flaherty intervened by telling the prisoner his show of bravado was designed to impress with a 'casual attitude towards the whole affair'.

Doherty did not appreciate the gibe and said: 'You can think what you like. I have nothing to lose, and nothing to gain.'

Cairns left the room and Flaherty continued the questioning, alternating between approaches designed to attack Doherty's estimation of self, and the gentle tactic of talking about his likes and dislikes.

An example of this technique occurred before 3.00 pm, when Flaherty suggested that the prisoner had a 'chip on his shoulder', as evidenced by his disgruntled attitude to society and expressed in his political rhetoric that morning. Doherty merely agreed that Flaherty could well be correct in his assessment of him.

The detective quickly left the topic and asked Doherty if he had hobbies or played sport. Doherty replied, 'No, not really.' That ended the interrogation session at exactly 3.40 pm.

Doherty was returned to his cell for refreshment and recalled to the interrogation room at 3.50 pm. His interrogators were now Detective Constables William Windrom and Stephen McMurtry. They began their session by engaging Doherty in a cross-questioning exercise. The transcript of that session demonstrates that only when Doherty's courage, or that of his comrades, was at issue was he willing to be drawn into a response, although he handled other questions in keeping with IRA policy.

Q:   You're not long out of jail, are you?
A:   November.
Q:   What were you in for?
A:   Bombing. I was caught with a bomb.
Q:   How long did you get?
A:   Twelve years. I only served six.
Q:   Will you recognise the court when this comes up?
A:   No.
Q:   Why?
A:   I don't know.
Q:   Do you think going to jail serves any purpose?
A:   I refuse to say.
Q:   Do you think going to court will be a waste of time?
A:   Refuse to say.
Q:   You were lucky to come out of that house yesterday.
A:   So I was told.
Q    Was yesterday the first time you were shot at?
A:   Refuse to answer.

The interrogators stopped briefly, because Doherty interrupted them to talk about his parents, their lifestyle, their hard-working approach to life and the various jobs his father worked at. It was Doherty's means of stemming the flow of questions and of giving himself time to relax, to think of his future responses and assess the men facing him. It was a tactic he learned during IRA training in anti-interrogation techniques. The detectives allowed him the opportunity to do this but proceeded with their short, sharp, predetermined line of questioning.

Q:   Are you grateful you are still alive?
A:   I suppose so.

*Q:*  Why did you not surrender to the army?

*A:*  Refuse to say.

*Q:*  Did you shoot yesterday?

*A:*  Refuse to say.

*Q:*  Were you looking after the hostages?

*A:*  Refuse to say.

*Q:*  Do you remember looking at the M60, Belgian rifle and another rifle and saying: 'There goes my baby'?

*A:*  Refuse to say.

*Q:*  Do you think you are brave men taking a house from a woman at gunpoint?

*A:*  Refuse to answer.

*Q:*  Are you afraid of the army? You are afraid to take them on in the streets.

*A:*  Are we? We'll get out our Chieftain tanks and tin helmets and see.

*Q:*  You weren't interested in anybody's safety when the M60 was fired. You could have killed four or five people walking about. Do you not care?'

*A:*  Refuse to say.

*Q:*  You wanted to live yesterday, that's why you surrendered.

*A:*  Refuse to answer.

*Q:*  Did the priest bring you out of the house yesterday?

*A:*  Aye.

*Q:*  Do you believe in God?

*A:*  No.

*Q:*  Well, why call out for a priest?

*A:*  Refuse to answer.

*Q:*  Do you believe that your beliefs could be put across in some way other than bombing or shooting?

*A:*  Aye. We could get the banners out, and march, and get shot at, and get the fuck kicked out of us.

*Q:*  What do you mean shot at?

*A:*  I mean rubber bullets and CS gas.

*Q:*  Are there any innocent people in Long Kesh?

*A:*  Sure. It's not a crime to shoot at someone in an opposite army.

*Q:*  So you think it's war?

*A:*  Aye.

*Q:*  You think to kill a member of the British army is not a crime?

*A:*  Aye.

*Q:*  Have you any training ground?

*A:*  Refuse to answer.

*Q:*  Why did you shout at people yesterday when you were being escorted along the Antrim Road – 'See you in thirty years'?

*A:*  Just for a laugh.

*Q:* When you are on the 'blanket protest' in prison will you smear the walls with your own excrement?

*A:* I'll have to.

*Q:* What do you mean you'll have to?

*A:* I want to. It's part of the protest.

*Q:* Do you want the Troubles to finish?

*A:* Aye. I'm fed up with them.

*Q:* Why keep fighting? What motivates you?

*A:* I believe in the cause.

*Q:* If the Troubles were over would you stop fighting and lay down your arms?

*A:* Aye.

*Q:* What would you do?

*A:* I'd get married. I'd go back to my job as a plumber, probably.

*Q:* What did you do yesterday morning when you got up until you were caught?

*A:* Refuse to answer.

*Q:* Why?

*A:* Why should I? I'm not going to tell you what time I got up or what hat I was wearing.

*Q:* What hat?

*A:* My wee black monkey hat.

*Q:* What gun did you fire?

*A:* Refuse to answer.

*Q:* Why?

*A:* It'll give you some more work in finding out.

*Q:* Is the M60 heavy?

*A:* Don't know. Refuse to answer.

*Q:* Were you involved in the hijacking of the van?

*A:* Refuse to answer. I suppose you think that after seven days of this I'll give in. It won't happen with me.

*Q:* Would you be honest with us?

*A:* I can't.

*Q:* Why?

*A:* Nothing to say.

The questioning was designed to find weaknesses in Doherty's character or his resolve, but none became obvious. Apparent stress in his demeanour only occurred when the courage or methods of the IRA were being chided or derided. When it was suggested that other methods could be employed to change society, he dismissed the civil rights approach of peaceful protest with the crude observation that such action would result in getting 'the fuck kicked out of us'. There was little room for manoeuvre in the police methods but they hoped that constant questioning and wearisome reiteration of issues might open a crack in his mental armour. Before the session ended at 6.15, Doherty talked again, keeping the discussion in his grasp, knowing the police would listen with expectation of a breakthrough. For his part, he was in control, and he talked of his previous imprisonment, internment, the manner in which he was treated at Girdwood Barracks, and his political philosophy. He was returned to his cell by his interrogators and uniformed personnel, and served dinner.

At 8.20 pm he faced his last interrogation session of the day, a short one, ending at 9.55 pm. It was undertaken by two detectives unknown to him, Detective Constable Derek McAllister and Detective Sergeant Jackson. Doherty began by refusing to answer any questions pertaining to the shooting of Westmacott but, when asked about himself, took the unusual step of discussing his love of sports including football and snooker. He contradicted earlier statements of that day – that he was not interested in sport and possessed no hobbies. Once again, Doherty was playing the interrogation game – searching out topics which halted the questioning and temporarily provided a diversion. His knowledge of football and snooker proved extensive and entertaining. His mood was lively, in marked contrast to the afternoon session with McMurtry and Windrom.

At 8.30 McAllister knew Doherty was playing for time. He and Jackson had seen a transcript of the earlier interrogation in which Doherty claimed not to have an interest in sport or hobbies. After affording his prisoner the luxury of discussing sport, McAllister changed the tone of the conversation. 'I suppose you expect a long sentence?' he asked. Doherty said he did and he would refuse to recognise the court.

The two detectives probed further and asked questions about the shooting. Doherty refused to reply. McAllister moved the discourse towards the prison sentence expected for the shooting of Westmacott and Doherty responded, admitting he believed it would amount to thirty years. Before the session ended, Doherty reminded McAllister and Jackson they were 'wasting time' talking about the killing and that over his seven days of interrogation he would not change his attitude to them. At 8.45 he admitted he was 'caught cold' at the shooting scene and for that reason there was little point in asking him questions about it.

The following morning at 11.10 Doherty was brought to the

interrogation room and, during a two-hour session, refused to reply to all questions put to him. As he walked from the room, one of the detectives asked why he was uncooperative. Doherty replied: 'It's a wee game I'm playing.' He played the 'wee game' in another period before tea, remaining silent throughout. He was asked to verify the transcript of those two interviews, and instead of signing them he wrote 'up yours' on the bottom of each transcript.

Detective Constables Windrom and McMurtry were in charge of those sessions and the notes they kept show how an experienced terrorist played the anti-interrogation game:

Q:   Why don't you talk to us?
A:   *Remained silent.*
Q:   Would you like to read more of the transcript of this session?
A:   *No reply. He held out his hand and appeared to read the page. Asked him to sign and he wrote 'up his'. He refused to read any more of the pages.*
Q:   You could have proved again you want to be involved in this process, so why not talk?
A:   *No reply.*
Q:   But you seem to want to get involved by reading the notes so why not talk?
A:   *Subject replied in Irish.*
Q:   Is that Gaelic you are speaking?
A:   *Subject nodded to indicate 'yes'.*
Q:   Why do you not speak in English?
A:   *Again replied in Irish.*
Q:   We do not understand Gaelic, so why make a reply in Gaelic? If you want to prove something speak in English.
A:   *Subject seemed to give a long answer in Gaelic.*
Q:   You know this will do you no good. We don't understand, and cannot record your answers, so will you talk in English?
A:   *Again answered in Gaelic.*
Q:   I suppose you think you're being smart with these stupid answers in Gaelic? This will not do you any good when it goes to court.
A:   I don't give a fuck.
Q:   If you say that why don't you give all your answers in English?
A:   *Again returned to Gaelic.*
Q:   Would you like to sign the notes in Gaelic?

Doherty maintained the tactic of replying in Irish until 4.45, when he was asked which gun he had used at 371 Antrim Road. He replied: 'The one with the trigger.'

At 7.45 pm Detective Sergeant Flaherty, now well known to Joseph Doherty, tried once again to break his man with the assistance of Detective Constable Hugh Hall.

Flaherty began gently by enquiring if the prisoner had been served tea and if he had enjoyed it. The detective proceeded in a traditional way to discover if the prisoner was considering a change of attitude to the shooting and a co-operative approach to police enquiries.

Doherty said he was thinking about it and the pending court proceedings, but he would not reverse his view or thoughts on the killings, and 'would change his mind for no one'. He added that there were matters which he was prepared to talk about. As the detectives listened intently, Joseph Doherty began describing an episode in his life which happened in 1974 in the New Lodge district. At that time his family were living at 25 Hallidays Road. One evening his parents and sisters were watching television when a bomb concealed in a creamery can was thrown through a front window of the house. The bomb was crudely made and incorrectly wired, and the blast went outwards towards the attacker and the family was uninjured. The blast caused considerable damage to the property and the house was eventually demolished. The incident resulted in the Doherty family moving to nearby 192 Spamount Street. Doherty attributed the attack to 'Prods'. The story was a further attempt by the prisoner to interrupt interrogation proceedings. Flaherty remained undaunted, and continued with his questions until after midnight, but to no avail. Once the bomb story ended, the prisoner refused to answer questions or be drawn into conversation. It was apparent that he was proving to himself and his interrogators that he was in control, and he would only talk when he regarded the moment judicious, and his choice of subject matter would be innocuous.

Doherty did not remain idle in those periods between interrogation sessions. He exercised, and strode up and down his cell to keep himself alert, and to seek a pattern of behaviour which he used to monitor time. It was critically important to him not to become disorientated, and IRA training had taught him that by assessing time and sleeping patterns, and through constantly regimented exercise, he could devise a time schedule much in keeping with the structures of daily life.

In subsequent interrogations in the days which followed he showed no sign of relenting on his committed refusal to answer pertinent questions. Occasionally he exhibited annoyance towards questions which undermined his self-esteem. McMurtry was steadily acquiring knowledge of those issues which tempted Doherty into delivering more than a one-word reply.

Q:　Why did you send for the police to surrender to them. Sure you're not friendly towards the police?

A:　We shouted out for a priest, not the police. The stupid Brit misunderstood and kept shouting to get the police. We told him not the police but a priest, minister, Pope, vicar, member of the church, for fuck sake.

Q:　How many people have the police shot in cold blood?

A:　But sure it's different for the police. We don't have jails and all that to keep you in if we catch you.

Doherty complained about the police and army shooting innocent men in the New Lodge area. He talked about his house being blown up with all his family in it. No one was hurt, but when his young sister ran through the back door she met an army foot patrol. He said the army gave clearance to the loyalists to carry out such bombings of Catholic houses and particularly to the Protestant Ulster Freedom Fighters (the military wing of the Ulster Defence Association).

Q:　What would you say if you had shot innocent civilians on Friday?

A:　Cat. I don't like the thought of killing or bombing.

Q:　But you will do it for your beliefs, will you not?

A:　Aye. I believe in the cause.

Q:　Do you believe violence solves the problem?

A:　I'm totally against violence unless it solves the problem. The problem is the British. If they were out there would be no problem.

Q:　Do you think that shooting a policeman or soldier will solve the problem or bring you closer to a United Ireland?

A:　I would rather negotiate for peace but it doesn't make my position any different. I'm going away.

The reference to peace negotiations provides an interesting, if confusing, insight into the mind of a terrorist such as Doherty. One could conclude either that he was lying or that he was a man under orders, whose personal views were of little relevance to his reality. I am inclined to the latter view, and it is a subject which impinges on any assessment of the life of Joe Doherty in the United States. Suffice it to say at this point that he was a dedicated member of the

IRA, a foot soldier who was tired, but there was no way out for him. He held an ideal, the IRA was his means of realising it, and his membership of the organisation demanded total obedience to IRA political policy. Doherty was caught up in a situation from which he knew he could not extricate himself, but yet he was curiously prepared to offer a personal opinion. I am drawn to believe that he was being truthful when he said that his opinion was of little importance because he was likely to spend the remainder of his life behind bars.

Five days after his arrest, at 2.30 pm on 7 May 1980, Doherty finally (judging from the transcript) showed signs of strain. The constant interrogation sessions were beginning to unravel some of the complexities of his personality. McMurtry and Detective Chief Inspector Dempsey began their search for answers by talking about the killing of Westmacott. They knew Doherty would react predictably by refusing to reply, and he did.

They quickly manoeuvred the conversation towards the one subject they knew their prisoner would not ignore – the prospect that the remainder of his life would be spent in prison. Both detectives sensed that Doherty was concerned about his family because he talked frequently of the hardship they endured. Could he be mentally weakened by confronting him with the effect his conduct would have on his next of kin? They began by reminding him that he faced at least thirty years for the murder of the SAS captain. Dempsey undertook the questioning and the following is a direct transcript. McMurtry was the note-taker:

*Q:* Do you know you are facing five times your last sentence?
*A:* So what? I'll do it.
*Q:* Why do a sentence like that?
*A:* That's what I'll have to do.
*Q:* If you make a statement it will be something for you to have at the court – to show you have some remorse about the incident.
*A:* I'm not making a statement.
*Q:* What about your family?
*A:* Leave my family out of it.

McMurtry recalls:

We went back again to having a general conversation about his life and how the IRA had not helped him in any way. We told him that as soon as he was off the streets another man would take his place. Doherty talked about his time in prison and how he was not looking forward to going inside again. He seemed to change his attitude to jail. He stated: 'I'll find it hard even doing another four years, never mind thirty years.' He said his mother would not like to see him inside again. We told him to think about his family and forget about the Provisionals as they weren't going to help him now. We told him to think about how many times he was going to see his family when he was in jail. He agreed with us that it was going to be hard on his family seeing him inside again and that a long sentence would probably kill his mother. It was pointed out to him that all we wanted was the truth, and would he like to make a statement about the incident? He seemed to think about it and then said: 'I'll make a statement, not for me, for my family. They've suffered enough, especially my mother.' We asked him to tell us about the incident and he stated that on Friday 2 May he went to 371 Antrim Road and took up position at the front of the house. The army drove up in a car and made an assault on the house. He added: 'I fired my weapon at the army and I don't know whether I hit anybody. I did it for the Provisional Irish Republican Army. I'm saying no more.'

Joseph Doherty signed the above statement without reading it and declined the offer of legal assistance. Before he left the interview room he reminded the two policemen that he had made the statement 'for the sake of his family'.

One of the factors which motivated Doherty's change of attitude to police questioning was to be found in the notes of an interview which occurred the previous night. Detective Constables McAllister and Malone were being constantly frustrated by the prisoner's negative approach until they both raised the issue of moral justification for violence. Doherty, who days earlier had denied belief in God, asserted that from a Christian standpoint there was no moral defence for IRA violence. He emphasised that he shared this view with the two detectives. He also defined himself as a Christian. Suddenly the policemen recognised a flaw in the previously immutable persona. They knew they were getting closer to that part of his personality which was vulnerable. His family background was that of a boy educated in a strict Catholic tradition, and his previous denial of God was a denial of his family. McAllister shifted the conversation towards family matters and pursued the question of the possible impact his actions would have on his mother.

Doherty broke down and wept. After several minutes he was composed, and stated:

I'm sorry for my parents. I've been thinking about it in my cell and when I was in jail; about getting married and settling down and that sort of thing. There's a girl – I suppose you have heard this type of story before – I've tried to break it up with me being in the movement. It wasn't on. They're always at you. I've tried to break it up but I've always ended up going back. She's special and I didn't want that. I'll tell you one thing – that soldier, it wasn't me. I have never injured anybody but I don't want to say any more. I don't really know how it all came about, none of the rest of my family are republican. They believe in a United Ireland but they always say 'that's terrible' if a soldier is shot or something like that. I grew up in a street that was Protestant, my friends were Protestant and I used to go along to the Orange procession on 12 July and never thought anything about it. I heard all the slogans like 'to hell with the Pope' and 'up King Billy' but they don't mean anything. None of my family is involved. My father would be a staunch trade-unionist but that's all. He has worked hard all his life. My mother has worked hard. He didn't come home drunk and beat us or my mother. He came home right enough with a few drinks taken. I don't know how it all started. I don't know why I'm saying all of this. I'm saying no more.

As far as the detectives were concerned, their prisoner was saying what they wished to hear. The veneer of the tough terrorist was suddenly stripped away. He was vulnerable after all, and his sensitivities about his family had not been blunted by his career as a gunman. The notes of that interview and an analysis of it by the team of interrogators provided the basis for the line of questioning by McMurtry and Dempsey – which led to Doherty making his statement of guilt.

One of the Crime Squad detectives told me that Doherty was a difficult subject. The interrogators knew they would probably fail to break him to the extent that he would admit to killing Westmacott or identify the guilty person. They were looking for a statement of his involvement in the actual shooting, as grounds for a murder charge in relation to acting in concert with the other gunmen in a conspiracy to kill. They achieved their goal by seeking out meticulously the only conceivable element of remorse in the character of a man who was an experienced terrorist. Doherty's interrogators knew he felt no guilt about the murder of a soldier, but his affection and sensitivity about his family was a recurring theme in his monologues during interrogation, and it was that element that they cleverly exploited.

How much truth is contained in those revelations about his family and the background to the conflict? A considerable degree of honesty emerged in those final interrogation sessions. His loyalty to the cause, meaning the republican ideal which his grandfathers held so dear, was in conflict with his loyalty to his parents and in particular the anguish he was causing his mother. If one simply viewed Doherty on that testimony, one would be inclined to recognise a young man who had been swept away in inherited ideals, the emotionalism of the late 1960s and early 1970s, and then controlled by an organisation which did not countenance betrayal. However, consider his personal commitment to that cause and his lack of remorse for the murder of Westmacott. Perhaps the answer lies in the events which occurred latterly.

Doherty admits that the days of interrogation concentrated not only on the gun-battle but on his family and his family background. He says he was also questioned about his political beliefs, the ongoing war, the post-British evacuation and whether policemen would ever face retribution or an IRA war crimes tribunal.

In the course of research I uncovered a story which illustrates the black humour endemic in the violent events of Northern Ireland. During an interrogation session in the early 1970s the Ardoyne commander, Martin Meehan, was badly beaten by British military questioners. In a lull in the proceedings Harry Patterson, a Special Branch officer, entered the interrogation room and requested a private conversation with a bruised and battered Meehan. Patterson was a priority IRA target but respected Meehan's toughness and resilience under what was a form of torture. He turned to Meehan and asked: 'Martin, when the war is over is there any place where officers like me will be safe?' Meehan peered at him through swollen eyelids and replied: 'Yes, Harry – the fucking sea of tranquillity.'

In 1984 Doherty told the US District Court, Southern District of New York, that the RUC interrogators did not torture him, but made threats against members of his family. When asked the nature of the threats he replied: 'The usual threats that are very common among the Special Branch and the British military forces; that is, is your father still working here and is your mother still working here, etc., and we will deal with them. The sort of sarcastic remarks about your family, bringing up your family life, etc.'

The US Attorney put it to Doherty that he spoke willingly about his family, and expressed concern to his interrogators in Northern Ireland that a prison sentence would have a detrimental effect on his family. Doherty responded with the lack of exactitude which was to become typical of his remarks in several court hearings in the United States: 'Yes. There was some sort of conversation in that line, but not the exact words as what you are talking about.'

The following is a transcript from the 1984 proceedings in New York and represents Doherty's retrospective analysis of his six days of interrogation. I include it to compare the lines of questioning and the diversity which emanates from it. The US Attorney for the Southern District posed the questions.

Q: Didn't you willingly speak about your family and the concern that your further imprisonment was going to have upon them?

A: Sorry?

Q: Didn't you mention to some of the police officers questioning you that you were upset for your mother and father, because you had been in jail for so long and this was going to have quite an impact on them, that you were going to be in jail some more, probably for what you thought was a long time, since you had been caught in the building?

A: Yes. There was some sort of conversation in that line, but not the exact words as what you are talking about.

Q: You expressed some remorse for the impact your actions were going to have upon your family, did you not?

A: Well, of course my family was going to suffer. My mother hadn't seen me for a number of years while I was in prison. Of course my mother takes it bad. She still takes it bad that I am still in prison. It's the same with the rest of my family.

Q: You talked about a girlfriend that you had, didn't you?

A: Well, of course. We all have girlfriends in Ireland.

Q: At one point while you were being questioned, Mr Doherty, you actually broke down in tears and expressed concern for your family?

A: Of course I have concern about my family. What do you think I am, an animal or something? You take it that you are locked up in a cell for seven days and the lights are on twenty-four hours, the temperature is kept at a very humid temperature. You are given no salt, and everybody knows what happens to you when you don't get salt, you feel eerie and depressed and things, I guess. It is not exactly fun being in the Castlereagh for seven days. It's very hard. Maybe, as I said, I didn't get physical torture, but I got what you call psychological effects, psychological torture. This is another part of the segment of the sensory deprivation, to isolate a person, to keep him awake twenty-four hours a day, etc., keep him on as minimum food as possible, don't give him water. Of course, after seven full days in a situation like this, you feel tired, you feel restless, you feel fed up. Of course. What do you expect?

*Q:*   Mr Doherty, didn't you tell some of the officers at one point that you had never injured anybody, and it was not you who killed the soldier?

*A:*   No, I am afraid I didn't.

*Q:*   You didn't say that?

*A:*   He asked me – they asked me did I kill anybody and I says 'no'. Of course, this is the attitude all volunteers take. You don't admit that you have killed anybody. You don't admit to jobs.

*Q:*   You didn't tell them specifically that it was not you who had shot at and killed the soldier?

*A:*   I didn't tell them that I shot the soldier, yes, correct.

*Q:*   You didn't say the opposite of that, that it was not you? 'I will tell you one thing, fellas, it was not me who shot the soldier'?

*A:*   No, that is a way that the police put it down, which wasn't true.

*Q:*   That was introduced at your trial, wasn't it?

*A:*   Yes, it was.

*Q:*   You are saying it didn't happen that way?

*A:*   It didn't happen in that specific way. They asked me did I kill anybody and I said 'no'. They asked me had I got any remorse. I said 'no', but I have sympathy with whoever his wife was, but the IRA have always expressed this, that the wives and parents of British troops or, of course, anybody who is killed in action, or killed by the IRA; but they blame the British Government. If the British Government wasn't in the North of Ireland, these people wouldn't get killed. After all, most of these British soldiers are from the same situation as ourselves. They are from big cities and, of course, unemployment, and the only employment is you join the British army. You join the British army out of somewhat false patriotism, whatever. They think it's their duty to go to the North of Ireland. They come to the North of Ireland in a war zone and they get killed. The fault lies with the British Government. Of course we don't take any fun in sending coffins of British soldiers back to their homeland. This lies with British policy in the North of Ireland. But if you are trying to say that I was actually sorry for the soldier, the soldier had a duty to do. The soldier came to the North of Ireland. He was killed in action and that's all that really could be said about it. But as far as –

*Q:*   Mr Doherty –

*A:*   Go ahead.

*Q:*   I thought you were finished. I'm sorry.

*A:*   No, I am just saying – you are trying to make out – as I say, it's already been expressed by the movement that these people should maybe put their false sense of duty behind them and go back to their own country. The fault lies with the British that most of these young men were killed.

Q:   Why did you make your written statement?
A:   I made a written statement to confirm that I was in the Irish Republican Army and had taken part in the operation. I fired my gun and I don't know whether I hit anybody or not.
Q:   You just wanted for the sake of the record to have said that in your written statement, is that what you are saying?
A:   Of course, after five or six days I felt very, very weary and I could say I was very psychologically damaged, as you could say it like that, and I think it was on the last day, the sixth or seventh day, they asked me to make a statement and I says, 'Okay, I will', and I made a statement, as you well know.

Whatever the truth of the account I have outlined, or Doherty's later evidence in New York, the RUC interrogation ended on 9 May 1980. Doherty was conveyed to prison to await trial, and uppermost in his mind was the prospect of thirty years behind bars. He was determined that no prison would hold him for long, because he was important to the IRA and they to him. Escape was his only way to fulfil his relationship with life and, as the American courts would later seek to prove, a continuing career in terrorism. (As regards the interrogation of the other three members of the IRA active service team no statements were forthcoming from them. Magee smoked incessantly during his sessions and, like Fusco and Campbell, persistently refused to reply to questions or remained silent. Fusco made one remark that as a Provo he could not speak to policemen.)

# 8

# The Great Escape

Joseph Doherty entered familiar territory when he was driven through the gates of Crumlin Road prison. It was his third visit to one of the most secure and heavily guarded prisons in Europe, situated half a mile from Belfast city centre in densely populated North Belfast. On the road opposite was the large imposing courthouse where most terrorist cases were heard. A tunnel running underneath Crumlin Road joined the two buildings. The prison housed terrorists awaiting trial and the tunnel ensured that they were led to the courthouse without risking a journey across a busy thoroughfare. When terrorists on remand were convicted, they were transferred from Crumlin Road to the Maze Prison, formerly Long Kesh. Crumlin Road prison proved a secure holding area and few terrorists managed to escape because of its tight security, its high walls, air-locking doors and the vigilance of a staff with a long history of dealing with many of the most dangerous prisoners in the world. As in all prisons in Northern Ireland there was always an awareness on the part of the authorities that the IRA was the most capable and clever organisation at planning escapes, because all IRA volunteers regarded themselves as prisoners of war with a duty to escape. They used prison as a means of causing disruption for the authorities, and they recognised the propaganda value accruing from successful breaches of prison security. The 4th Battalion, composed of prisoners in Crumlin Road and the Maze, constantly issued statements about prison conditions and prisoners' opinions on events in the outside world. Statements were smuggled out of the prison and communications from the IRA hierarchy found their way into the prison. In some instances prison officers were bribed, blackmailed or physically coerced into assisting the IRA.

When Doherty arrived in Crumlin Road prison he was assigned to A wing and was one of 200 republican inmates. On his first day, like all volunteers, he was obliged to report immediately to the IRA battalion commander. He was ordered to write an account of the Westmacott operation, and the subsequent police interrogation. The purpose of the exercise was twofold. First, the IRA required to know if an operation had failed so that it could attribute blame, or assess whether the operation had been compromised by someone in its ranks. A detailed account of police interrogation offered, through subsequent analysis, an indication of interrogation techniques and the type of intelligence the policemen required for their questioning of a suspect. IRA intelligence officers minutely examined volunteers' reports of their interrogation sessions in the hope that a detective's line of questioning might reveal something of his knowledge of terrorist methods and operations.

The IRA also made use of such reports in shaping anti-interrogation techniques. Terrorists were, and still are, held for questioning for seven days under the Prevention of Terrorism Act. During that period the IRA has virtually no access to them, and cannot determine if they have 'broken' under interrogation, and perhaps compromised other volunteers or future terrorist plans. The written account when a terrorist enters prison is the IRA means of assessing damage to its cause. The only way in which both republican and loyalist organisations circumvent the law is by using sympathetic solicitors who visit arrested terrorists, and then report back to terrorist leaders. The second dimension to IRA prison policy in 1980 was that a volunteer's 'confession' was passed to IRA internal security who assessed whether he had contravened IRA rules during an operation or during his interrogation. In the event that they deemed him to have acted irresponsibly, not in keeping with his orders, or that he divulged sensitive information to his interrogators, or carelessly endangered the lives of his comrades or innocent people during the operation, they were entitled to recommend a suitable punishment, or a court martial, which could be held within the prison.

Doherty completed a written account of events at 371 Antrim Road, his interrogation, and why he made a voluntary statement not permitted by IRA policy. His co-accused refused to make statements to police, but he was fortunate that his was a brief admission of his membership of the IRA and his part in the shooting. He argued that he made the statement merely because he had been caught red-handed, and added that he did not identify who fired the guns at 371.

The confessional records of Doherty, Fusco, Campbell and Magee were smuggled out of prison. They were written in typical IRA style in minute print on rolls of toilet paper. While the four waited for the IRA to analyse their written accounts they were not allowed to hold rank within the prison, or to be privy to the workings of the 4th Battalion.

Within two weeks the IRA commander in the prison received a communiqué from the Belfast Brigade saying the four were 'cleared volunteers'. The commander approached Doherty and told him he was appointing him the 4th Battalion publicity officer in the prison. The job necessitated the drafting of statements for the press on matters such as conditions in the prison, prison policy and support for IRA actions on the outside.

It was an important role because IRA prisoners in the Maze were 'on the blanket'. This was an ongoing protest against an attempt by the authorities to criminalise terrorists by forcing them to wear prison clothes and to undertake prison work. The Government was determined to eradicate the memory of Long Kesh and the status of paramilitary inmates as prisoners of war. The IRA believed the clothing issue was the beginning of a process which would lead to its men being perceived as ordinary criminals. It preferred the earlier Long Kesh model where prisoners behaved as political prisoners of conscience and were distinguished from ordinary inmates because they wore civilian clothes, did no prison work, had their own command structures and treated their prison surroundings as a parade ground. In protest at Government attempts to change the rules, IRA prisoners wore only blankets, refused to leave their cells, smeared cell walls with excreta and refused to allow their hair to be cut. This soon became known as the 'Dirty Protest'. The IRA demands were supported in the outside world by a grouping known as the National H-Block/Armagh Committee. It was an amalgam of republicans, left-wingers and professed liberals who organised rallies, newssheets and press conferences to highlight the plight of the dirty protesters in the H-Blocks.

In Crumlin Road prison there were several prisoners 'on the blanket' in support of those in the Maze. Doherty constantly wrote statements about the sympathy protest. He was also made director of education with responsibility for co-ordinating lectures and debates, as well as acquiring books requested by other inmates. He says the education classes were 'pretty basic', and included the history of the republican movement, all struggles against the British, constitutions such as that of the United States of America and the general history of Europe. Those subjects were taught by IRA officers in separate lectures. Doherty organised debates among the men about the building of a new Ireland, the 'post-British evacuation' and the formation of economic and social policies. His explanation for the education classes was that the IRA in prison 'must be kept alive, the men are combatants and must educate themselves to the full'.

Within three months he was appointed to the Escape Committee, the most secret IRA body within the prison. The decision was probably taken because of Doherty's long prison experience, his trustworthiness and obvious dedication to IRA ideals. The responsibility for such a decision lay not only with the battalion commander but with the Army Council, the highest IRA authority in the outside world. The Army Council Director of Prisons communicated with all battalion commanders behind bars. In respect of the Maze and Crumlin Road he employed the resources of the Belfast Brigade as a conduit for his communiqués or orders. Doherty's elevation to the six-man Escape Committee was indicative of the IRA's esteem for his loyalty and ability.

We were formulating about three or four escapes. We had a few ideas. Some were to go over the wall. There were another couple of ideas for digging tunnels. Security was so tight that the tunnels, and plans for going over the wall, were out. A volunteer suggested to the committee that maybe we should go out the way we came in, and that was to go out the front gate.

The latter concept was accepted and Doherty assigned volunteers to what he termed 'intelligence duties'. They were ordered to map out the security measures throughout the prison and the position of remote-control cameras. The vital task was to listen for codes or passwords used by the prison officers when they were handing over duties or locking and unlocking doors. On many doors there were emergency buttons which, if pressed in the events of an escape, led to the entire prison being electronically sealed.

The Escape Committee spent three months analysing the

volunteers' intelligence reports before determining the viability of the plan and recommending its implementation. Doherty says: 'This was a tough one – so a lot of intelligence had to go into doing this, because we had to base it on a military operation; co-ordination, timing, synchronising of watches, just like you really see in the movies.'

In 1990, in the Southern District Court of New York, Doherty, in reply to questions from the US Attorney Otto Obermaier, offered an insight into his role in Crumlin Road prison in 1980:

| | |
|---|---|
| *Obermaier*: | I would like to know first of all, were you directed to break out? |
| *Doherty*: | No, Your Honour. The prisoners organised a battalion. They call it the 4th Battalion of the Belfast Brigade. Each prison is organised in a battalion because we are recognised political prisoners. In the sense of the structure of the prison, there is a big difference between the New York Metropolitan Correction Centre and the prisons in the North of Ireland. |
| *Obermaier*: | There is some sort of self-government? |
| *Doherty*: | Yes. You have the battalion staff, the PRO, the education officer, the training officer, etc. Within that you have an Escape Committee, and they meet just like the educational committee. They meet once a week to form escape procedures. They take ideas from the political prisoners, and they organise getting ropes or tunnels or guns through the prison. |
| *Obermaier*: | And the prison authorities permit the Escape Committee to meet every week? |
| *Doherty*: | No. It is a quasi-secretive – it's a sort of secretive committee. The authorities in the prison know the IRA command. They approach the command within the prison if there is a problem between officers and volunteers. In Long Kesh I was a quartermaster, a staff captain in C Company. I dealt with staff, maps, everything. The Governor or Warden, as you say over here, would approach our commanding officer. In other words the authorities reckon the structure. With the exception of the Escape Committee, the IRA command structure is well known and accepted by the British authorities. The Escape Committee meets secretly within a cell or prison yard. |

Doherty also offered Obermaier an accurate account of the way in which the prison authorities dealt with those entering prison. It illustrated his point that the prison hierarchy liaised closely with the IRA command within penal institutions.

You are designated to a particular prison where you are segregated off. You go to a block which is 300–400 member blocks. The commanding officer will ask you are you republican or loyalist, and you will say 'I am an Irish republican'. Whether you are IRA, or someone associated with the IRA, you will be accepted into that block as a political prisoner by the Governor or Warden.

Doherty rightly described how the paramilitaries were influential in deciding where a prisoner resided within the actual prison. As soon as a terrorist arrived in prison, one of the first people he met was a terrorist commander, who alone determined the politics of the inmate and to which part of the prison he should be confined. It was exactly that procedure that the authorities were seeking to eradicate with their criminalisation policy in 1980. The conflict between the dirty protestors and the Government was about to impact on Doherty and his plan to escape from what the former British Prime Minister, Margaret Thatcher, once described as one of the most secure prisons in the world.

While the plan was being formulated, seven IRA H-block prisoners in the Maze began a hunger strike on 27 October, to try to force the authorities to reinstate special-category status for IRA prisoners. The special category which had been in force from the outset of internment, allowing terrorists to be regarded as political prisoners, had ended almost five years earlier. Its ending signalled violence and the dirty protest. By 27 October 1980 the IRA believed a hunger strike was the only method of forcing Margaret Thatcher and her Government to relent but they underestimated the tenacity of Thatcher and her formidable image. By 18 December, the IRA was persuaded to end the hunger strike in the belief that the British would agree to concessions. The IRA proved itself naïve. The late Irish Cardinal Tomas O'Fiaich travelled to Rome to solicit the Pope's intervention during the hunger strike, and interceded to no avail with the British Government. The strike ended because the IRA wrongly interpreted documents presented to them by the British Government. Those documents indicated the basis for negotiation if the hunger strike was ended, and if the IRA agreed to terms. The IRA later felt it was duped by the British, and that may well be a fact of history.

By Christmas, Doherty and his Escape Committee, who were following events in the Maze, sent their escape plan to the Belfast Brigade, proposing that fourteen prisoners should be involved. While they awaited a reply, the situation in the Maze appeared to be resolved. The IRA, believing it had grounds for a settlement with the authorities, ordered men on the dirty protest to wash and shave, and relatives were requested to come to the prison with clothes for those men. On 20 January 1981, prisoners' relatives arrived at the Maze but the authorities refused to pass on the clothing. The IRA responded by resuming the dirty protest and wrecking cells. Another hunger strike was advocated.

Meanwhile the Crumlin Road Escape Committee received approval for its plan with a proviso that only eight volunteers should participate. The Belfast Brigade named those it wished to see on the escape list. Doherty believes he knows the factors which led the brigade to make its particular selection:

It must be volunteers, experienced volunteers, prestige volunteers. He could be a brigade or divisional commander, somebody very important, particularly to us. I wasn't a commander. I was just an ordinary foot-slogger, but the case of the SAS shootout brought a lot of publicity, where we actually fought the SAS head-on, and the case was very famous. So they wanted myself and the three other volunteers who engaged the SAS to be on the escape.

Irrespective of Doherty's self-deprecating description of himself as 'a foot-slogger', he was now an important figure in IRA thinking. The prospect of extracting the four members of the M60 gang appealed to IRA propagandists, but the escape plan was overtaken by other events.

On 1 March, Bobby Sands, the IRA officer commanding in the Maze, began a hunger strike which gradually brought world attention to the republican cause. Doherty's escape group received a communication from the Belfast Brigade, and Doherty as the publicity officer personally took possession of the directive. He says:

The communication read 'Urgent'. This was a lengthy communiqué stating the policies of the republican movement outside, the IRA on the outside stating that Bobby Sands and the other lads were on hunger strike in the H-Blocks. The brigade felt the escape should be suspended because there was ongoing negotiations in the H-Blocks. There were representatives from the Pope, the United States, Amnesty International, the European Parliament and the Southern Irish Government. They were trying to convince the British to make some sort of negotiation with Bobby Sands. They thought that by our escape we could jeopardise these very, very touchy negotiations which were going on on the outside, so they told us to suspend the escape plan.

What Doherty really means was that the IRA could not afford a publicity disaster. They were successfully controlling propaganda, and support was being expressed from across the globe for the hunger-strikers. Sands was elected to the Westminster Parliament while he lay dying in his prison cell. A prison escape in Belfast would have highlighted the danger posed to prison security by determined terrorists, and would have overshadowed the hunger strike. The IRA knew the authorities would make political capital out of a successful prison break and use it to undermine the hunger-strikers' demands. On 28 April President Reagan said the USA would not intervene in the hunger strike, but he was 'deeply concerned about the tragic situation in Northern Ireland'. The Pope sent an envoy to meet both Sands and British Government representatives. The envoy returned to Rome believing the British were uncooperative. Sands died on 5 May, the sixty-sixth day of his fast. His funeral was attended by 100,000 people, many of them not supporters of the republican cause. Seven days later, a second hunger-striker, Francis Hughes, died.

After four deaths the Belfast Brigade contacted Doherty. He says they pointed out that the IRA now knew it 'could not put the British in a corner' and the escape plan was to be accelerated. This latest communiqué stressed the need to put more work into the plan: 'They told us in a footnote to go over the plans again because it was important for the escape to come off as the morale in the country was very low.'

The IRA on the outside was inextricably linked to the hunger strike, which would claim the lives of six other men. Doherty confirms an interesting historical point that the IRA knew the hunger strike was a failure at an early stage, but could not extricate themselves from it. The IRA needed a morale booster, an operation which would improve the morale of its own men and embarrass a government which was immovable on the prison issue.

The escape plan appeared simple, yet it demanded operational requirements inside and outside the prison. The Escape Committee, with Doherty a central planner, believed that a cell block in the middle of the prison could be commandeered prior to the escape. The block was set aside by the prison authorities for supervised interviews between lawyers and prisoners. Inside were 'holding areas', where prisoners were held prior to the arrival of their legal representatives. Alongside the holding areas were interview cubicles, or 'bullpens', as they are known in the USA. Solicitors sat with prisoners in the cubicles, while prison staff maintained scrutiny at a polite distance. The escapers' objective was to take over the block, arrest prison officers and lawyers and put them in the holding cells. Doherty was specifically assigned to remove the clothes of a prison officer and dress in them. The eight escapers would then pose as solicitors and prison staff. They knew they would have to act convincingly to negotiate a route through three air-locked gates. Those posing as solicitors would remove the briefcases from the lawyers and carry them. The eight would also be in possession of the prison passes handed to each lawyer who entered the holding area. The passes were intended to identify visitors leaving the prison so that the authorities could maintain an accurate check on all people entering and leaving Crumlin Road jail.

Doherty knew that once outside the prison they would not be safe. The courthouse across the road was heavily guarded. If a prison alarm was sounded at the moment of breakout, security forces personnel at the court would quickly rush to the prison gates. Speed, and the provision of getaway vehicles, would be essential. The Belfast Brigade informed Doherty that adjacent to the courthouse, and 30 yards from the prison, was a car park where several cars would be placed by IRA active service personnel. The make and registration of those cars would be conveyed to the Escape Committee prior to the breakout. The cars would be hijacked on the escape morning. Because of intensive security measures in the vicinity of the prison and courthouse, only a few IRA active service personnel could be used in a back-up role near the car park to cover the escape. Guns would be smuggled into the prison and the escapers would, if necessary, shoot their way out of the prison and away from the vicinity. Those selected for the escape were all capable of using weapons and of dealing with a gunfight inside or outside the prison. The only matter which was not resolved was the date of the escape. The IRA quickly defined a major obstacle. The trial of Doherty, Fusco, Campbell and Magee was about to begin and would mean that they would be in the courthouse on weekdays and under intense security. If the trial ended quickly and they were found guilty and sentenced, they would be removed to the Maze Prison, and they would not be part of the escape.

The trial of the four began on 27 April 1981. After three days, Doherty, under IRA orders, dismissed his lawyers and refused to recognise the court, ensuring the proceedings were lengthened. That suited the IRA, which was uncertain about the nature of the hunger strike and preoccupied with finding a way out of it. Towards the end of May, with five hunger-strikers dead and the trial coming to a close, it became crucial for the escapers to be given a specific date for their plan. The Lord Chief Justice completed the taking of evidence and announced that he was ordering a recess to allow him time to reconsider the evidence and reach a judgement. Doherty and his co-conspirators knew that time was not on their side. He says that two small .25 calibre pistols were already concealed in the prison. He has always been vague about these weapons – which suggests that they were smuggled into the prison either two weeks beforehand, twenty-four hours before or on the day of the escape. The Belfast Brigade learned that the Lord Chief Justice, the Honourable Mr Hutton, intended to deliver his verdict on 12 June, and in response set the breakout date for 10 June. Doherty says this was after the last hunger-striker died, but he is incorrect, since the hunger strike did not end until October 1981. This suggests that by June the IRA was desperately aware of the futility of the process and was keen to seek a morale booster and a reverse of its propaganda losses.

According to Doherty, on the morning of 10 June the eight prisoners selected for the escape were told there were to be no casualties, and the breakout would coincide with the visit of solicitors and barristers. Sixteen prisoners, including the eight selected for escape, requested visits from their legal representatives. These were scheduled to begin mid-afternoon, and the prison authorities arranged to transfer four prisoners at any one time to the cellular holding/visiting block.

Senior Prison Officer John Patrick Bell, who was assigned the role of professional visits officer on that day, recalls that he was in position at the main gate at 3.00 pm. His task was to accompany solicitors and other legal representatives to the cell block. At 3.05 pm he met two solicitors, Oliver Kelly and John Rice. Kelly, who was Doherty's lawyer, told the prison officer that Mr Steele, a clerk in his law firm, would shortly arrive to assist him. Prison Officer Bell assured Kelly that he would hurry Steele to the visiting area on his arrival at the front gate.

Bell and several other prison officers began the process of removing prisoners from the holding area known as 'search-box short-term visits' to nearby adjoining cubicles, where they were presented to their solicitors. Kelly and Steele conducted business with Campbell, Magee, McKee and Fusco. In adjoining cubicles, solicitors Peter Forde, William McNulty and John Rice were dealing with other prisoners.

At 4.00 pm Senior Officer Bell was standing in a passageway close to the cubicles, discreetly observing proceedings, when Doherty, Sloan, Magee and Campbell indicated that their visits were ended and they wished to be returned to the holding area. Bell says Magee was the first to leave a cubicle and he walked into the passageway followed by Sloan, Doherty and Campbell. Bell adds: 'Magee was in front of me, Sloan was alongside me and Doherty and Campbell were behind me. We were followed by Prison Officer Tweed.'

None of the prisoners was searched on leaving the cubicles because Bell believed in the security of the system. Prior to being taken from their cells to the visits area, prisoners were searched but maybe not thoroughly enough. The positions chosen by the prisoners on their exit from the cubicles was prearranged. Magee turned towards Bell and in one sudden movement raised his right hand to reveal a pistol which he levelled beside the officer's left temple. This grouping was now stationary outside number 3 holding room and Bell, aware that other prison officers were in that room, decided to test Magee's willingness to use the pistol. Bell made to move towards the room but Magee pushed the gun tight against the officer's head and said: 'You'd better stay where you fucking are and do nothing.'

Bell quickly recognised the threat and interpreted his position as acutely dangerous. He moved back against the wall of the passageway just in time to see Joseph Doherty waving a pistol at Officer Tweed. Doherty forced Tweed alongside Bell and told them to remain still and silent.

Magee walked to the door of holding room 3 and released Fusco, Sloan and McKee. Prison Officers Bell, Tweed and Muir were escorted into the room by Doherty, who levelled his gun at them. Other prison staff from two other holding rooms and the visiting area were rounded up by Doherty, Magee and Campbell and ushered into holding room 3.

Bell remembers solicitors Kelly, Rice and Steele being pushed into the room by Joseph Doherty and a fellow prisoner, Michael Ryan. He says: 'The solicitors did not speak to me. I saw Anthony Sloan grab solicitor Rice and told him to come on. Rice said: "No, I'm having nothing to do with this." ' John Rice, under the threats, was pushed into the room with the other hostages.

Officer Tweed remembers Campbell warning him not to do 'anything stupid', and Doherty ordering him to remove his cap, tunic, baton and whistle. These were finally pulled from him by other prisoners. Other officers were also told to remove their uniforms, which were given to prisoners who in turn removed their civilian clothes and dressed as prison officers. Doherty was one of those chosen to play the role of a prison officer.

Everything appeared to be working according to plan. All the prison officers in the bock were subdued by the threat posed by firearms. The escapers were fortunate that no one was in a position to raise the alarm, but they needed to gain access to an area designated 'B Division', which led to the front gates. Their path was blocked by a door locked from the outside. The door was guarded by Prison Officer Richard Ian Kennedy, who was large in stature, and fearless. His role was to search prisoners entering the visiting area: prisoners were accompanied by another prison officer who requested admittance, and it was left to Kennedy to slide back the heavy bolt on the door and usher them into the block.

Kennedy provides a graphic description of how he was unknowingly drawn into the escapers' plan and how he tried to resist:

I went to a post known as 'search-box short-term visits', which is located on the ground floor at the bottom of a set of wooden stairs, which led in the direction of B Division. My duty was to search and record the movement of prisoners to and from short-term visits. The area used for this purpose is a big room of which the search-box is a sealed-off section. At approximately 4.05 pm I admitted a prisoner known to me as 'Quigley', who was accompanied by Prison Officer Worbey. I completed a search of the prisoner who was carrying a paper bag containing assorted items of confectionery which had been purchased at the prison Tuck Shop. Nothing unusual was found. I looked through the flap of the wooden door which had direct access to the visiting area and having satisfied myself that everything was correct I slid the bolt across and opened the door. Both prison officer and prisoner passed through and out of my view. While in the process of closing the door an inmate whom I know as Fusco burst through the door and I noticed immediately that he was carrying an officer-issue baton and what was unusual is that he held it upside-down in his left hand. In the space of a few seconds he was joined by another inmate whom I know as Campbell. He was carrying a small automatic pistol in his right hand.

Kennedy's huge frame must have intimidated the prisoner because Campbell pulled back the sliding carriage of the pistol, ejecting a round into the chamber. He pointed the gun at Kennedy and told him: 'Kennedy, this is no fucking joke. We are taking you as a hostage.' He grabbed the officer by one of the lapels of his tunic and demanded the keys for doors to the block. Kennedy replied that they were in the possession of another officer. The prisoners, one of them holding the back of his collar, pushed him towards the holding rooms. He felt the gun pressed tightly into his body below his right shoulder blade. As he walked along the passageway towards holding room 3 he saw Officer Worbey ahead of him, looking round, a look of helplessness on his face.

Kennedy entered the room and walked towards a concrete pillar in the middle of it. He used the pillar to swing his body round to face his captors and simultaneously drew his baton and struck Campbell twice on the side of the head.

His show of bravery was calculated to deal first with the man who posed the greatest threat with the firearm, but Kennedy did not know that the prisoners possessed two weapons. As Campbell reeled, stumbling, from the baton blows, Kennedy was struck on the head from behind by a blunt instrument, probably the other gun. As he fell to the ground he was repeatedly punched and kicked. Kennedy says he has a clear recollection that, as the attack ceased, a calm authoritative voice said: 'Don't shoot him, or we won't get out.' Another voice ordered that he be 'left, lying on the floor'. That order was not complied with and he was dragged from the room. Officer Bell recalls the prisoners bolting the door of the holding room. He looked out of the top portion of the door and saw several prisoners dragging the battered and seemingly un-conscious officer along the passageway. He also saw McKee drag another officer into a room opposite.

Everything was now working according to plan. The Escape

Committee had organised the prison arrangements to ensure, in the first place, that the eight selected were all at one time in the visiting area. To this day no one is certain whether the guns were smuggled from cells, or were concealed in the holding area, or in the vicinity of the visiting cubicles. Officer Kennedy thoroughly searched all prisoners entering the block and feels that the guns must have been in the block when the prisoners arrived. No one may ever resolve the matter of the guns, but it is worth noting that they were .25 calibre, small and easily hidden.

All accounts of the takeover of the block state that several of the prisoners were seen carrying pistols. That may well be due to prisoners handing their weapons to fellow inmates, while rounding up the prison staff and the solicitors. Doherty and Campbell appeared prominently in eyewitness accounts as the two prisoners most frequently seen with weapons in the initial part of the escape.

The escapers were now faced with the task of convincing prison staff at the exits that they were prison officers and solicitors. While some of the escapers wore prison officers' tunics, others carried their lawyers' briefcases in an attempt to look like members of the legal profession. With their hostages securely sealed in the holding rooms, the eight made their way into the prison yard. They were faced with two gates which were 15 feet apart, separated by what is termed an 'air-lock', a secure area which could be electronically sealed. The first gate led directly to the main gate, which opened on to a short laneway facing Crumlin Road and the courthouse. The first gate in the air-lock was a wicket gate which opened by means of a key held only by the officer in the air-lock. Prison staff referred to the inner gate as Golf 2 and the main gate as Golf 1.

As the escapers approached Golf 2 they came to the attention of Officer Thomas Perrit, who was in charge of that location. He was not fooled by those prisoners who were posing as solicitors but the sight of 'prison officers' in their midst delayed his reaction.

I observed a group of men walking towards me from the reception area. The group was led by inmate Anthony Sloan who was dressed in a civilian jacket and carrying a black briefcase. Behind him was Joseph Doherty dressed in a prison officer's tunic, cap and tie. He was walking with his head down and I didn't realise it was him until later. These men were walking in a rounded group and I could see different persons dispersed throughout the crowd wearing prison officers' clothing. My first impression was that a group of prisoners was being escorted by prison staff.

The group made its way to Perrit, and Sloan stepped forward and handed him a brown prison pass used only by solicitors. He tried to push past to gain access to the air-lock but Perrit realised what was happening and tried to restrain him. Michael Ryan, disguised in a prison officer's uniform, stepped forward and stuck 'a blunt instrument' in Perrit's back and ordered him to open the gate. Perrit complied in the belief that the blunt instrument was a loaded gun. Ryan told him to 'make no noise'. Officer Perrit opened the gate and was pushed into the air-lock, followed by the escapers. Doherty levelled a pistol at his face and warned: 'Keep that door locked or I'll blow you away, you bastard.'

The closing of the wicket gate ensured that the escapers were in the air-lock, a small area which sealed them from the main prison buildings, and prevented prison staff from gaining access to them. Provided they could overpower the officer at Golf 1, the main gate, they would be free to negotiate a path to the escape cars parked nearby. If they failed to take Golf 1 the air-lock would be activated and would hold them in the tiny area between the two gates.

Forty-six-year-old David Batchelor was on guard at Golf 1, and his role was to check the identity of people entering or leaving the prison. Every day at 4.00 pm officers who had completed duty left the prison by a visitors' gate beside the main gate. At 4.15 pm he was standing sideways to the visitors' gate when the escaping group approached. The first person to pass him was a man in a prison officer's uniform, carrying a briefcase. His attention was drawn to that person because part of the prison tunic was irregular. The man was wearing brown trousers and not the regulation navy-blue trousers of prison staff. He scrutinised the man's face and, on recognising him as Joseph Doherty, rushed to seal the visitors' gate. As he fumbled to close it he heard someone shout 'Get him!' He was 'chopped on the back of the neck' and fell to the ground.

Suddenly the eight escapers were above him and he was scrambling on the ground. He intentionally tripped one of them but the prisoner quickly rose to his feet and rushed through the visitors' gate with the others.

As the escapers ran from the prison, an alarm was sounded, attracting the attention of the security forces personnel at the courthouse. Full-time Reserve Constable David Studd was on duty at the courthouse when the prison alarm sounded. The sight of a group of men running from the main gate of a secure prison was sufficient to encourage him to action. He noticed that two of the men were carrying batons and were dressed as prison officers. They all ran along the Crumlin Road towards the nearby car park which was attached to a health centre. Constable Studd set off on foot in pursuit of the men and saw them enter a car park. He momentarily lost sight of them until he also reached the car park, and saw the escapers positioned behind two cars. He took out his Walther pistol, levelled it at them and called upon them to halt.

One of the men pointed what Studd judged to be a .38 special revolver and fired several shots at him. Studd returned fire with one shot and saw the gunman raise the revolver again and release several more rounds. He suddenly discovered that shots were being fired from behind him by other police officers and he was in danger of being caught in the crossfire. As the shooting continued he holstered his gun, dropped to the ground and crawled out of the line of fire.

In his initial pursuit of the escapers Studd had failed to notice a police car travelling citywards along the Crumlin Road. The occupants were Constables Patrick, Tynan and Thompson, who were off duty. Patrick was 100 yards from the prison when he saw eight men running towards the car park at Court Street. He accelerated into Court Street and he and his colleagues alighted from their car, their guns in their hands. At the same time another police car mounted the pavement in Court Street alongside a 3ft-high wall which surrounded the car park. The officers in this car took cover behind the wall. Constable Patrick knelt behind the front offside wing of his car in time to witness one of the escapers firing a handgun. Patrick, who was armed with a powerful Ruger revolver, fired back.

Three detectives in a car driving past the prison also observed the breakout, but the fact that several of the escapers were dressed in prison uniforms created confusion in the policemen's minds. One of those detectives, Samuel Hamilton Curry, provided this account of the escape:

I was sitting in a police Ford Escort with Detective Sergeant Herron and Detective Constable Logan when I saw a number of males running out of the prison, followed closely by three or four prison officers. They ran across the road diagonally towards the health centre. One of the prison officers had a baton, holding it in the air with his left hand. I thought these were civilians who had assaulted a prison officer, and we drove up the road to render assistance. This group of men appeared to be authentic as they ran across the Crumlin Road. The prison officers jumped over the car park wall at the end of the courthouse. Our car pulled to a stop at the junction of the courthouse railings and I heard a number of bangs. A number of shots were fired. One of these shots hit the bonnet of our car.

Detective Curry was getting out of his car when he saw one of the escapers firing at him and realised that his colleague, Detective Logan, was standing in a vulnerable position at the car park entrance, four yards from a person dressed in prison officers' uniform.

The person dressed in prison officer's uniform had a gun in his hand and had it pointed at Detective Constable Logan. Logan called to this prison officer, and told him he was a policeman. The prison officer took aim and fired two shots at Detective Logan. There were other shots being fired and I fell to the ground and took cover.

The bogus prison officer who fired at Detective Constable Logan was Michael Ryan. The three detectives later considered themselves to have had a lucky escape. Logan also fired at his assailant before diving for cover but was unsure if his shots found their target. The majority of security forces personnel who surrounded the car park were members of the RUC, though one soldier, Corporal John William Younger, ran to the car park perimeter and discharged four rounds at the IRA men.

Doherty and his fellow terrorists, in the middle of a gun-battle, were almost surrounded, and knew that time was running out for them. He says that as many as a hundred shots were fired, though official estimates put the number at fifty or less. Doherty claims the firing was 'sporadic'.

In 1984 he gave an account of the escape aftermath to a New York court, and his description of events conflicted with the official version. He said the escapers fired their weapons because of the overwhelming numbers of police and soldiers surrounding them, and the superior firepower ranged against them. It is true that there was a large number of security personnel on the scene but, as I have discovered, the majority were police officers. It was the responsibility of the RUC to guard the courthouse. His claim that the firepower of his adversaries was superior was also true, except that Doherty deliberately overestimates its quality: 'Of course when you have maybe fifteen or sixteen military and police firing Heckler & Koch rifles, Belgian FN machine-guns, pistols, you are going to return fire.'

That gross exaggeration of the weaponry used by the police was Doherty's justification for the use of weapons by the escape team. If such powerful automatic rifles were used, it is doubtful that any of the IRA volunteers would have been so brazen as to stand and fire at Detective Logan or other policemen present. The policemen were all armed with pistols; the exception was the army corporal, who had a rifle. It seems to me that Doherty didn't need to exaggerate the seriousness of what was a crazy gun-battle, but he sought to demonstrate to an American court that the IRA team were obliged to defend themselves because so many bullets were being directed at them from high-powered weapons. In fact he alleged that the IRA escapers were 'returning fire for the sake of return fire, to make possible the escape'. That assertion conflicts with numerous eyewitness accounts which illustrated that the escapers were directing their fire at targets, and not into the air.

Doherty also gave the American court a description of the outside of the courthouse which was a vivid example of his tendency to exaggeration: 'This is one of the most security-tight courts in the world. It has pill-boxes, machine-gun posts, and outside the front gate you usually have a platoon of soldiers in place.' 'Usually' was a convenient word to indicate either that 'sometimes' there was a platoon, or that as a matter of policy there was always a platoon. In my experience of the geography of Crumlin Road, I have never known the army – usually, regularly or occasionally – to station a platoon at the front gates, or inside the front gates, of the courthouse. He talked of pill-boxes and machine-gun posts which have never existed at that location. There has always been tight security around the courthouse, but not of the nature conveyed in Doherty's account. If his account were true, the IRA team would never have made it to the car park, let alone out of the area. He alleged that the gun which he used during the takeover of the prison jammed while he was in the car park, and that another volunteer tried to fix it. His testimony in the United States did not identify him as firing that gun at any time during the escape. I am not inclined to believe him because of the central role he played in the proceedings. However, he was willing to concede that several armed, active service IRA volunteers were waiting in the car park to give covering fire, and did indeed discharge their weapons.

In the midst of the gun-battle, when the escape looked doomed, it was left to Doherty to resurrect IRA fortunes. In an incredible show of bravado, self-assurance, some would say courage, others foolhardiness, he took the initiative and stopped police firing with one gesture.

There was an active service unit round the cars to give us armed back-up. A mass gun-battle started. We were crouched behind a car. The police and army were at the trunk of the car. We were trying to get into the car but there was too much firing. We only had two guns, one is operating but the other is jammed. I don't know whether it was just nerve. I stood up and put my hand up and told them I was a police officer. This totally confused them because of the prison officer's dress. I jumped up and said, 'Police, police, don't fire.'

The stunt did indeed confuse the security forces and they temporarily lowered their weapons. That was sufficient for some of the escapers and the back-up IRA men to jump into their cars and drive away. In seconds, the police realised they were being fooled. Some of the IRA men, among them Doherty, made off on foot. Constable James Patrick fired at the departing cars, shattering the rear windscreen of one. Some of his colleagues followed his example and the cars were peppered with bullets, but the damage was not enough seriously to impair the vehicles or their passengers. Afterwards the examination of the scene of the gun-battle revealed a large number of cars with bullet holes, and the presence of many vehicles in the car park was a likely reason why there were no dead bodies at the scene.

When Doherty was asked to account to a New York court for his movements after the escape, he replied that he made his way to Catholic West Belfast, and handed himself over to his IRA superiors. That was not entirely true, and the events which followed the gun-battle were as remarkable as the prison escape itself.

The car park was on the periphery of the Shankill Road, one of the staunchest loyalist strongholds in Northern Ireland. Hundreds of little streets provided a network of thoroughfares which linked the Shankill and Crumlin Roads. Doherty and his fellow terrorists were in the heart of enemy territory, the centre of loyalist terror group operations. To reach the Catholic Falls area of West Belfast, they faced crossing through the Shankill area, and even at that they were still obliged to find their way to the Falls Road. Every policeman and soldier in Belfast was alerted to the escape, the identity of the escapers, their form of dress and the registration numbers of the hijacked cars.

Doherty says that three of the original eight escapers were in one of the cars which left the scene, that others ran, and that he met up with two or three of them later in the Shankill area. An internal police memorandum, from Detective Chief Inspector Kidd to the RUC hierarchy, offered an account of what happened. It was based, I believe, on police inquiries and eyewitnesses who were residents of the Shankill.

Prisoners made good their escape on foot into the Shankill estate. Various items of clothing were discarded in the streets as they ran off. They entered a house at 3A California Close where articles of clothing were also discarded. All eight prisoners left this house by the rear on to the Shankill Road. Blood at this house indicated that at least one of the prisoners was injured.

The police report was incomplete but in at least one respect it was accurate. The blood belonged to McKee, who had a gunshot wound to the head. It was not sufficient to incapacitate him and he was medically treated later that day by a doctor sympathetic to the IRA.

A later police investigation was more forthcoming and revealed that the two hijacked vehicles were abandoned in streets off the Shankill Road. It also recorded that three prisoners entered a house at California Close in the Shankill area, discarded their clothing and ran to the Shankill Road, where they hijacked a car at gunpoint and drove it to the Children's Hospital on the Falls Road and abandoned it.

Three other prisoners were witnessed abandoning a vehicle damaged in the shootout, and hijacking another at Shankill Parade. This car was also found in the Falls area.

Doherty, audacious as ever, was among several IRA men who made their way on foot to the safety of the republican stronghold of Lower Falls. He was one of those who discarded the prison officer's tunic as he ran through the maze of tiny side streets linking the Crumlin and Shankill Roads. The final part of his journey across the Shankill was made in a casual fashion, along the main thoroughfares of Agnes Street and Northumberland Street, to the Falls Road. Within hours of the breakout, the escape became known as 'The Great Escape' and the escapers as the 'A Team'.

A hurried prison investigation into the escape of the eight

dangerous men unearthed additional information. Prison Officer Christopher Worbey identified Doherty as one of the three men who had assaulted Officer Kennedy, causing head wounds which required thirty-eight stitches. He also heard one of the escapers say they should shoot Kennedy on the floor.

Senior Prison Officer Colin McPike said he ran to the main gate to prevent the escape and was confronted by Campbell, who told him: 'Get back you bastard or I'll shoot you.' Other officers saw the escapers firing their guns as they ran towards the car park. It was assumed that this was a tactic to prevent pursuit by prison officers and policemen. The prison officers' evidence confirmed the scale of the IRA operation inside the prison. In the cell block more than ten officers were taken hostage, and on the way from the prison at least ten officers who attempted to prevent the escape were deterred from doing so by determined and life-threatening gestures from the eight terrorists.

Solicitors John Rice, Oliver Kelly and Kelly's assistant, Ciaran Paul Steele, were arrested under section 12 of the Prevention of Terrorism Act and detained for questioning at Castlereagh interrogation centre. Another solicitor, Peter Forde, told police he was interviewing a prisoner when a firearm was produced and he was forced into a holding room which was locked. Forde's assistant, William McNulty, suffered a similar fate and was locked up with Steele. Rice, Steele and Kelly satisfactorily answered police questions and told how they were also held at gunpoint. They were subsequently released from custody without charges being preferred against them.

Doherty revealed his views on the escape four years later in a New York court. He was not forthcoming about the means used to smuggle firearms into the prison, nor did he mention the vicious assault on Officer Kennedy. In 1990, in the same court, when asked about the assault, he talked about the officer being 'rushed' after he struck Campbell. In an effort to justify the assault, Doherty described the threat posed by Kennedy: 'It took four of us to hold him down. In doing so he was hurt but did not lose consciousness and he was put into a cell.' It was not an apt description to account for Kennedy's injuries, or the fact that he was dragged, bleeding, from a holding area along a passageway. When pressed by the US Attorney, Otto Obermaier, to explain the brutality of the assault and the implication that it was not intentional, Doherty, without revealing his involvement, commented:

There was no intention to hurt any of the guards. The rest of the guards complied with the orders. When I stated that they were under arrest, I told them to take off their uniforms. I told them in a dignified manner. We didn't have any problems with the guards. They knew we were an organised IRA unit. They knew that nothing would happen to them. Mr Kennedy had taken it upon himself to attack one and that is his problem.

Doherty's choice of language when describing the behaviour of the prison officers was ludicrous if not bizarre, particularly his assertion that 'they knew nothing would happen' because they were faced with an organised unit. The reality was that they were made to believe they would be shot if they stepped out of line.

At the 1990 hearing, Obermaier pressed Doherty to account for the number of shots exchanged between the escapers and their pursuers. Doherty's reply, as was frequently the case in his 1990 testimony, was designed to shift blame to the security forces for the firing. He told the US Attorney that at least a hundred shots were fired and only two of those were discharged by IRA volunteers. That was untrue, and he showed once again his tendency to distort the evidence to support a personal thesis.

However, in his 1984 New York court appearance, he gave a more precise account of the moment which triggered the escape.

I was in the bullpen [cubicle] when we got the codeword. A certain prisoner had to say something. I think it was 'It's going to be raining tomorrow', and I replied, 'Well, let's get our umbrellas.' This was the codeword that the escape was on by that time. So the prison guard opened the door. I pulled a weapon and told him he was under arrest. Officer Campbell who arrested the other prison guards told them the Irish Republican Army had taken control of the block.

When I examined that statement I was puzzled and have not satisfactorily resolved the questions it posed. Why at that moment was the escape given the go-ahead? What information triggered the decision to allow it to proceed and, in the confines of the cell block, who was in possession of information which finalised the decision? Doherty, understandably, has not provided the answers.

Whatever the truth, at 6.00 pm on 10 May 1981 he celebrated his escape with officers of the Belfast Brigade while bonfires and street parties heralded the 'Great Escape'. In the Maze Prison, hunger-strikers were preparing for death, but their plight was temporarily forgotten. Joseph Doherty was fulfilling his threat that no prison would hold him, but he was nevertheless a worried man. He believed that he was top of a security forces' hit-list, and that the SAS would seek revenge for the death of Westmacott. He knew he could not hide for long in a republican area which was constantly under surveillance. The likelihood that he would be shot on sight necessitated swift action to spirit him to safety.

That night, the RUC sent the following security bulletin to all police and army personnel:

The following 8 persons escaped from Crumlin Road Prison at 1610 hrs 10/6/81. They are at present on trial in connection with the murder of police and army personnel.

(1) Paul Patrick Magee, last known address: 6 Glenalina Gardens, Belfast. 5ft 6ins, DOB 30/1/48, fresh complexion, dirty fair hair, slim build and face, born in Belfast, has a moustache, scar on his left lower arm, mole on left lower arm, scar on back of neck, scar on his left lower leg.
  IN FOR MURDER

(2) Robert Joseph Campbell, 21 Ballymurphy Crescent, Belfast, DOB 7/8/53, 5ft 6ins in height, fresh complexion, dirty fair hair, hazel eyes, medium build and face, born in Belfast, scar on back of right hand, 2 scars under left arm, scar on both knees.
  IN FOR MURDER

(3) Michael Anthony McKee, home address, 53 New Barnsley Crescent, Belfast, DOB 24/3/56, 5ft 4ins in height, fresh complexion, light brown hair, has a tattoo on lower right arm 'Patricia and Mark', tattoo on lower left arm 'B Love', scars on his forehead and mole on left shoulder.
  IN FOR MURDER

(4) Angelo Fusco, home address, 80 Slieveban Drive, Belfast, DOB 2/9/56, 5ft 5½ins in height, fresh complexion, brown eyes, slim build and face, born in Belfast, tattoo lower right arm of Shamrock, tattoo lower left arm of heart with dagger and LOVE, scars palm of left hand and scar on the front centre of his body.
  IN FOR MURDER

(5) Anthony Gerard Sloan, home address, 27 Summerhill Drive, Belfast [Twinbrook], DOB 15/6/54, 5ft 5¼ins in height, fresh complexion, black hair, blue eyes, medium build and face, born in Belfast, occupation taxi

driver, has a moustache, has a scar on his lower right leg, scar on his left knee, vaccination mark on upper left arm.

IN FOR MURDER

(6) Michael Thomas Ryan, last residence, Battery Bar, Ardboe, Coagh, DOB 6/7/55, 5ft 7ins, dark brown hair, fresh complexion, hazel eyes, medium build and face, born in Ardboe, vaccination mark on upper left arm, scars on both knees, fisherman.

IN FOR MURDER

(7) Gerard Sloan, home address, Westview Pass, Belfast, DOB 21/4/53, 5ft 4½ins, medium build and face, fresh complexion, dirty fair hair, blue eyes, oval-shaped face, born in Belfast, barman, appendix scar, vaccination scar on both knees.

IN FOR POSSESSION OF EXPLOSIVES

(8) Joseph Patrick Doherty, 192 Spamount Street, Belfast, DOB 28/1/55, 5ft 8½ins, fresh complexion, dirty fair hair, hazel eyes, medium build and face, born in Belfast, plumber, 3 vaccinations on upper left arm, small scar on bottom lip, slight moustache.

IN FOR MURDER

*These Persons Are In Possession Of At Least 3 Prison Uniforms. Copies Of These Descriptions Should Be Immediately Taken To Police On Duty At Road Stops.*

# 9

# 'Ruthless and Highly Dangerous'

The 'Great Escape' lifted the republicans' gloom surrounding the deaths of the hunger-strikers. Bonfires lit the streets of West Belfast, parties were held in the open air and republican sympathisers celebrated the freedom of the escapers, the 'A Team'. The eight had been dispersed to safe-houses in the Falls, Andersonstown and Turf Lodge districts of Catholic West Belfast. They were told to remain in hiding until plans were finalised to ferry them to safety across the border to the Irish Republic. The IRA knew the authorities would swamp nationalist neighbourhoods with police and soldiers, and would conduct massive search operations. The houses chosen for the concealment of the eight belonged to republican sympathisers, and not IRA families or supporters known to the security forces. Doherty says he was put in a house and told to remain there until further notice. A woman in the house congratulated him and said everyone had been solemn, and morale had been low until the escape. She believed the IRA's Belfast Brigade was right in ordering it. 'It was essential', she remarked, 'to get people back on their feet to struggle against all the odds.' She then walked through the streets, observing the merry-making, and returned to give Doherty a detailed account of the parties and the elation of adults and children alike.

IRA history is littered with stories of escapes, and, as Doherty recalls, his adventure quickly found its way into IRA folklore:

That very night they made up a name for this escape – they called it the Great Escape. Escapes are very important to the war, to the campaign as well as to IRA prisoners. We contribute a lot to the war effort. So the escapes bring great publicity to the movement. The very first escape I remember was on the *Maidstone* prison ship, where seven volunteers swam across Belfast Lough and got away. They were called 'The Magnificent Seven', after a western movie. There were songs written about it, bonfires in the streets, and poems. The next one was when prisoners playing football jumped over the wall at Crumlin Road Prison. They called them 'The Crumlin Kangaroos'. There was a song made about that. After that there was an escape where a helicopter landed in the prison yard at Mountjoy in Dublin and removed prisoners. They were called 'The Whirlie Birdies'. Each escape has a particular name or culture behind it.

Doherty's first meeting with his IRA superiors took place on the night of the escape, and he was placed under the control of officers of the IRA's 2nd Battalion based in the Lower Falls area. They were responsible for his safety and ensuring he did nothing to jeopardise the security of the safe-house in which he was hiding. At 7.00 pm high-ranking officers from the Belfast Brigade visited and congratulated him. They asked him to write an account of the escape and record details of injuries suffered by the prison staff, police and military, and whether there were any mishaps in the escape plans. That was part of normal IRA procedure, and similar statements were requested from the other escapers.

Those statements were later given to IRA internal security, as well as propagandists. A collective account of the escape was written in a colourful form for the IRA newssheet, *An Phoblacht*, and the escapers' evidence was used to counter official claims of brutality towards prison officers, and reckless firing on Crumlin Road and in the car park.

Doherty remained in the house for five days and watched television reports of the efforts of the security forces to find him. Border areas were virtually sealed off by the British army in the certain knowledge that the IRA would attempt to smuggle the eight out of Northern Ireland, where their risk of capture was increased by a large, constant security presence. On the fifth day the IRA's Northern Command, which controlled all the Northern Ireland brigades, told Doherty they were taking responsibility for his welfare, and plans were in place to move him to the wild, rugged countryside of South Armagh close to the Irish border. He would be handed over to a border battalion whose members lived in the countryside and knew every hedgerow and laneway linking the Irish Republic with Northern Ireland.

Doherty says he was transported, without a hitch, to the border battalion, who guided him through mountains to the South of Ireland. The other escapers were also conveyed to South Armagh and to a safe haven in the Republic. South Armagh was an ideal area for conducting the movement of the wanted men. It was given the description 'bandit country' by the British army, because of its history of lawlessness. The terrain was such that it offered a myriad labyrinthine routes through mountains, unapproved roads and ditches to the Republic. The British army consistently regarded it as the most dangerous and lethal area of operations in Ireland. Many British soldiers and policemen lost their lives in the lanes and ditches in that area where the IRA proved a match for the army. Over the years, the SAS and other undercover soldiers spent days and weeks hiding in ditches, or carefully concealed holes in the ground, to counter the threat, but the IRA's battalion had the advantage of knowing every stone and coppice. The IRA volunteers in South Armagh had been born there, and their families had lived there for generations.

When Doherty crossed the border to safety, he was told he was now under the command of General Headquarters Staff and would receive orders directly from them. He learned that his fellow escapers were already in the Republic, being dispersed to towns and villages. The IRA knew the British Government would put huge diplomatic pressure on the Irish Government to track down the eight, and hand them over to the Northern Ireland security authorities. The dispersal of individual escapers reduced the risk of all of them being caught in one search operation. There were thousands of IRA safe-houses in towns, villages and remote parts of the Irish countryside, and little prospect that the Irish army and police would mount search operations on the scale normally undertaken by the British army in Northern Ireland.

It was also vital to the IRA that the escapers be moved to places far from the border, and that factor was dictated by a fear of the SAS. Doherty admits he was frightened that SAS teams would be sent to find and eliminate him and his fellow escapers, particularly those involved in the murder of Westmacott. The IRA agreed with him on the basis that the SAS were known to operate illegally in the Republic on what was technically foreign soil. Throughout the history of the conflict, the Irish Government has made repeated protests to the British Government about British army incursions, and has regarded the operations of the SAS on its territory as a serious violation of sovereignty. There is a wealth of evidence linking the SAS, and *agents provocateurs* run by British intelligence, to crimes in the Republic. At one point in the early days of the Troubles, criminals employed by British intelligence carried out robberies and terrorist-type operations. The SAS were known to have kidnapped republicans and transported them across the border to Northern Ireland. In 1982 surveillance operations were conducted by British military undercover teams on republicans living in border towns in the Republic, such as Dundalk and Monaghan. Available evidence suggested that murder was carried out in the Republic by British military intelligence undercover squads, and by the SAS. There was also evidence to connect bombings in the Republic to loyalist terror groups, and members of the British army's Ulster Defence Regiment.

In the light of Doherty's fear, and IRA knowledge of SAS tactics, it was felt the escapers should not know each other's whereabouts, and should be confined to places away from prying eyes, and where SAS retaliation would prove impossible. The IRA's GHQ Staff believed the SAS would view the killing of one of its men as personal and would seek revenge. It was likely that, if members of the SAS had discovered the whereabouts of Doherty or his accomplices, they would have tracked them down and killed them.

Doherty viewed his speedy departure from Northern Ireland as a sign of the Belfast Brigade's willingness to relieve themselves of the acute responsibility of hiding and protecting the 'A Team':

When I crossed the border I was told to lie low and keep a low profile. It was to make sure that we didn't get recaptured. There was the initial propaganda of getting the prisoners out, but to the British we were prestige targets. If they could get us back it would have taken the whole thing of the escape away. If they recapture a prisoner it is bad for morale for the Irish Republican Army and the population as a whole, and it is a great boost to the British. So the Northern Command of the IRA, they didn't want us. We were hot bricks, we were too hot. It we were situated in West Belfast and the British army knew our location, they would send 1000 troops just to go in and get me. If they go in to get me, they get arms and other volunteers who are on the run. So the Northern Command sent us to GHQ. It was like passing the buck. They were getting rid of us. We were of no further use in the North as yet.

Doherty offered that analysis of IRA thinking when giving evidence in New York in 1984. His use of the word 'no further use in the North as yet' implied it was the IRA's and his own intention that he return to operational active service in Northern Ireland once the heat had died down. It would be reasonable to conclude that the 'A Team' were of no use languishing indefinitely in the Republic, and that their killing ability would eventually be put to better use against the British security forces. Such a conclusion fits the history of IRA men who were sent to the Republic to lie low when high on police and army 'wanted' lists in Northern Ireland. The IRA rested such operatives, and encouraged them to carry out operations in Northern Ireland from the safety of bases in the Republic. South Armagh was one area chosen as a favourite operating zone. If specialist attacks were required in Belfast or Derry, volunteers were ordered to leave the relative safety of the Republic and return to those cities. The 'A Team' were primarily a valuable propaganda asset but, as Doherty pointed out, their presence in Northern Ireland would have led to unrelenting searches, which in turn would have temporarily compromised other IRA plans. In order to deter the searches, the IRA made it known publicly that it had safely ferried the escapers out of British jurisdiction.

Doherty was not idle in the weeks or months following his escape, and his low profile did not remain a feature of his existence. He presented officer-training lectures, as well as showing volunteers how to fire weapons, and use urban and rural guerrilla tactics.

In his absence, the trial judge proceeded with the sentencing of some of the escapers, particularly those involved in the killing of Westmacott and the original M60 gang who murdered Constable Magill.

The Honourable Justice Hutton, now Lord Chief Justice, dealt first with the case against Fusco, McKee, Anthony and Gerard Sloan and Magee. Sitting alone without a jury, as is the procedure in terrorist cases, the judge addressed himself to the evidence of James Kennedy, Northern Ireland's first 'supergrass'. He said that while he was satisfied that Kennedy did not willingly move weapons it was probable that his mind was not so overborne by fear that he could successfully plead duress as regards the movement of weapons at Dalebrook Avenue. He considered Kennedy an accomplice and felt it safer to treat him as an accomplice. The judge publicly warned himself as any judge would normally warn a jury about accepting the uncorroborated evidence of an accomplice. The nature of the warning was in respect of legal precedent from a 1954 British appeals trial. He quoted the warning from that case thus:

In such a case the issue of 'accomplice *vel non*' is for the jury's decision; and a judge should direct them that if they consider on the evidence that the witness was an accomplice, it is dangerous for them to act on his evidence unless corroborated; though it is competent for them to do so if, after that warning, they still think fit to do so.

'I gave that warning to myself,' the judge told the assembled lawyers and spectators, 'and at all times I bear it in mind, and the weight which must be attached to it.' This type of personal directive may appear absurd to those who have not witnessed terrorist trials in Northern Ireland. However, the absence of juries, because of the risk that jurors could be shot or threatened, means that judges sitting alone are required to behave as though a jury were present. A judge will, in effect, talk to himself, repeating to himself those warnings or recommendations which he would normally give to jurors.

Justice Hutton said he regarded Kennedy as a truthful and accurate witness and believed he sought to give 'honest and truthful evidence' from the witness box.

Under prolonged and skilful cross-examination he did not alter in any material respect the evidence he gave when examined in chief. Having watched him give evidence, and be examined skilfully and at great length by three senior counsel, and bearing in mind at all times the danger of convicting on the uncorroborated evidence of an accomplice, I found myself totally convinced at the end of his evidence that the account he gave of the involvement of the various accused in the various incidents he described was true and accurate, with the exception of the accused Ronald King.

Ronald King was found by the judge to be wrongly accused of imprisoning Kennedy on the night when Sloan took him to Ballymurphy to be interrogated by a member of the IRA. Kennedy had identified King at a police suspects' parade. Justice Hutton said he doubted the accuracy of Kennedy's identification and as a result was obliged to dismiss the case against King. In respect of the evidence against the others, the judge relied on his observation of Kennedy's behaviour when giving his evidence.

First there was his demeanour and manner in the witness box, particularly under the most searching, prolonged and skilful cross-examination. From watching him in the witness box I am satisfied that he had come to tell the truth and not to give false and concocted evidence. Secondly, he gave his evidence in an immensely detailed and consistent way, which I consider is only consistent with a witness describing what he had actually seen happen.

The judge augmented his assertion by reminding the court that different defence lawyers had concentrated on various aspects of Kennedy's evidence: they had asked him to repeat it, and expand it, and they probed deeply, but always the witness recounted his story with consistency. A third point made by the judge in reinforcing his view of the supergrass related to the way in which Kennedy, without hesitation, added detail or an explanation which he could not have prepared in advance or a moment's whim. The judge turned to the crucial issue of Kennedy's reasons for becoming an informer, and the allegation by defence lawyers that it was for personal gain. It was Justice Hutton's opinion that Kennedy felt he was being implicated in murder, and was being dragged deeper into IRA crimes, and he gave evidence to halt that decline in his life.

The judge turned to the defence allegations which questioned Kennedy's sincerity as a witness. These included an assertion that he gave false information because of a grudge against Anthony Sloan and a conceived hatred of Angelo Fusco, and was a paid police informer who wished to avoid prosecution. Justice Hutton recalled a defence submission that Kennedy was an inveterate liar. He had told lies about his past before entering court, dishonestly claimed state benefits and committed dishonest acts. His credibility was such that it would be dangerous to convict on his evidence, and that a court replying on his evidence could not be satisfied of the guilt of the accused beyond a reasonable doubt. He was also significantly an accomplice.

The judge singled out points made by Donnell Deeny, a highly experienced lawyer who represented Anthony Gerard Sloan and Gerard Michael Sloan. Deeny relied on proving that Kennedy was a man of bad character. The defence arguments were, in the opinion of the judge, unconvincing. However, one of the defence allegations to which the judge paid particular attention and which, to a limited degree, he accepted was Kennedy's support for the IRA.

It was suggested that he had been a supporter of the violent methods of the IRA or sympathised with those methods. These included suggestions that he asked a friend to join the Fianna with him; that he expressed the view some years ago that the IRA could easily blow up premises in the centre of Belfast; that he had more knowledge of weapons than he admitted to having; and that he was happy to drive about Angelo Fusco and Lucas Quigley whom he knew were active members of the IRA. I think that prior to September 1979, when his car was first hijacked by the IRA, that he may have had some sympathy with the IRA, which may have extended to some sympathy with some of its activities, but I am satisfied that from April 1980 when Constable Magill and the civil servant were murdered, and it may be from an earlier date, that Kennedy had become totally opposed to the violence carried out by the IRA.

Justice Hutton recognised that Kennedy was putting his life and his parents at risk by becoming a prosecution witness, and would be obliged to leave Northern Ireland, possibly not to return. This, said the judge, was not the behaviour of a man who was merely motivated to impress people, or because of a grudge. Therefore, even in the absence of supporting evidence, he was deemed a credible witness.

The judge publicly 'reminded' himself that the critical test for accepting the uncorroborated testimony of an accomplice rested in a 1916 English test case, *Queens* v. *Baskervile*, which stated: 'We hold the evidence in corroboration must be independent testimony which affects the accused by connecting or tending to connect him to the crime. In other words it must be evidence which implicates him, that is, which confirms in some material particular not only the evidence that the crime had been committed, but also that the person committed it.' Kennedy's history of involvement with the M60 gang was such as to fulfil, in the court's view, the test laid down in that 1916 judgment.

In order to clarify the position further, the judge quoted from a 1977 case presided over by the Lord Chief Justice of that time, Lord Widgery – regarded as infamously inadequate by the nationalist Catholic community in Ireland in his inquiry into the killing by the army of thirteen innocent Catholics in 1972 in what became known as 'Bloody Sunday'. (It was perhaps ironic that the words of Lord Widgery should echo in a courtroom in Belfast eight years later in a crucial case against republican killers, and not killers from the Parachute Regiment, whose activities on 30 January 1972 also provided Widgery with problems of identification and corroboration. No soldier was ever charged with unlawful killing, what Bishop Edward Daly of Derry described as 'unadulterated murder'.) It was to Widgery's legal mind that Justice Hutton turned for legal precedent.

When, in the judgment of the trial judge, the quality of the identifying evidence is poor, as for example when it depends solely on a fleeting glance or a longer observation made in difficult conditions, the situation is very different. The judge should then withdraw the case from jury and direct an acquittal, unless there is other evidence which goes to support the correctness of the identification. This may be corroboration in the sense lawyers use that word; but it may not be so if the effect is to make the jury sure that there has been no mistaken identification. For example, X sees the accused snatch a woman's handbag; he gets only a fleeting glance of the thief's face as he runs off but he does see him entering a nearby house. Later he picks out the accused at an identity parade. If there was no more evidence than this, the poor quality of the identification would require the judge to withdraw the case from the jury; but this would not be so if the house into which the accused was alleged by X to have run was his father's.

Justice Hutton directed his attention to alibi evidence, which was presented on behalf of some of the accused to show they were elsewhere when the M60 was fired at the army foot patrol, and at Constable Magill. He found the majority of alibi witnesses untruthful, and refused to place any reliance on their evidence. He preferred to accept Kennedy's evidence with the exception of where it related to Ronald King. There were two flaws in Kennedy's identification evidence: the first related to King, whom he wrongly accused of being the IRA man who interrogated him; the second was that he identified the wrong man at one identification parade which was designed to select a person named Carmichael who was alleged to have hijacked his car in September 1979. The judge, however, accepted Kennedy's explanation that he had wrongly identified another person because that person's appearance had significantly changed by the time the parade took place.

The judge turned to the court and announced his verdicts, first in respect of the attempted murder of the soldiers in February 1980. He singled out Anthony Sloan as the leader of the gang in possession of the M60 and sentenced him to twenty years in prison and his brother Gerard to eighteen, with Fusco and McKee each receiving a twenty-year sentence. For other offences relating to the incidents, the accused were sentenced to no less than ten years on each charge, with Angelo Fusco receiving a life term for the attack on the soldiers.

The judge reserved a different view of the participation of Emmanuel Fusco, and his part in the events leading to the death of Constable Magill. Emmanuel Fusco, unlike his brother, was in court to hear his sentence.

Now, Emmanuel Fusco, you have pleaded guilty to manslaughter of Constable Stephen Magill. It was your breaking into the Stewartstown Road library which lured the police Landrover there. By accepting your plea to manslaughter, the prosecution have accepted that you did not break into the library with the intention of bringing about the death of a police officer, and that you did not fully understand what was planned, but I am satisfied that you knew this was no ordinary burglary, but that it was a burglary connected with the IRA, and I think you suspected that something sinister was afoot and you played a part in bringing about the death of the constable. I take into account what has been said on your behalf, that before this offence you had a criminal record in respect of crimes like burglaries and other offences of dishonesty, and that you were not connected with the IRA. But on the evidence that I have heard I consider that, as regards this offence, you did it for the IRA knowing that it was for the IRA, and I sentence you to ten years' imprisonment for manslaughter, and six years for the burglary.

With respect to the murder of Constable Magill, the judge did not return 'guilty' verdicts on murder charges, but declared Angelo Fusco, McKee, Magee and Anthony Sloan guilty of possessing weapons with intent to endanger life on the day of the constable's death. The sentences for that offence ranged from sixteen to twenty years.

Ronald King, who was wrongfully accused, was discharged from the court, a free man, and the judge turned to the killing of Westmacott. He pointed out that, although Doherty, Fusco, Magee and Campbell were not present, he was entitled in law to pass sentence on them. He described Doherty, Fusco and Campbell as 'ruthless and highly dangerous men', and said that Magee might not have fired a weapon at 371 Antrim Road but it was probable he too was a highly dangerous man.

As regards Doherty, Fusco and Campbell I recommend to the Secretary of

State that in sentencing each of them to life in prison, the minimum period which should elapse before he considers their release should be thirty years. I recommend that the minimum period which should elapse before Magee is considered for release is twenty-five years.

News of the sentences reached Doherty, who realised that if he was recaptured he would be in prison at least until the year 2011 when he would be fifty-six years old. His fear of recapture was accentuated when the three other 'ruthless and highly dangerous men' were seized by security forces in the Republic. Robert Campbell and Paul Magee were arrested in 1981 and Angelo Fusco in January 1982. The four hit-men initially thought they were safe in the Republic, but the search for them was unrelenting because of British diplomatic pressure on the Irish Government, and the embarrassment caused to that Government by the obvious presence on its soil of such a notorious gang. The IRA began to suspect that an informer within the ranks of the organisation in the Republic was supplying information on the hiding places of all the escapers, but most notably the killers of Westmacott. Those four were the prime targets for British intelligence surveillance in the Republic, and for the Irish army and police. The recapture of Fusco convinced the IRA that it was only a matter of time before Doherty's hiding place was revealed to the authorities. The arrest of other members of the gang was damaging IRA morale, and it illustrated to other active service personnel that the organisation could not safely conceal or ever guarantee the freedom of volunteers on the run.

The safety of men on the run was of paramount importance to IRA morale, and the maintenance of their campaign. It was vital to have an area of the island of Ireland where men could conceivably hide without facing the constant risk of capture, where they could recuperate, and prepare a return to active service, or leave the country from remote fishing ports or from Dublin airport. The IRA in Northern Ireland was always assured of support from people in the Republic, irrespective of their political affiliations. Prior to 1969 the IRA ran all its operations throughout the island from Dublin, and all arms training rook place on remote hillsides along the west coast. The violence of 1969, and the creation of a new IRA, eventually led to IRA resources being placed at the discretion of those organising the violence north of the border, and much of the decision-making process was delegated to the Northern Command. The IRA Army Council and General Headquarters Staff remained in Dublin, but the bulk of their members were men from Northern Ireland who had experience of violence. The Dublin Government rarely arrested members of the Army Council, even though they knew their identities: in 1970, while travelling through Dublin, I saw a Provisional IRA leader driving a car along O'Connell Street, the city's main thoroughfare. Dublin was an ideal centre for the planning of overall IRA strategy; for negotiating arms deals with Middle East contacts; and for harbouring fugitives. By contrast with Belfast there was no war in the Republic; there was a tacit approval of IRA ideals, a dislike for the British, and less police scrutiny.

Northern Ireland, on the other hand, was a war zone with constant roadchecks, searches, computerised files on all households, informers, undercover surveillance squads, and a military presence with an ever-growing knowledge of IRA operational methods and activists. The security forces in the Republic displayed an ambivalence about the presence of IRA men on their soil, while some policemen (Garda) and soldiers provided IRA men with logistical support. In the late 1970s and 1980s there was a gradual change in attitude, and successive Irish Governments ordered a clampdown on IRA activities, and the arrest of men wanted by the British. Prior to that change, towns such as Dundalk and Drogheda, just inside the Republic, resembled 'wild west towns'. IRA men on the run openly carried guns, swaggered round the streets and bars, and led a life free from interference. An IRA officer from Ardoyne showed his displeasure at the result of a horse race by producing his pistol in a Dundalk hotel and shooting a television screen which displayed the winning horse. The Irish Government eventually changed all that, and the IRA equally told its men to seek a less public profile. There remained, however, a support for the Provisionals at all levels of society, but particularly in rural areas where republicanism was traditionally a feature of the history. In areas of the west and south-west, people were unaware of the nature of the conflict and viewed it simply in terms of the age-old Irish–British struggle. That ensured there were always safe-houses for men on the run.

The lifestyle of those on the run can be judged from an account given to me by a former IRA officer:

Every IRA man in the North knew that the Republic represented freedom, in the sense that it was a liberated part of Ireland. People in all walks of life supported us there, and would give us shelter when we were on the run from the Brits. Life on the run was not the great lifestyle that many volunteers expected. Some guys thought that once you were over the border you could drink, walk about and pick up a few girls. That was the good old days of the early seventies, and it was gone. If you were on the run in Northern Ireland whether you'd escaped from prison, or they were searching for you because of a particular operation, there were few hiding places in the North once the heat was on. The Brits and RUC could just swamp an area with men, seal it off and search it house by house, ditch by ditch. On the run in the North was more stressful because freedom of movement was virtually impossible. Guys lay under floorboards for days, pissing into plastic containers with no room for movement, and unable to talk to each other except in whispers. The stench of stale urine, filthy bodies and constant fear of detection made life unbearable.

This had to be endured until the movement planned your journey to the Republic. Often men were transported in coffins in car boots or in disguise on public transport. Sometimes a woman and her kids would accompany a volunteer to a border area in the North where a local IRA unit would take over and arrange the cross-border part of the journey. That unit would know the terrain and would be armed so that in the event of running into an SAS patrol, or ordinary army or police, they would provide covering fire while the wanted man escaped. Once across the border, another unit took over and ferried you to a safe-house. It was here you were debriefed about your escape, what, if anything, went wrong, or simply what operations you were involved in north of the border. They knew all about the attitudes of men on the run and the fact that many of them didn't know the kind of life they were about to lead. You were given ground rules about personal security in the Republic, ways of evading detection by the Garda, and the manner in which you dealt with people who would be offering you shelter.

Personal security determined that you tried to get rid of your northern accent and developed one which could be easily taken for the typically Irish accent. Disguise was essential, because the Brits would send wanted photographs of you to the Irish police and Special Branch. That meant that you grew a beard, shaved one you already had, dyed your hair and wore clothes in keeping with city or rural lifestyles. Politics was never to be discussed openly and public places were to be avoided unless it was essential for travelling from one safe location to another. The word 'inconspicuous' was constantly used in lectures about personal security. Each volunteer on the run was given a weekly subsidy of £10 or more for cigarettes, or personal items, and the occasional drink. Clothes were provided by the people who harboured us. I was told, like most men on the run, never to discuss my identity, my IRA history, or any family details with people sheltering me. This was to safeguard them and me. I was given an identity by the IRA, but told that as I changed location the identity would also change, which would make it difficult for people to trace me.

One of the most important ground rules was to avoid having any sexual contact with females in safe-houses, particularly married women. The IRA knew from experience that an affair could lead to a husband turning informer, or to a perception amongst other families that IRA men were a sexual risk in their houses. That was a strain, because the women were always at home and they were people with whom you had the most contact. There was an intimacy between a man on the run and the woman of the house which was unspoken and rarely realised. All of us knew it could be a fatal attraction. It was difficult especially if you'd spent years in prison masturbating and dreaming of real sex. Every woman looked good, and the fact that there was a no-contact policy added to the stress of life on the run.

Daylight was often spent indoors, in an upstairs room, a loft or a hayshed. At night it was possible to walk the fields. In moving from one house to another I sometimes spent days lying under hedges waiting for a local unit to pick me up. Nobody liked being too close to the border because we all knew that the SAS made incursions across the border and lifted wanted men, shot them and dumped the bodies in Northern Ireland.

The SAS was not concerned about the sovereignty of the Republic. Ordinary army patrols constantly crossed the border and claimed it was due to a map-reading error. The SAS were different, because their job was to go in to eliminate someone, but they wouldn't do the hit in the Republic for fear it might be discovered and an international incident created. Sometimes they lifted someone south of the border, took him to the North, handed him over to the RUC, and claimed he was lifted within Northern Ireland territory. It was safer to be in the west, in Donegal or Leitrim. Kids in safe-houses were well learned in acting as lookouts, running errands and keeping quiet about your presence. They grew up with this sort of thing and enjoyed the secrecy and being able to help. Nobody wanted to be a hero but people regarded you as one and that was difficult because you looked more like a tense, tired man.

The IRA talked to every man about his commitment, his intentions towards the movement, and his future. Sometimes they arranged for a wife or kids to travel from the North to meet him. This was never easy to arrange because British intelligence kept surveillance on families, and friends of wanted volunteers, in the hope of tracking them on a visit to a safe-house. The most important thing was for a volunteer to decide whether he wanted to return to active service, to leave the IRA, the join the political side with Sinn Fein or to leave the country to recuperate, or to get engaged in operations in England or abroad. Initially, 'on the run' meant volunteers resting, getting themselves readjusted, and having time to consider their lives. Escapers, or men on the run from operations, faced a similar problem. Both types suffered from different types of incarceration. Men from prison needed to readjust to life, to understand what it was like in the real world. They were not ready for active service – some of them required retraining. In most cases their propaganda value as free men was their most precious commodity. They were the prime concern of the IRA because their recapture devalued their success in escaping. They were jealously guarded or moved out of the country to safety. The active service volunteer who was constantly on the run while doing operations in the North also needed time to recuperate. He was either in the Republic resting, or he was genuinely on the run because his cover was blown. In the second instance he needed time to decide whether he was willing to return to active service knowing the risks to him would be greater.

In some cases active service volunteers were allowed to remain in the Republic and operate with cross-border units. These would operate from either side and co-ordinate their resources. If you chose to leave the country, that could be arranged with a passport and new identity. In America there was a network of safe-houses organised on the same basis as Ireland. It did not mean you necessarily leaving the movement. The arrangement was that you left until the heat died down. You were under orders, and the IRA could recall you at any time. The option of leaving the country required a lot of planning and was only undertaken for people who were top of the Brits' wanted list.

There was an emerging view in IRA circles that Doherty was 'too hot to handle', an opinion parallel to the one expressed by the Northern Command the previous year. The search for Doherty, in particular, was generating too much scrutiny in the Republic, where the IRA preferred a low profile in order to maintain a safe haven in that part of Ireland. The status of the IRA was linked inextricably, some would say ineradicably, with the history of the Republic.

An indication that the IRA was careful about its behaviour in the Irish Republic was to be found in the way in which terrorists operated from that jurisdiction and the internal IRA rules governing the organisation's attitude to the authority of the Irish state. When the IRA executed informers or agents in the Republic, it dumped the bodies across the border in Northern Ireland. The reasons for transporting bodies to another jurisdiction were twofold. First, acts of violence were not therefore judged to have happened within the jurisdiction of the Republic and, second, the security forces in the Republic were not directly involved in examining such crimes, or closely investigating IRA involvement in them. It was a ploy which guaranteed a virtual stand-off with the ordinary police in the Republic, and the tactic was part of IRA policy which prohibited any military action against the Republic's security forces and controlled and governed all behaviour by volunteers, to prevent conflict between the IRA and the Irish state. That policy was set out in the IRA rulebook, 'The Green Book', under General Order No. 8, which I have quoted earlier. The introduction of General Order No. 8 in the 1950s had convinced Irish politicians that the IRA posed no threat to the Irish state, but solely to British-occupied Northern Ireland. When the Provisional IRA was created in 1970, that order became enshrined in its constitution; the IRA assured a sovereign Irish state that its intentions in relation to that state were benign; that it would not act against Irish security forces and would not seek publicly to compromise the legality of the state; that its activities and intentions were aimed only at the British and that volunteers would always seek to conduct IRA affairs with secrecy, so as to avoid confrontation with Irish police and soldiers. The Provisionals, like their predecessors, needed the territory of the Irish Republic as an operational base for attacks across the border, and for training, concealment of weapons and as a haven for men escaping British law. From the outset of the present conflict, members of the IRA Army Council have resided, often openly, in the Republic.

The continued failure of extradition arrangements between Britain and Ireland has always facilitated IRA strategy. For many years no extradition arrangements existed until, in a European context, extradition laws linked Britain and Ireland. Such a new arrangement did not often lead to the participation of both parties. It was automatically assumed that terrorists who committed acts which offended against civilised behaviour would be extradited, and in some instances, particularly where the evidence identified a person guilty of bombing or shooting innocent civilians, extradition worked. Problems inevitably arose when someone was sought for the killing of soldiers or policemen and, as in many countries, such crimes attracted the definition of 'political offence exception'. In the history of Ireland, the conflict with the British, which resulted in freedom from British rule for part of Ireland, resulted in a politico-cultural mentality which was vulnerable to the 'political offence exception', and remains so to this day. An additional problem for the Irish courts was a genuine belief since 1969 that British justice frequently failed to present balance and fairness towards the Irish.

Internment, the Widgery tribunal report on Bloody Sunday, the campaigns to release the 'Guildford Four' and the 'Birmingham Six', convinced successive Irish Governments that it was unwise to hand over IRA personnel to British courts. The controversial shootings by the SAS and RUC in the 1970s and 1980s, in what many hold to be a shoot-to-kill policy, served to heighten general Irish antipathy to Britain's sense of justice where Ireland was concerned. In a climate of bitterness, recrimination and suspicion, extradition tended to collapse under the perceived view that acts which were collectively regarded as 'political' accorded a person status as a prisoner of conscience. Although that may be a simplification of a complex political/legal difficulty, nevertheless it illustrates the broad parameters of the problem, and the public perception of it. Whether or not Doherty would have succeeded in fighting a successful anti-extradition case is debatable, though the aftermath of the hunger strike, which ended in the autumn of 1981, might have generated sufficient anti-British sentiment within the Irish legal system to prevent him being returned to a Belfast prison. If such a legal battle had taken place and was extended further into the 1980s, when allegations of a British security forces' shoot-to-kill policy were beginning to surface, Doherty might have capitalised successfully on a growing disillusionment with British policy and justice in Northern Ireland and Britain. In 1982 the IRA could afford neither to risk such a legal case nor to suffer the indignity of the fourth member of the 'A Team' being caught.

By the middle of January, Doherty's position was untenable. News reached him from the IRA leadership in Dublin that six of those from the 'Great Escape' were in custody. He met an IRA leader who stressed that this was 'a bad record' and that the likelihood was that the two remaining volunteers would be recaptured within four or five months. Doherty says this meeting took place in a safe-house in the 'middle of a mountain'. There was a woman and children present when a member of the 'IRA Army Command' arrived and told him that adverse publicity was being created by the arrest of six escapers. He said Doherty was one of the most 'privileged' of the escapers. 'He told me, "You got to stay away", because the protest was still going on in the H-Blocks, and it looked pretty bad when it came on the news that an IRA escaper had been recaptured. It made headlines in the British newspapers and on the British news that night that these people had been captured.'

Doherty was a prestige target, and was correct to emphasise his importance to the British Government and, little did he know then, to the British Prime Minister at the time, Margaret Thatcher. She was proud of her stand on terrorism, but was personally proud of the SAS. The killing of Westmacott and the escape of his killers angered her. Doherty was the only one unaccounted for, and eventually would become so important that she would demand to be personally briefed about him. In January 1982, Joseph Doherty and the IRA knew that security forces on both sides of the Irish border were determined that he should be recaptured quickly in order to restore faith in security policies in Britain and Ireland. Thatcher believed that his recapture would enhance relations between Britain and Ireland, and repair the damage to security in Northern Ireland arising from the 'Great Escape'. Doherty remembers Margaret Thatcher publicly declaring she 'wanted these people back'. Neither the IRA nor Doherty needed to be convinced of her intentions, or her determination to see them fulfilled, but they were unaware then of her growing personal interest in him.

The IRA leader told Doherty that preparations were being made to send him to the United States of America. In 1984 Doherty told a New York court that he interpreted the IRA decision to move him out of Ireland as 'a directive'. In other words, he was given an order to leave Ireland and volunteers were obliged by IRA rules to obey orders.

If I had approached the issue saying I want to stay on . . . I am a volunteer in the Irish Republican Army. I take orders. When the IRA says you go to the United States for two, maybe two and a half years, stay cool, and we will approach you for coming back, I do not disobey orders.

# 10

# Under IRA Orders?

Doherty says he was 'somewhat frightened' to go to New York, because he was 'from a small country' and 'possessed no experience of foreign travel or life in large cities'. True, he had spent most of his life in the backstreets of Belfast, or in prison or in hiding in remote parts of the Southern Irish countryside. Nevertheless, the IRA was an organisation skilled in smuggling weapons and people, and would have briefed him on his trip, on the people he would meet in New York and on the nature of IRA support systems in that city. Nor would they have dispatched him to the United States without briefing him on his personal security, and the lifestyle he would be required to lead. The procedure would have been similar to that undertaken with men on the run in the Republic, and they would also have assured him that IRA contacts would take care of his security and needs on the other side of the Atlantic.

The moment when he was ordered to leave Ireland is a crucial part of the Joseph Doherty story, and it impinges on his subsequent life in the US, and his relationship with the IRA. He clearly admits that he was given a directive, and as a volunteer he obeyed orders, but confusion arises over his IRA status prior to leaving Ireland – not in respect of his willingness to comply with 'the directive' or the preparations made for his departure: he says there was the prospect of being recalled by the IRA within two or more years, which suggests a degree of IRA control. Confusion was, however, created by testimony he gave in the US in 1984 which implied that he resigned from the IRA before departing Ireland. That is a matter which I will deal with in a later chapter, but it is necessary that I outline some of it at this point, so that one has the opportunity to interpret the issue as the Doherty story unfolds in an American context. The following is a transcript of part of the cross-examination of Doherty by the US Attorney in 1984. He was trying to establish whether Doherty had entered the US as a member of the IRA.

Doherty:   You don't come to the United States as a member of the Irish Republican Army. This is a neutral country.

Attorney:  Why was it necessary for you to sever your membership, suspend your membership?

Doherty:   Because I couldn't come to the United States as a member of the Irish Republican Army. . . .

Attorney:  Are you saying that you were told to resign your membership and you were ordered as a good IRA soldier to do something, that is to go to the United States, even though you were no longer a member of the army, even when you had resigned, you were subject to the command discipline of the army?

Doherty:   Well, when I resigned from the Irish Republican Army back home, they said I would be going as a civilian but could be called back, much like you would say the National Guard or the reserve in the United States where they are told to go home and you could be called back in a national emergency. Maybe that's a bad example, I'm not too sure.

His reference to 'being called back' is a crucial element in determining whether he was a member of the IRA prior, and subsequent, to his departure from Ireland. If he had resigned, the IRA would not have possessed the authority to 'call him back' two years later, because his 'resignation' would have determined he was no longer under their control. Where are the ingredients in his story prior to his proposed departure which would formally have encouraged his resignation? How could he survive outside Ireland without the support of the IRA in acquiring the contacts necessary for him to establish a new identity, several thousand miles from home? True, the IRA never conducted violent operations in the United States, in much the same way it did not do so in the Irish Republic *vis-à-vis* operations which could directly threaten the state or its civilians. In that respect Doherty was not sent to the US to act in the fashion for which he was already infamous. The IRA's history of operations in the US has always related to weapons procurement, fund-raising and propaganda, so where would

Doherty have been useful in any of those contexts? As an active service operative, he would have been told there was no role for him in the United States. Was he told, however, that there would eventually be a role for him in Ireland when the heat subsided? Was he told that he might have a role in weapons procurement in the US if he established a new identity there? Whatever is true or close to the truth, none of those options would have forced him to resign from the IRA. One is obliged to ask why the issue of resignation became an important feature of his story.

I believe he was briefed that if caught in the United States it was vital that he denied being a member of the IRA; that the US legal system would accept him being a republican, but its stand on terrorism would militate against him if he admitted to active service membership of a terrorist organisation. He accepts that his IRA superiors told him that, if apprehended in the United States, he would have access to very good legal advice.

Perhaps they also told him about the 'political exception principle', and that if he pleaded only former membership of the IRA he could seek sanctuary as a political prisoner of conscience. The IRA is a clever organisation with a long history of dealing with the law in other jurisdictions, particularly the United States. Doherty both attended and gave lectures on the US constitution to IRA prisoners in Long Kesh/the Maze. Resignation from the IRA is a complex business, and nothing in his career before he left Ireland would have prompted him to resign. Was it a ploy? In 1984, in reply to the US Attorney, he said: 'I did resign, but they told me to go to the United States and resign, but I could have resigned and said you have no authority, and I want to stay in Ireland as a civilian. But I took my orders and I don't question them to the extent as what you might think.'

He was never a man to question orders throughout his IRA career. Members of the IRA are entitled to resign, but he claims he was given an order to resign 'in the United States'. That serves to reinforce my contention that he was instructed to go to the US and, if the matter of his membership ever arose, he was to say he had 'resigned'. The paradoxical nature of a directive to resign is illogical when related to historical IRA orthodoxy and rules, but is understandable in the light of the organisation's knowledge of US legal processes. The IRA was really giving Doherty the authority to deny membership of a terrorist organisation in the event of his arrest in a neutral jurisdiction. Although volunteers who denied membership were court-martialled, they could be granted permission to do so: the IRA plays fast and loose with its own rules when it knows that an orthodox policy response is detrimental to the interests of the organisation. A familiar example is when IRA volunteers appear before the courts. If IRA analysis of a volunteer's legal defence is that it is futile, the volunteer is ordered to refuse to recognise the court. If there is a probable chance of a successful legal defence which would result in a volunteer being freed to continue his terrorist activities, the IRA orders him to recognise the court and to challenge the prosecution case. The latter position is in direct conflict with IRA policy which dictates non-recognition of the British judicial process. Like all terrorist groupings, the IRA often regard the war as more important than individual policy guidelines. I believe that this is exactly what happened in the Doherty case.

He told me that I had to resign from the Irish Republican Army as we treat the United States as a neutral country and, of course, I could not go there as a volunteer. He told me I was to go as a civilian. He told me to keep low, enjoy myself and wait on further orders or when the coast was clear, or I was a forgotten name, then maybe I could go back in two, maybe three years, whatever the situation was.

The crucial piece of evidence in the above testimony of 1984 is contained within the line: 'He told me to keep low, enjoy myself and wait on further orders . . .' 'Further orders' clearly defined that Doherty was to remain subject to IRA orders while in the United States. The only people within the republican movement who could be so directed were members of the Irish Republican Army. Such orders as were given to Doherty were also given to 'sleepers' – volunteers sent into England with instructions to establish a new identity and to wait for orders which would activate them operationally. Volunteers employing those tactics were 'active' only in so far as they remained 'active volunteers' by membership; when orders for an operation were delivered to them they then engaged in 'active service'. The IRA constitution defines all volunteers as 'active': the reason lies in the organisation's desire that all volunteers be subject to orders and therefore 'active', with the prospect that at any time they can be told to fulfil an 'active service' role which, in reality, means to assist or participate in bombing or killing.

At the beginning of February 1982, Joseph Doherty was given a forged passport and a one-way airline ticket. He was placed on a plane at Shannon airport to begin a new life in the United States as Henry J. O'Reilly. A new chapter in his life was about to begin and it would be no less controversial than his history in Ireland.

He arrived at Kennedy airport and was safely processed by an immigration official. The name 'Henry J. O'Reilly' was typically Irish, and the passport 'genuine'. He was met in the arrivals lounge by IRA sympathisers; they drove him to Brooklyn, to meet others who were preparing his new life. New York was the IRA choice of destination, because they reckoned Doherty would find it easy to adapt to that society. The IRA told him he would 'receive a good education' there. They would remain in touch with him through 'secret communications', habitually done by means of letters sent to sympathisers, or notes via republicans travelling to New York from Ireland. Doherty claims a member of the IRA's ruling body, the Army Council, told him: 'You are going to New York as a civilian. Do what you want to do.' He was told he was even free to join the New York Police Department, if he so wished. I am not inclined to believe that the IRA really intended him to become a policeman, although such a suggestion has frightening dimensions. It may well have been the IRA's black but humorous way of indicating that he was entitled to select a career, any career, which he believed best suited his talents. Of course, they also said he might choose a different occupation, such as a job in the New York Sanitation Department. In a firm fashion they told him: 'When we get in touch with you, we will get in touch with you.'

His departure from Ireland was, he alleges, a final severance from the IRA. Despite his claim to have resigned from the organisation, he offered all the reasons why the IRA was not saying 'adieu'. They were prepared to recognise that he needed to live a different life for a time – but not without IRA approval, advice or contact: he could communicate with them by posting a letter to people in Ireland who were known to the IRA. That implied that the IRA were also intent on establishing a form of direct contact with their volunteer, rather than by way of sympathisers already in the country, or other IRA volunteers in hiding in the United States at that time. Doherty was briefed, prior to his departure from Ireland, by a member of the Army Council who had spent some time in America, and was familiar with cities such as New York, Boston and Philadelphia. He told Doherty that the IRA frequently sent volunteers 'on the run' to the United States for rest periods. The IRA regarded Doherty as an important activist and were not going to risk his being compromised by introducing him to other activists.

Doherty denies the presence of an IRA structure in the US. The organisation's ability to place him in another country, provide him with a new identity and eventually a job was a *de facto* indication of a network of people prepared to assist IRA operations. The dispatch of a leading IRA operator to New York and the presence of 'sympathisers' at the airport were proof of planning and a definite link between the IRA in Ireland and the US. The word 'sympathiser' has several connotations: people who vocally support the IRA; people who raise funds; who procure arms; who secretly assist the IRA by providing a safe haven for wanted terrorists. Within those categories there is probably no one who is an actual member of the IRA. Many of those people, however, could be validly defined as 'republicans' of the Irish persuasion. Some might even be members of the republican movement, a term used broadly to define all the groupings, the IRA included, who shape and promote the republican ideal of a United Ireland, with the specification that the 'armed struggle' of the IRA is central to achieving that ideal. Therefore, the umbrella term 'republican movement' is politically and intrinsically linked to the IRA. Not all those within the republican movement, whether they be members or supporters of the political party Sinn Fein, are necessarily volunteers in the IRA. They are, however, part of the 'war effort'. Sinn Fein is the political cutting edge and the IRA the Sword of Damocles. The two are inseparable in the central thesis that the only way to achieve a United Ireland is to wage armed struggle to force the British out of Ireland

Those people who helped Doherty in New York were part of the overall IRA structure, and thus part of the 'war effort'. In the early 1970s, support for the IRA within the United States was important to the 'armed struggle'. The IRA set up a network in the country to smuggle arms to Ireland. Fund-raising also provided a much-needed supply of cash to sustain the development of the emerging Provisional IRA. The traditionalist thinking of the Provisionals was attractive to Irish Americans steeped in orthodox republicanism. They were the inheritors of the romantic nationalism of the men who sacrificed their lives in 1916 in Dublin to achieve Irish independence. The loyalist pogroms against Catholics in 1969 and the subsequent heavy-handedness of the British towards the nationalist population in the early 1970s generated increasing support for the Provisionals in the US. By the late 1970s and 1980s, arms procurement from the US was made too difficult by the work of the FBI, and the IRA turned its attention to the Middle East and discovered an unlimited supply of guns and explosives from Libya's Colonel Gadaffi. The US remained important in respect of fund-raising, and as a safe haven for IRA activists. In another respect, it still held the prospect of providing the opportunity to acquire the ultimate weapon for the IRA arsenal – the surface-to-air missile, which the IRA believed could change the war against the British in the border areas of Ireland. A surface-to-air missile could make impossible the use of helicopters to ferry soldiers to and from barracks, and prevent surveillance planes photographing rural areas where the IRA hid weapons or conducted operations.

Therefore the network in the US was in place when Joseph Doherty arrived in New York, and it remains in place today. The term 'IRA structure' was rejected by Doherty, and he may have been correct in so far as it narrowly defined the network as being the Irish Republican Army with the corollary that all the partici- pants were IRA 'volunteers'. On the other hand, he may have had a more important reason for rejecting the term. His own denial of membership of the IRA in the US dictated that he could not attach the letters 'IRA' to republicans there. It seems feasible that he was told that, if captured, he should declare the US a neutral country in much the same way as General Order No. 8 defined IRA policy within the Republic of Ireland.

The US was much too useful for its facilities to be jeopardised by an admission that the armed wing of republicanism was in the country. If the US Government was publicly faced with a declar- ation that the IRA was on its soil, namely in the person of Doherty, it would be forced to act more decisively against the organisation. The IRA has always known the importance of having a US network which legally acts in support of the armed struggle. But would the IRA's principle of neutrality apply if British servicemen were stationed there? Holland and Germany are no longer regarded as neutral soil: in recent years British servicemen have been killed and army bases attacked in Germany, and servicemen shot in Holland. Perhaps the IRA would never act in such a fashion in the US because of the bedrock of overt and tacit support. Equally, the US Administration has always been timid about the powerful Irish vote, tangentially Irish nationalist or republican in character, and which often exercised its traditional aspirations by providing money for IRA front organisations. In recognition of the need not to disturb a delicate political balance, the IRA and the US Administration tone down their rhetoric. Thus Doherty was instructed in the ground rules before he left Ireland.

He told me I was going to New York. I says: 'What in the event I am arrested?' He says: 'Well, I doubt if you will be arrested. It is a big city and don't go with such a negative approach, but if you are arrested then you can try and fight somewhere. You have plenty of support in the United States and there are people ready to stand by you and fully understand your situation in the North of Ireland and there are pretty good lawyers in New York, probably the best in the world.' He said: 'Go over and get your head cleared.'

That advice from the Army Council member who briefed him was apparently reassuring for Joseph Doherty, who quickly settled into a new life as Henry J. O'Reilly. He says he was not obliged to stay in New York, and was offered a choice of Colorado, Baltimore or San Francisco, but he liked New York and decided to remain there. I suspect his choice was informed by the network of people in New York and their ability to mould him into a typical inhabitant of a New York suburb. He was given money, was provided with accommodation and a job, and settled in Bensonhurst, Brooklyn. His first job was with a construction company, HRA, which was renovating the Union Carbide building on Park Avenue, later the Chase Manhattan Bank. He says that, although the people who assisted him knew he had 'some trouble with the British', they were not members of the IRA.

People in the IRA passed the word to them. That goes back hundreds of years to many people who are here in the US, grandfathers and great-grandfathers came here from the old country, and when I was approached in Dublin and given a passport, the IRA said, 'We are going to send you over in a week', and sympathisers took over. On the record there is no IRA structure in the United States. They said there were plenty of sympathisers who would help me along, like thousands of other young people who come here – they are just young fellows off the farm or something and I was part of the many thousands who have been coming, particularly to New York City, for the past one hundred to two hundred years.

It was easy for Henry J. O'Reilly to fit into the Irish community. A trip to the Gaelic Park in the Bronx acquaints the visitor to New

York with the large numbers of Irish who have arrived in the city, even within the past two decades. Young Irish people arriving for the first time find support and advice from those who regularly congregate in the park for Gaelic football matches. It resembles in all its character a small piece of Ireland, and is a warm and reassuring place for first arrivals to be able to meet Irish people who already have an intimate knowledge of New York. Joseph Doherty was not typical of the thousands of young Irish people he refers to as 'young fellows off the farm'. He was hiding a deadly secret; he possessed an alias – and it was vital that he constantly used deception to sustain his new identity. As an IRA volunteer he was skilled in avoiding detection, but he was none the less required to fashion a past for himself which was entirely separate from his history. The fact that so many young Irish resided in New York made it easier for him to blend into his surroundings. Before long he had a girlfriend, and visited places where the Irish congregated for sport and entertainment. He was simply regarded as Henry J. O'Reilly, 'a lad over from the old country'. Sympathisers 'fixed him up' with an apartment and took him on trips through Manhattan and the other boroughs to give him a thorough knowledge of his surroundings.

They showed me how to get into Manhattan. They showed me Yankee Stadium, etc. They were sort of escorting me around. They put me on to people who could get me a job. You go to the Irish-American clubs and dances, you meet up with union members, people who know somebody in the union, and you tell them I would like to get a job and they ask if you have the skills. They came back and told me I could go into mason-tending. They knew I was illegal.

Doherty says those people may have guessed that he had escaped from a British prison, but they never asked questions about it. He explains the tacit understanding of sympathisers by offering a description of how people in Ireland react to IRA men running from the law.

When you are on the run and you stay in people's homes, they will either call you Sean or Pat and not call you any surname. When I got up one morning I patted two kids on the head. They turned around very maturely and said: 'What would you like us to call you?' I said: 'Call me Joe, that's my name.' They understood that there are a generation of persons on the run and you don't ask them any questions. A man is sleeping there in the barn, in a back room. That is a sort of cultural thing with the Irish because we have always been rebelling against the British. It is a part of everybody's culture that you don't ask questions when someone is in trouble.

Getting a job was one thing, but a job which would legally fit with the apparent authenticity of his alias was a pressing problem. His passport was stamped with a visitor's visa and it was too dangerous to attempt to use it to fill out the forms necessary to acquire a social security number. He overcame that difficulty by seeking advice from 'a sympathiser'. From the end of March 1982 he used the number 076–50–0652, a social security number belonging to someone else.

Doherty paid his federal and city taxes and worked in several jobs, from shoe-shining to a part-time job as a bellboy. He also worked in Clancy's Bar in Manhattan and was paid a daily fee of $25 or $50 plus tips. He was determined to earn money so that he and his girlfriend could move to New Jersey. According to Doherty he went of his own volition to the bar to seek work, although he admits that Alan Clancy, who owned the bar, was known to him as 'a sympathiser'. Contrary to IRA advice that he should keep a low profile, Doherty worked in a place known to the FBI as a haunt of IRA sympathisers. In 1983 he moved to Davison Avenue in Kearny, New Jersey, in the belief that his new identity was firmly established – and unaware that the security forces on both sides of the Irish border were now convinced he was no longer in Ireland.

The RUC guessed that he had gone to the United States, and asked Frank Schulte for FBI assistance to trace him. The request presented a daunting task on account of the many cities where IRA sympathisers were willing to hide a fugitive. In New York, the FBI department with responsibility for counter-terrorism and, in particular, Irish terrorists, both republican and loyalist, sought advice from their informants within the Irish community. One of Schulte's informers pointed the finger at a relatively recent arrival, Henry J. O'Reilly, who worked occasionally in Clancy's Bar. Schulte became personally involved because of his interest in the M60 theft, and he placed undercover surveillance in and within the vicinity of the bar for one week. He was concerned that if the FBI seized the wrong man there would be a political backlash within the community, and a consuming embarrassment within the Bureau.

The RUC provided a detailed file on Doherty which included a series of photographs, one of which was taken before the escape. His physical description was given as '175 cms, slim build, oval face, pale complexion, brown hair, brown eyes, Belfast accent'. The description fitted FBI observations of Henry J. O'Reilly, except that he was older than his portrait in the RUC file. Ironically Doherty did not change his appearance, as might have been expected of a terrorist in hiding. Perhaps he felt too comfortable with his New York lifestyle, too casual in the knowledge that after February 1983 he encountered no problems in shaping his new identity. He admits he was wrong to remain for too long in New York. Maybe his acquisition of a house in New Jersey, his relationship with a girlfriend, tied him to the place. In any case, the FBI had decided he was their target and discovered he worked at Clancy's every Saturday.

Early on the morning of 18 June 1983 Doherty arrived at the bar, oblivious of the presence of two FBI undercover teams sitting in cars, parked discreetly nearby. At 9.10 am two agents, dressed as construction workers, entered Clancy's and saw him standing behind the bar counter. They ordered drinks and scrutinised him, mentally comparing him with his RUC profile. They were careful not to create suspicion and behaved in a congenial manner. They finished their drinks and moved forward to seize him, saying he was under arrest on a warrant claiming he had entered the United States illegally. The warrant had been issued the previous day by the Immigration and Naturalisation Service, as an order to show cause and warrant of arrest. Doherty admits now that, when the FBI agents walked into the bar and ordered drinks, he should have known that construction workers did not normally order drinks at such an early hour. He told them he was Henry J. O'Reilly, because he believed they were unaware of his true identity and were arresting him as an illegal alien. He was taken to FBI headquarters at Federal Plaza in Manhattan where he agreed to be fingerprinted. He was interviewed about his identity and recalls a casual atmosphere prevailing in the FBI office:

Fifteen minutes into the interview they got me a cup of coffee. They were reading the Irish newspapers and sitting around gabbing and I looked across the table and I seen one of the guys had a British 'Most Wanted' photograph of me. So I knew that they knew I wasn't Henry O'Reilly. So I said excuse me, my name is Joe Doherty. They said: 'We know.'

Doherty's recollection of the precise time when he admitted his true identity has been legally disputed because he signed an FBI document with a Henry J. O'Reilly signature at 9.45 am on 18 June and a receipt for $120.81 which was removed from his coat.

It is reasonable to conclude on available evidence that he revealed his true identity at some stage that day, although he continued to sign documents with his alias for one week after his arrest. He says, however, that he told his lawyers his true identity from the outset of their meeting.

Within days there was little doubt that Doherty faced serious legal problems; few people, however, could have forecast that they would prove so complex and time-consuming, and would provide such a rare examination of the US legal system. Before long Joseph Doherty, alias Henry J. O'Reilly, would be the subject of one of the most intriguing politico-legal sagas in American history.

# 11

# Prisoner of Conscience?

On 18 June 1983 the arrest warrant charged Joseph Doherty only with failing to show the time, place and manner of his entry to the United States. The District Director of the Immigration and Naturalisation Service (INS) ordered he be held without bond (in custody). Doherty's lawyers, from the firm of Somerstein & Pike, with offices at 401 Broadway, requested a hearing before an immigration judge, in the hope of arguing that their client should be freed on a bail bond. A hearing was set for 27 June, but, behind the scenes, the British and American Governments were closely examining the prospect of returning Doherty to the United Kingdom, and I have been told the British Government demanded that the US respect extradition arrangements between the two countries. The insistence of the British was a primary indication that they would henceforth be unrelenting in their pursuit of Doherty and would constantly put pressure on the US Administration to resolve what soon developed into a legal complexity. British Government legal analysts believed extradition proceedings should be immediately initiated to prevent Doherty and his lawyers proceeding with a strategy which could prove lengthy and tortuous, would almost certainly generate Irish-American support for him, and would thwart British ambitions to return him to the United Kingdom.

On 27 June an immigration judge heard Steve Somerstein of Somerstein & Pike argue for a bond redetermination in favour of his client. The hearing was interrupted by a US Attorney who served Doherty with a provisional arrest warrant so that he could be dealt with in accordance with the law, terms and requirements of the extradition treaty between the USA and the United Kingdom.

Doherty's lawyers responded by asking the immigration judge, Mr Blackman, to relieve himself of the bond hearing and he agreed, with the proviso that he would refer the matter to the Associate Regional Commissioner for Eastern Operations. Their argument was that the hearing was compromised by the untimely presentation of an extradition request, and should be reset in a more conducive atmosphere. The INS lawyer replied by requesting an end to the bond hearing on the basis that extradition proceedings took precedence, and that the bond application should be suspended pending a resolution of the extradition issue.

In keeping with legal practice, a United States District Court Judge of the Southern District of New York ruled that all international extradition cases required a person to be held in custody in abeyance of proceedings. Doherty was handed over to the United States Marshal for the Southern District of New York, and was removed to the Correction Center in downtown Manhattan. He was about to begin life as a prisoner wearing prison uniform, undertaking voluntary prison work, with a prison number and an address: D Block, Main South, Metropolitan Correction Center.

Before he was removed from court to his new abode, his lawyers sought an assurance that the Immigration Service would not seek to initiate deportation hearings against him on their warrant until a decision was given in the extradition case, and that was agreed.

Doherty travelled along the corridor between the courthouse and the Correction Center aware that the extradition warrant from the British proved they were taking a personal interest in his life. He did not know they would persevere with their efforts until he was returned to them.

The extradition treaty required the British Government to present the US with a formal request for his extradition, but, ironically, they had left it to the very last date required by the terms of the treaty. I was privately informed that the lateness of the request was due to the British assessing their line of argument, examining the merits of their case and waiting to see which way Doherty would proceed legally. They were determined that there should be no flaws in the presentation of their case against him; and they believed that, if everything was in place and they were successful, the return of Doherty would represent a body blow to IRA propaganda, would indicate that the United States was tough on terrorism and its soil no longer a safe haven for wanted IRA personnel. The British viewed the case as part of the European fight against terrorism, and intended to demonstrate a developing closeness in tactics and policy between the US and British Governments, and impress countries such as France, which was at times weak on the issue.

Margaret Thatcher took a personal interest in Doherty, because she believed his return would highlight her public demands that all countries show a common will to provide 'no safe haven'. The IRA was her main terrorist problem, and the Doherty case was central to her being able to display her ability to seek out terrorists wherever they were hiding. Her Government's formal request for Doherty's extradition was made on the forty-fifth day after he was served with the provisional warrant.

On 12 October 1983, Steve Somerstein presented another bail application. A hearing took place before Judge John E. Sprizzo, who rejected the application in favour of a prosecution argument that Doherty was 'a very big bail-flight risk'. That argument was to become a central feature of the US Administration's subsequent legal strategy which I shall deal with in due course. However, it is worth noting the nature of Sprizzo's reasoning:

People are human and it would certainly not be irrational for Doherty to think, 'I am not going to roll those dice. If they come up the wrong way I am going back to England and I don't want to go back to England', especially if he does feel he is engaged in an insurrection against England, which I am sure he does believe. I would be greatly surprised if Mr Doherty were bailed, if he did not exercise what I would think would be a very rational judgment perhaps to disappear.

Before I began researching this book, people said the Doherty case was significant from its outset but lacked evidence to support their contention. I learned that behind-the-scenes discussions took place between representatives of the US Administration and the British Government in advance of the bail hearing of October 1983. Confidential memoranda prove that contact between both Governments was quickly established after Doherty's arrest, in order to plan a joint strategy to ensure his return to British custody. Documents show that Margaret Thatcher viewed American support for Doherty as a dangerous trend, which could only be halted if he were extradited.

Thirty days after Doherty's arrest and only twenty days after he was served with the extradition warrant, a meeting took place on 18 July in the United Kingdom which was specifically labelled

'Doherty Extradition Case'. Those present included representatives of the British Foreign and Commonwealth Office, the Home
Office, the Northern Ireland Office and the RUC's Legal Adviser. It
was a high-powered meeting, with the majority of those present
representing the central arm of British policy-making.

The meeting was held on the basis that 'the extradition application should proceed and the United Kingdom's written submission – or part of it – should be made to the US authorities by
their deadline of August 11.' A classified document recording the
points raised at the meeting read as follows:

(i)     The procedure involved the submission of a 'statement of facts'
        and a 'statement of law' together with supporting personal
        statements. It would be necessary for the Northern Ireland Office
        to receive these in final form from the RUC (for certification and
        conveyance to New York through the Foreign & Commonwealth
        Office (FCO) ) at least a week before the deadline, since the FCO
        would have to involve the US Embassy in the exercise too. The
        defence would then have about two months to respond in writing
        before oral evidence was taken. Oral hearings could therefore
        start in October or November.

(ii)    It was not known how the Quinn case, which awaited an appeal
        hearing, would affect this application since *inter alia* the San
        Francisco District Court's judgment that his offences were
        unrelated to the civil uprising in Northern Ireland was not
        binding on the New York District Court. (It was not of course
        helpful that the case was to be held in New York at all.)

(iii)   Doherty's defence could not dispute the facts and could only be
        based on a claim that his offences were political in character.

(iv)    The fact that the soldiers had been in plain-clothes was double-
        edged: on the one hand the defence would try to show that this
        was typical of the tactics of the SAS and other agents of the British
        'occupying forces', but on the other hand *our American attorney*
        [my italics] might be able to show that the murder of someone in
        civilian clothes, which followed the taking of hostages, was a
        typically indiscriminate act of IRA terrorism.

(v)     It would be important to show that Doherty and his colleagues
        had been under surveillance, because they were moving
        weapons which had been used in a number of murderous
        attacks, and that the security forces were anxious to catch as
        many terrorists as possible in the operation, so as to protect
        society as fully as possible.

(vi)    The offences which would be the basis of the application would be all those for which Doherty has been convicted, or was wanted for trial, save that of escaping from custody (which was not extraditable).

(vii)    If Doherty were extradited, he would probably not be prosecuted for his firearms offences, since he was already under a life sentence, but this was not of course a point to be offered in evidence.

(viii)    If he were not extradited, he would probably be returned to the Republic as an illegal immigrant where he would be amenable to extradition proceedings, or to prosecution under the reciprocal legislation, so there was a fall-back position.

(ix)    Our attorney would probably be able to make use of the clear wish of both Administration and Congress to more narrowly define the characteristics of an offence which was political; it would not be possible, however, to apply any new legislation retrospectively, even if it were enacted before a decision in Doherty's case.

(x)    It would be prudent for the Northern Ireland Office during the period leading up to the defence's response to our depositions, to give thought to possible witnesses on the general situation in the Province at the time of Doherty's offences. It would be important for any such witness to be disassociated from the British Government, and for him to be able to paint a picture of declining violence and impartial law enforcement and judicial procedures. While such high profile figures as Conor Cruise O'Brien, Gerry Fitt or Robert Kee could be difficult to land, the bigger the 'fish' the better. It was unlikely the American attorney would want to use an RUC officer on this occasion.

The above document showed the seriousness with which the British Government viewed Doherty, the ensuing legal battle, and American thinking on the matter. The degree of collusion between the two Governments was clear in the repeated use of the words 'our attorney'. In revealing this material my intention is to clarify the workings of law at an international level and to highlight the importance with which the British Government viewed the need for international co-operation on terrorism, and how the Doherty case symbolised the way in which such co-operation could be displayed. In 1983 a central aim of Thatcher policy was the defeat not only of the IRA but of international terrorism, and subsequent meetings of high-powered figures took place to realise that ambition. The Doherty case placed Thatcher's strategy in jeopardy: the risk of Doherty being deemed a 'political offence exception' threatened her public denunciation of the IRA as 'thugs, murderers and terrorists'.

The document referred to a 'fall-back position', which was the belief that, if extradition failed, deportation would succeed, since there was incontrovertible proof that Doherty was an illegal alien. Those present at the London meeting rightly suspected that, in the event of a deportation order, Doherty would choose the Irish Republic rather than the United Kingdom, but they knew privately that the Irish Government was becoming flexible in its extradition arrangements with the UK. The evidence to support such a view was in the Irish response to a British request for the return of one of the most notorious republican hitmen, Dominic McGlinchey, who was in custody in the Republic of Ireland. McGlinchey led a breakaway IRA grouping and was acknowledged to be responsible for the murder of at least thirty soldiers and policemen, as well as innocent civilians, the majority of whom were Protestant. He operated across the border from the safety of the Republic, but was caught by the Irish police and army during a gun-battle. The British authorities wished him returned to Northern Ireland to face charges connected with the murder of a civilian. They hoped that having him extradited and finding him guilty would illustrate growing co-operation on terrorism between the two Governments and, as in the Doherty case, prove there was no safe haven for the IRA. A guilty verdict in Northern Ireland would also return McGlinchey to a British prison for life. The Irish Supreme Court agreed to extradite him on the basis that the crime for which he was sought, the killing of a civilian, was a crime which offended civilisation, and could not be treated within the 'political offence' exception. Proof that the McGlinchey case had a bearing on Doherty is contained in an RUC document prepared for the US Attorney: 'Prior to the Republic's Supreme Court decision in the McGlinchey appeal against extradition, there was no point in seeking extradition for terrorist-type offences. The McGlinchey decision was after the escapers were arrested in the Republic.'

Ironically, if Doherty had been arrested with the other escapers before the McGlinchey verdict, the RUC would not have sought his extradition, because they believed it futile to do so – his offence was 'terrorist-type'. A corollary is that the prosecution case against McGlinchey failed in Northern Ireland, and he was returned to the

Republic, where he remains in prison. However, the Supreme Court verdict to send McGlinchey back to Belfast to face charges offered hope that, if Doherty were returned to the Republic, he too would be successfully extradited to the UK. One has to ask why there was British optimism in that matter. I think the answer is to be found in paragraph (vii) of the record of the British Government meeting of 18 July 1983: 'If Doherty were extradited, he would probably not be prosecuted for his firearms offences, since he was already under a life sentence, but this was not of course a point to be offered in evidence.'

Why not offer it in evidence? In the event of a successful extradition, there would be little point in prosecuting him for a firearms offence because he would be returning to prison to serve his life sentence. If extradition failed, however, and deportation followed, it was important that a subsequent tactic be available to the British Government. If Doherty were returned to the Irish Republic, the British would be obliged to proceed with a request for his extradition. They would be unlikely to achieve it unless, as in the McGlinchey case, they could prefer charges against him which were not of a directly political nature.

The British knew the Westmacott killing would be judged a 'terrorist-type' offence. Was there a firearms offence which was not within that definition, the type of offence which clause (vii) did not detail, yet recommended should not be mentioned? There was such an offence, and it related to the prison escape. Charges could have been fashioned to relate to the holding of hostages, some of them lawyers, the attack on Prison Officer Kennedy, and the endangering of civilians during the gun-battle on the Crumlin Road. Any of those actions could have been defined as 'assaults' or 'life-threatening attacks on non-combatants'. In July 1983, those present at the meeting were keen that Doherty's defence should not know that there was such a 'fall-back' position. They did not wish his lawyers to know the legal tactics which might eventually be employed against their client in the United States or the Republic of Ireland.

Progress in the Doherty case appeared slow, and 1984 arrived without indication of when the extradition hearing would take place. On 15 February, a secret meeting was held in London to convince the US Government of the significance of the case, and its importance to both administrations. Two days later, a classified British Government memorandum precisely recorded the motives of the Assistant Secretary of the Northern Ireland Office who chaired the meeting:

The meeting was held so that the Northern Ireland Office could be updated as to the present state of the case and, in the main, to formally put Her Majesty's Government's particular interest in the extradition of Mr Doherty to the United Kingdom.

The US Administration was represented by Patricia Gunn of the Justice Department, who heard reasons why it was imperative that the extradition case succeed. She was told that the Prime Minister, Mrs Thatcher, took a 'personal interest' in the proceedings and had asked to be briefed at all stages.

On 17 February, another secret memorandum from the RUC's Legal Adviser outlined instructions received from the Assistant US Attorney. This document was forwarded to Senior Assistant Chief Constable Whiteside at RUC headquarters; it was marked 'NICRO 69/1033'.

The Assistant United States Attorney (AUSA) in charge of the Doherty case recently received instructions from the Judge who is scheduled to hear it, that he should provide details on a production request to defence lawyers. I have attached the book of interrogatories for your information – the relevant question that requires answering is at page 3 No. 10. The question relates to the Crumlin Road escape of 10 June 1981 – eight men including Doherty's three co-accused in the M60 murder escaped. All three men, bar Doherty, I understand have been captured in the Republic. I would need to know the dates and resulting court decisions. More particularly, I would need to know why we did not attempt extradition in respect of Campbell, Magee and Fusco for the M60 murder of Westmacott and other related offences.

One further matter: the AUSA requires the total background to Joseph P. T. Doherty. The AUSA would require to know of any Special Branch or other factual material collected on Doherty.

It is the AUSA's intention to attempt to drive a wedge between Doherty and 'the cause' – in the main to show that Doherty is a hanger-on, and that he is simply a terrorist. A Special Branch pen picture relating to Doherty's past history would in my view be sufficient.

Finally it would prove useful if we could obtain particulars leading up to the shootout between the late Captain Wesmeath's team [the incorrect spelling of Westmacott is part of the document] of undercover soldiers and the terrorists on 2.5.80. Such details will of course remain solely in our possession and will be treated as secret. Special Branch may be able to assist in this answer.

Several features of that memorandum require scrutiny. First, the RUC Legal Adviser appeared oblivious to the fact that the reason why no action had been taken to extradite Doherty's co-conspirators in the Westmacott murder had a bearing on the Doherty case. If extradition were sought it would rely on a tactic which would expose the 'fall-back' position: the secret of employing ordinary criminal offences to achieve extradition. The Legal Adviser was present at the meeting in London on 18 July 1983, and yet his own document did not reflect clause (vii) of that meeting. I am inclined to deduce that he was, perhaps, unwilling to declare his hand to the RUC hierarchy until the extradition took place. He may have been under orders not to reveal details of the secret London meeting. It may be that his document was a reply to an RUC enquiry which did not oblige him to fully reveal the strategy. Another explanation is that as a lawyer he was acting with propriety, by suggesting that, if such a ploy should eventually be used against Doherty, someone might ask why it had not previously been applied. The answer to such a question would have revealed, and possibly compromised, the plan to employ the 'fall-back position'.

His document clarified the Assistant US Attorney's scenario – which was a naïve analysis. The AUSA should have known that Doherty's history of commitment to the IRA would provide conclusive evidence of his commitment to the republican cause, and that the tactic of describing him as a 'hanger-on' would be futile. Portraying him as a terrorist in an international context offered wider and more achievable results. No one understood that by trying to link both they would weaken their case against him. The assumption that a Special Branch 'pen picture' of Doherty's history would be 'sufficient' was another example of simplistic reasoning. This thinking took no account of how Doherty would personally portray his life, exploit the mythologised view of the conflict that existed within the US, or the likelihood that the killing of an SAS captain might well come within the 'political offence' exception. There was detailed evidence, if they had just known about it, which could have shown Doherty to be still a member of the IRA, and could have portrayed him as a terrorist. They did not possess a detailed knowledge of the rules and policy governing the behaviour of IRA volunteers, the nature of membership and the guidelines related to resignation from the organisation.

Finally, the last paragraph of the document confirmed the status of the RUC when faced with questions about SAS operations. It was clear that the police force was not privy to the *modus operandi* or the motivation for SAS actions, because the Legal Adviser stressed that if information on the SAS activities was made available to him it would be 'treated as secret'. One would assume that such information should have been freely available to senior RUC figures and that a guarantee of secrecy should not have been required, but such are the vagaries of undercover operations in Northern Ireland that even senior RUC figures are required to give undertakings before they request information on elite military groupings. Uniformed police and detectives in the Criminal Investigation Branch are never given access to the plans or policies of undercover groups, particularly the SAS. Special Branch remains the only arm of the RUC with access to classified information. It owes authority and allegiance to the upper echelons of the intelligence community, and not the police force to which it is linked. The Legal Adviser tentatively suggested that Special Branch 'may be able to assist', and his use of language implied that even he remained unsure whether assistance would be forthcoming.

In April 1984, Doherty appeared before the United States Southern District Court of New York in Manhattan, and gave an account of his life. Under cross-examination by the US Attorney he offered an outline of his general thinking, which, he hoped, would answer the prosecution case that he was a hostage-taker, a terrorist without a moral code.

We did not take hostages because civilians are not part of the war, plus we see ourselves as an army. The IRA has a military code of ethics. Of course this contradicts the general British media that tries to say we are terrorist thugs, Leninists, murderers. This is just a screen to the outside world so people won't fully understand what's going on in the North of Ireland. People in the United States, if they went to Belfast and understood the situation, seeing the strife that was there and came back to the US, and tried to do something about it through their congressmen or senators, would fully understand. But the IRA, we recognise ourselves as an army. We recognise ourselves that we have some moral justification in the war. We have moral justification in the war.

The US Attorney did not ask the pertinent question – why was Doherty referring to the IRA as 'we' when he had already told the court he had resigned? Maybe the Attorney was confused by a plethora of statements by the Irishman concerning a situation that seemed complex in the minds of most US citizens, or maybe he was oblivious to what could have been a more productive line of cross-questioning.

It was eight months before a review of the evidence from both parties resulted in a decision favouring Doherty. On 12 December, Judge John E. Sprizzo denied the British request for Doherty's extradition. He held that the case fell within the terms of the 'political offence' exception 'in its most classic form'. He accepted that Doherty had killed Westmacott, and as a prisoner of war had exercised his duty to escape from enemy captors – a duty enshrined by the international law of war and the US Military Code of Conduct. He also conceded that while Doherty was in the United States, 'a neutral nation not occupying his country and with whom he was not at war', he had made no attempt to escape. He regarded Doherty as a political offender and not a common criminal, and concluded that his crimes did not violate international law, nor were they inconsistent with international standards of civilised conduct.

Doherty's lawyer later summarised the judge's view of the British Government's attempt to define Doherty as a hostage-taker:

Not only were there no civilians killed or injured during the course of events on the Antrim Road – and Judge Sprizzo so stated – there was no evidence of threats to do so. None were used as shields or as bargaining chips to compel the British authorities to allow Mr Doherty to escape once the building was surrounded by the army. The object of Mr Doherty's mission, an attack on a military convoy, clearly did not involve the use of hostages to advance or publicise his political agenda.

The utilisation of these particular premises in urban warfare did not in any manner involve hostage-taking, either in violation of American or international law.

Sprizzo also dismissed as 'trivial and irrelevant' attempts by the US Attorney to imply that Doherty's indiscretions as a youth represented a criminal propensity that undermined his assertion that he was a political offender.

The case presented by the US Attorney did not have the cogency it required. The British objective of 'driving a wedge' between Doherty and the 'cause' failed, and attempts to present him as 'a hanger-on' or common criminal appeared vexatious. The defence lawyers from Somerstein & Pike were clever in their handling of Doherty, and in schooling him in delivering his testimony. He succeeded in destroying what was an uninformed and naïve approach to the substance of the case. The British Government was angry and dismayed. It regarded the verdict as a moral victory for Doherty and the IRA, and a body blow to British attempts to turn the American legal system to the advantage of Margaret Thatcher's declared war on international terrorism.

A senior member of the Justice Department summarised his and the British view of the verdict as 'outrageous'. His comment generated a bitter tirade which ended with an editorial in the *National Law Journal* on 19 December 1984.

The style of their comments about the judge – whose decision was fully supported by the facts and the law – gives us great concern. For the head of the Justice Department's Criminal Division to express such outrage and make sarcastic comments is to demean the judicial process and the Justice Department itself.

The rebuke was warranted, but the statement evoked the outrage of the British and the US Administrations, who passionately believed they had the case won before it went to court. It also confirmed the significance of the Doherty matter to US–British foreign relations. The British were most aggrieved because they had placed the case at the top of their agenda and defined its success as central to the political relationship, and co-operation on terrorism, between themselves and the US Administration.

The British extradition warrant had effectively expired by the time of Sprizzo's judgment, but Doherty remained in custody because the Immigration and Naturalisation Service warrant for his deportation was outstanding. Doherty decided to oppose it by seeking political asylum. The Sprizzo judgment sparked off one of the most remarkable and long-running series of hearings and appeals in American history. It redoubled the resolve of both administrations to secure Doherty's return, and left his lawyers with a legal complexity which baffled the average citizen. The ensuing legal war, with its myriad battles, encapsulates the extraordinary tenacity with which the US and British authorities pursued Doherty at all levels, and how the matter was transformed into one of the most important issues disturbing British–American foreign relations.

Sprizzo's judgment delighted the IRA: it reinforced their claim to be freedom fighters; defended their right to escape from British justice; and defined them as prisoners of war. The judgment accepted Doherty's assertion that the IRA regarded and treated the US as 'neutral territory'. Such a declaration, and from a leading judge, excited IRA expectations that the United States could remain a safe haven for IRA men fleeing the British, and gave the IRA an international status as an acceptable army with a political mandate to use violence.

In London there was dismay, because the judgment not only undermined Thatcher's strategy but strengthened the IRA's position. She was not ready to allow the Americans to concede defeat on extradition, and she told the executive branch of the American Government to take the unprecedented step of seeking 'collateral review' of Judge Sprizzo's verdict. In seeking the overturning of his judgment, the US executive would be obliged to seek 'declaratory relief from it'. Whatever language jurisprudence cites as correct, the obvious perception of a casual observer was that the US Administration was being asked to disturb the proprieties of its own judicial system by questioning the ruling of one of its own judges. Doherty's lawyers decided to attempt to negotiate bail for their client by pursuing a redetermination of bond, while the US executive branch, on orders from the British, developed a two-pronged strategy: an action to overturn the Sprizzo verdict, and the recommencement of deportation hearings.

Doherty appeared before an immigration judge and was delighted to discover that freedom from custody was achievable. The judge set bail at $200,000, but the Irishman's hopes were dashed when lawyers for the INS filed an immediate appeal to the Board of Immigration Appeals (BIA). The appeal tactic resulted in an emergency stay on the judge's bail decree and ensured that Doherty remained in the Correction Centre.

On 4 March 1985 the BIA listened to the arguments presented by Doherty's lawyers and those opposing bail. It found in favour of the INS, overturned the immigration judge's ruling and ordered Doherty to be returned to his cell. The BIA cited the risk of flight as central to their judgment and said:

The prison term awaiting him in Northern Ireland provides a substantial incentive for him to avoid returning to his homeland. Further, the respondent's escape from prison demonstrates that he will go to great lengths to avoid that imprisonment. He made good his escape in a hail of gunfire; he might very well have been killed. In comparison, the consequences that might be expected from absconding to avoid deportation seem inconsequential.

The respondent's record demonstrates that he has the ability and resources to simply disappear. Although he has testified in his extradition proceedings that he resigned from the PIRA to come to the United States, a neutral country, he also testified that he is subject to being recalled into service. He stated again and again that he takes orders from the PIRA. We have no reason to believe PIRA could not or would not assist him in absconding in the future as it has in the past.

The BIA verdict was a loose arrangement of uncorroborated assertions. The risk of flight was a decidedly important element in the judgment and I believe unproven, yet it was to remain a wearisomely reiterated argument without substantive evidence. The claim that 'he stated again and again that he takes orders from the IRA' was not confirmed by his 1984 testimony. Their use of the present tense implied that the immigration team was convinced he was still 'taking orders', but they did not show proof to enable them to make such a judgment. Suddenly a second decision in his favour was questioned, and quickly overturned. Doherty's lawyers chose not to seek a judicial review of the BIA ruling, because they were busy preparing themselves to contest deportation.

On 25 March 1985 Doherty, accompanied by counsel, arrived in a court presided over by the immigration judge, Howard I. Cohen, to discover that the INS was adding six extra charges and twelve factual allegations to the original charge which appeared in the 1983 warrant. It was a delaying tactic to permit time for the executive to resume extradition at Thatcher's request. The pursuit of extradition was more important to her than deportation. It was central to the relationship between the two countries, and represented a broader and more effective weapon against the IRA. Thatcher and her advisers knew that at a future date a member of the IRA could enter the US legally, and if extradition were not properly in place it would be futile to seek his return to UK custody.

The INS presentation of additional charges forced Doherty's lawyers to seek an adjournment in order to analyse the import of the 'new evidence'. They were granted a month's adjournment and discovered that 'neither the additional charges nor the allegations were based on new information that had not been available to the Government as far back as June 1983.'

Somerstein & Pike also took the view that the INS was acting in violation of assurances given to Doherty that his deportation would not be pursued until the extradition matter was settled, and notice to seek relief from Sprizzo's decision was proof that extradition proceedings were still an option. The defence viewed the INS behaviour as contrary to a BIA precedential decision, and with that in mind they went back to Judge Cohen on 18 March 1985 and pleaded for a stay of deportation hearings until the following matters were dealt with:

(1) a final determination of the US Government's declaratory judgment action collaterally attacking Judge Sprizzo's decision in the extradition case;
(2) resolution of two separate actions Doherty brought pursuant to the Freedom of Information Act;
(3) until Doherty's Counsel had an opportunity to consider and meet the additional charges relating to his deportability.

The INS told Judge Cohen it required time to consider Doherty's request to have a stay of deportation proceedings. The judge agreed to an adjournment to 15 April, but both parties consented to 20 May 1985. On that day, Judge Cohen found in favour of Doherty and, despite INS protests, ordered deportation proceedings to be suspended until there was a decision in the action seeking relief from Sprizzo's judgment.

On 26 June 1985 the legal war against Doherty reached another critical point for the US and British Administrations, when the Honourable Charles S. Haight Jr dismissed the US Government's campaign against the Sprizzo verdict. Judge Haight declared that the complaint against the Sprizzo verdict 'failed to state a cause of action'.

The US Government's executive branch indicated its unhappiness with Haight, as it had done with Sprizzo, and said it would appeal. Suddenly two American judges were at odds with the will of their Government – damaging to the judicial process.

A subsequent notice of appeal against Haight's verdict bore a familiar resemblance to the appeal against Sprizzo, in that it was not filed until 26 August 1985, which represented the fifty-ninth day of the sixty-day period permitted the Government for noting appeals. One can only speculate whether the precarious appreciation of timing was deliberate, unnecessary, simply a matter of indecision, or a delay to allow for detailed consultation with the British Government

On 13 March 1986 the United States Court of Appeals found that Judge Haight was correct in his judgment. A panel of three appeal judges were unanimous in affirming his verdict, and expressed incredulity at the US Government's refusal to accept the rulings of two senior judges, namely Sprizzo and Haight. The appeal judges described the behaviour of the Government as utterly without foundation, and an attempt to escape from the 'long-held principle that when an extradition magistrate acting under 18 USC 3181 refuses to certify a person sought to be extradited under an extradition treaty, the Government's sole resource is to submit a request to another magistrate'. It was more than 'a slap on the wrist': it was a severe reprimand to the executive arm of the Government that it should not interfere with the rule of law. The Appeals Court believed the executive had breached the rules when it questioned Sprizzo's judgment, and did so because it feared another judge might also find in Doherty's favour – which is exactly what happened when Haight examined the case.

The Appeals Court panel used 'startling' to characterise the Government's behaviour, and Judge Henry J. Friendly noted: 'The Government has not cited and we have not been able to find a single case in which a declaratory judgment was used in a manner resembling that which the Government proposes here.' He also pointed out that the US Government, in seeking to escape from the earlier rulings, was running *counter not only to fifty years of history but to the evident purpose of 18 USC 3181 and of the Declaratory Judgment Act itself* [my italics].

Too few people in the United States were sufficiently informed about the nature of the Doherty story to recognise that the legal battle was central to US legal precedent, and dangerous to the normal workings of the judicial system. It was also of major significance to the relations between two administrations, who were prepared to seek any recourse, even if it compromised the US legal system. The Appeals Court ruling was a damning indictment of the executive's behaviour.

The executive responded by filing a motion asking that all

members of the Appeals Court be gathered to rehear the case. That was rejected two months later, but, at the time the motion was prepared, the executive indicated that it would seek a ruling on the Appeals Court verdict by proceeding to the United States Supreme Court within ninety days. It never pursued that strategy and neglected to inform Doherty or his lawyers that it had abandoned it in favour of other means.

Why did it not proceed to the Supreme Court at that stage? It may have feared that, if a review against the Appeals Court ruling was dismissed, the whole case against Doherty would have been perceptibly weakened. Perhaps it also knew that another attempt to question the judicial system, its authority and intellect might engender too much animosity and elevate the Doherty issue to a level where public and political awareness would be heightened, and the US executive and its British partners open to scrutiny.

By any standards the legal battle became a farce which threatened to make a mockery of the right of judges to act with freedom from executive interference. Sprizzo's judgment was questioned, an immigration judge's ruling was overturned, Judge Haight's decision was appealed, and recourse to the Supreme Court was threatened to overturn the Appeals Court ruling. Those actions by the US Administration illustrated the tenacity of a Government under pressure to get a result at all costs, even if it embarrassed judges and weakened their freedom to act within the judicial system. It was a US Government willing to take orders from the British to exploit any means to thwart one man. What no one knew was that behind the scenes Mrs Thatcher was putting pressure on President Reagan to deliver on the extradition issue, and to ensure that any legal decision which favoured the IRA man was contested and overturned. Reagan admired Thatcher, shared her campaign against terrorism and was indebted to her for support for his foreign policy. He was not in a position to ignore her advice or demands.

At a political level, events took place to ensure that, irrespective of what transpired at the US Appeals Court, the Sprizzo verdict would be overturned. By June 1985 an amendment to the extradition treaty between the two countries had been drafted to deal with Sprizzo's ruling on the 'political offence' exception. On 25 June 1985 an amendment to the treaty, 'a supplementary treaty', was signed by both Governments. The US Senate ratified it on 17 July 1986, and after receiving the sanction of the British House of

Commons it became operative in December 1986. The emergence of the new treaty may have been the reason why a petition to the Supreme Court was not sought. No matter in what way one chooses to analyse the sequence of legal and political events, both Governments were not prepared to let the Sprizzo judgment stand. The British saw it as 'opening the door' to other IRA men being defined as 'political prisoners', at a time when the British were branding them 'thugs, murderers, common criminals, animals, madmen and terrorists'.

Article 4 of the new treaty, the so-called 'supplementary' to the existing treaty, declared that 'the political offence exception relied upon by Sprizzo, to prevent extradition, was eliminated retroactively, allowing Doherty's extradition to the United Kingdom where he faced a life sentence'.

The emergence of a supplementary to the extradition treaty showed that, if the American legal system was not prepared to deliver up Doherty, other means were available to both Governments. The supplementary was drawn up on the instructions of Margaret Thatcher. I learned that she told a senior Foreign and Commonwealth Office official that the US courts 'were not to be trusted', and power politics were required to seal Doherty's fate. The new treaty had the effect of ordering the return of Doherty and ensuring that the political offence exception would never again be granted to a member of the IRA in the United States. Thus Sprizzo's ruling was erased.

Doherty's lawyers anticipated the passage of the new legislation, and it is important to look at some of the legal events which took place between the decision of the Appeals Court in June 1986 and the activation of the new treaty on 23 December 1986.

On 3 September, twenty-four hours after the expiry date for a Supreme Court petition, Doherty's counsel contacted Immigration Judge Howard Cohen, and asked that deportation proceedings be recommenced without delay. Doherty's lawyers pointed out that 'the executive branch of the US Government had consumed 20 months 24 days with its baseless and futile attempt to obtain a collateral review of Sprizzo's verdict, and as a consequence Doherty was now 38 months 18 days in prison without bond.'

On 5 September Judge Cohen acceded to a request from Doherty's lawyers to convene a 'conference' between the warring legal parties, particularly the INS. The defence argued that the purpose of the 'conference' was to put an end to the 'seemingly interminable litigation'. Their client would agree to be deported, and would designate the Republic of Ireland as his destination. If one looks at this legal battle as a chess game, the defence move was very clever. It possessed the properties of offence and defence. It anticipated the ratification of the new extradition treaty, which would dictate that Doherty be returned to the United Kingdom, and it offensively ensured that the opposition would be drawn into a separate legal argument, namely whether the Republic of Ireland was a suitable destination for Doherty, an argument which would go to the very top of the US Administration. Doherty made it clear to judge Cohen that he was prepared to withdraw his application for political asylum, and be deported to the country of his designation, namely the Irish Republic. His lawyers said the Irish authorities were prepared to accept him as an Irish citizen under articles 2 and 3 of the country's constitution which claimed jurisdiction over Doherty's birthplace of Northern Ireland. Those articles in the Irish constitution deeply disturbed the British Government and the Protestants in Northern Ireland, since they enshrined the Irish Government's belief that it possessed sovereignty over the British state of Northern Ireland, and defined 'the Irish nation' as 'all the people on the island of Ireland'. Therefore a Catholic such as Doherty, though born a British subject in Northern Ireland, had the right to claim Irish citizenship and to hold an Irish passport.

The INS immediately objected and asked for an adjournment to consider Doherty's offer; the prosecution case was a legal procedure controlled by different organisations all tied to the executive branch of the US Government, which in turn felt obliged to consult with the British before any legal decision was taken, or agreement reached with Doherty's lawyers. It was a cat-and-mouse game, except that the mouse was not easy to catch, and anticipated the dangers, sometimes even changing the rules of engagement.

Judge Cohen resumed the hearing on 12 September and agreed to formal pleadings, so that an order of deportation be entered on Doherty's request. Doherty admitted four of the accusations which formed the central thread of the deportability warrant. The INS tried to reintroduce the additional charges, but Judge Cohen regarded such a move as 'silly', because Doherty was agreeing to deportation, and it would serve no purpose to prolong the hearing. The INS responded by stating a previously argued opinion that if Doherty was deported he should be returned to the United Kingdom because 'deportation to the Irish Republic was prejudicial to the interests of the United States'.

No evidence was presented to prove that the Irish Republic was, by implication, an unsuitable destination for Doherty. I believe the US executive knew that if that issue were to be debated openly it would have raised matters dangerous to relations between the Irish and US Governments, and might have angered Irish-American opinion. The INS would have been obliged to prove that Irish–British relations were bad, and that there was no hope of the British recovering Doherty if he were sent to the Republic. In the event of presenting such an argument, the INS would also have revealed that its opinions and actions were shaped by British attitudes, and the Irish Government would have been obliged publicly to defend its position on extradition *vis-à-vis* Britain, an issue then and still a long-running political battle between the two countries.

The INS chose a familiar tactic: they opposed the deportation order and asked for a third adjournment to consult with the US Attorney-General, Edwin Meese III.

Seven days later, the protagonists once again faced Judge Cohen, who ignored the Government's opposition and ordered that Doherty's wish be granted. The INS presented no further evidence, but pointed out that it was opposed to Cohen's verdict. A British memorandum on that hearing defined it as 'important' but did not specifically mention British interests.

On 19 September 1986 the INS argued that deportation of Doherty to the Republic of Ireland would be prejudicial to the interests of the United States in its conduct of relations with foreign nations in connection with their attempts to combat terrorism. The INS also advised the immigration judge that this matter was of great concern to officials at the highest level of the Government and that the matter was still under consideration. Immigration Judge Cohen rejected the INS arguments, and refused to grant any further extension of time, and ruled that the deportation of Doherty to the Republic of Ireland would not be prejudicial to the interests of the United States.

Judge Cohen in delivering his verdict remarked that the Government had attempted to delay his decision. He had grounds for being suspicious, because seven days later the INS filed a notice of intent to appeal his deportation order.

Cohen was the fourth judge to find his ruling being appealed, and made his anger known to his colleagues and the Administration. Somerstein & Pike were now familiar with their opponents' manoeuvrings, and on 23 September they filed a writ for a petition of habeas corpus, alleging that an INS intent to appeal Judge Cohen's order was 'frivolous', and the 'Government was pursuing the matter with an improper motive, i.e. to delay proceedings in the hope that a new extradition treaty between the United States and the United Kingdom would be approved'. Doherty's lawyers, Steve Somerstein and Mary Pike, correctly read political events, although there was no hard evidence to prove that delaying tactics were being used to facilitate the ratification of the new treaty, and a return to the extradition issue. My reading of the case is that Doherty's lawyers were right in claiming there was a conspiratorial element to the legal battles, but they did not understand the significance of Doherty to both Governments, and/or the political wheeling and dealing behind the scenes.

On 25 September, Judge Peter K. Leisure dismissed a habeas corpus writ, remarking that Doherty had failed to show that the Attorney-General was acting frivolously, or deliberately delaying proceedings. On 30 September, Doherty's lawyers saw another legal route, one they knew well. They asked the Board of Immigration Appeals to overturn the INS appeal against Judge Cohen's verdict. The year 1986 ended with Doherty still in custody, and the subject of an unresolved legal battle which was steadily bringing him to the attention of the American public, and senior political figures sympathetic to Irish-American attitudes.

The New Year started with Doherty's lawyers optimistic that the BIA would accept their arguments about the validity of Judge Cohen's ruling on the Irish Republic as the designated country, and reject the INS attempts to interfere and reverse his decision. However, the INS and others were busy planning Government strategy and, with a view to the BIA hearing, they filed an affidavit in support of their motion on 19 February 1987. The affidavit was from Stephen J. Trott, Associate US Attorney-General, and it outlined policy considerations arising from the order to deport Doherty to the Irish Republic and Doherty's criminal background. An additional affidavit was provided by

Terrell E. Arnold, Deputy Director of the Office for Counter-Terrorism and Emergency Planning at the Department of State. The document was not new, having previously been submitted to oppose Cohen's judgment. Its re-presentation was designed to show that two important officials shared the same view.

Seven days before the BIA verdict was due, the INS discovered that the BIA was not in possession of the supplementary evidence, namely the two affidavits, and issued notice that it would appeal whatever decision was reached by the BIA.

The BIA met on 11 March and drew attention to the manner in which the INS had delayed the Cohen hearings by presenting additional charges: 'The Immigration and Naturalisation Service's contentions are without merit. An immigration judge is not obliged to allow the Service to waste valuable time and resources proving superfluous charges. A respondent is no more deportable on seven charges than two.'

The BIA also upheld Cohen's decision, and agreed to the country of designation as the Irish Republic. It made an interesting observation that no clear evidence had been presented by the INS to support its view of the Irish Republic as 'unsuitable territory'. The BIA remarked: 'The Service was granted a continuance to allow it to secure evidence of such interest, but it has produced none.'

Two days later the INS moved for a stay of the BIA judgment on the basis that the BIA had not received the affidavits of Trott and Arnold for the 11 March hearing, and asked for a reopening of deportation proceedings because of the importance of the supplementary evidence.

The BIA met again on 22 May 1987 and reaffirmed its March decision by a majority vote. It rejected the concept that an affidavit from a senior official at the Department of Justice, namely the Associate Attorney-General, Stephen Trott, proved that the Attorney-General disapproved of the Republic of Ireland as a designation prejudicial to US interests. The BIA reserved its strongest rebuke for the failure of the INS to submit its affidavits at an earlier stage, and levelled swingeing criticism at the US Government: 'The glacial pace at which any tangible proof of the interest of the highest levels of government was furnished seems to belie any sense of urgency or responsibility on the part of the Government to proceed promptly in this case.'

Two members of the five-man Board of Immigration Appeals

dissented from the judgment. They were the chairman, David Mulholland, and James P. Morris, and they recorded their disagreement in the following way:

The record does not reflect that the Service was at fault in failing to obtain the affidavits. Despite two short continuances the Service had actually only a few days in which to secure evidence in opposition to the respondent's designation of the Republic of Ireland as the country of deportation. The first indication in the record that the respondent would concede deportability and designate the Republic of Ireland appears in the record of September 12 1986, only seven days before the immigration judge had rendered his decision. Previously the respondent had contested the Government's every move against him. It is not surprising that the Service was unable to secure an affidavit from the Office of the Attorney-General at such short notice.

Time was not a factor in relation to the Trott affidavit because the Attorney-General's Office was fully acquainted with the Doherty case and an affidavit could have been prepared in forty-eight hours. The question was whether it was considered judicious to do so and whether there was a cogent argument to oppose the Irish Republic as a destination. The official difficulty lay in offering evidence to prove the INS case without damaging Irish–US and British–Irish relations. After all, the BIA pointed out in its judgment of 11 March that there was *no new evidence*, and it reiterated that point on 22 May. The affidavits hardly constituted evidence – merely an assertion of policy and opinion. Were they, therefore, introduced in the knowledge that the BIA would dismiss the INS motion, and because it was important to show, for the record, that evidence had been proffered? Certainly, subsequent US Government documents dealing with the matter relied on the fact that supplementary evidence had been presented to the BIA, in support of the assertion that the Irish Republic as a designation was contrary to the interests of the United States. It may have been a ploy by the US Administration to place on record evidence to show the British Government that it was making every effort to fight all aspects of the case.

I contend the INS deliberately used them as a tactic to interrupt the flow of proceedings which was in Doherty's favour. The INS was, in effect, providing the US Administration and its British counterparts with the necessary time to re-examine their gradually failing strategy. Once again the judgment of a judicial body was questioned because there was a risk that if Doherty was deported to the Irish Republic he might escape British justice. There was no guarantee the Irish courts would eventually extradite him if the 'fall-back' charges were preferred against him in that jurisdiction.

It should be pointed out that the duration of the proceedings and the bureaucratic nature of the US Government ensured that, at lower levels of decision-making, new personnel were constantly being introduced to the case, and people experienced in the history of it were being promoted to other roles or jobs. The British Government was angry that its representatives were dealing with constant changes of legal personnel, who required time to learn the complexities of the case, and adapt intellectually to its changing characteristics. The US Administration was powerless to halt the natural flow of professionals in the US Attorney's department. It was inevitable that the most able would not remain with the Doherty case, because of its introverted, time-consuming and seemingly endless nature.

On 29 May 1987, the INS decided to break the stalemate by appealing directly to the Attorney-General, Edwin Meese III, to reverse Cohen's deportation order. The appeal was made by the INS Acting Commissioner, and was followed by a letter from Doherty's lawyers reminding the Government of the duration of his confinement. On 28 October the Attorney-General formally agreed to review the case, giving Doherty until 1 December to file a brief. (That date was later extended at the request of the defence.)

Doherty and his lawyers were more concerned about events on the other side of the Atlantic. On 1 December the Irish Government signed the European Convention on the Suppression of Terrorism, which effectively linked it as a European partner with the British. Somerstein & Pike realised that if Doherty was deported to the Republic he would automatically be handed over to the British. Thatcher, they perceived, had again used power politics to undermine the US court decision allowing Doherty the designation of his choice. In encouraging the Irish Government to sign a European treaty, which effectively linked Britain and Ireland on the suppression of terrorism, she had created an arrangement which, she believed, ensured that Doherty would not escape British justice. The new treaty permitted the US Administration, through its legal channels, to argue that Doherty might as well be returned to the United Kingdom, because Ireland and Britain were partners to extradition arrangements which rendered irrelevant the European country of designation. Thatcher and her advisers were hopeful that the new treaty would convince US courts that Doherty's return to British soil was not a political issue, but judicious. The linking of Britain and Ireland within the European treaty negated Doherty's right to select the Irish Republic, and, at any rate, his offences were committed in Britain. Thatcher was sure that if the tactic succeeded it would represent a victory in her war against the IRA, and effectively rule out the Republic as a safe haven. A clever strategy, it was designed to prevent the IRA from ever having a safe haven in two jurisdictions, the US and the Republic of Ireland. Somerstein & Pike speedily asked the BIA to reopen the deportation hearings, and reinstate Doherty's right to apply for political asylum in the US. They quoted the BIA's use of the 'glacial pace' of the Government as justification for deciding that deportation was no longer an option for their client, though they also pointed to 'a conspiracy' which forced them to once again revert to 'political asylum' as Doherty's only retreat:

On 1 December 1987, the Extradition (European Convention on the Suppression of Terrorism) Act 1987 was implemented. Under its terms Mr Doherty's deportation to Ireland would be the equivalent of his extradition to the United Kingdom. Thus the glacial pace at which the deportation proceedings were conducted by the INS and the Attorney-General ensured that even were Judge Cohen's order to be ultimately executed, such eventuality would *de facto* achieve the result denied the Executive branch by the immigration judge's ruling and by the District Court.

Behind the scenes, however, some British officials were not entirely persuaded that the new extradition arrangements would work, because the Irish were insisting that the English Attorney-General provide a detailed outline of the evidence in respect of each person he sought. That demand angered Margaret Thatcher, and her early optimism was dashed within twelve months, when the Irish refused to extradite Father Patrick Ryan, a Roman Catholic priest, whom the British alleged was an IRA bomb-maker. The Irish motive for refusing the British request was based on the British media's virtually declaring Ryan 'guilty' before he could even be charged in an English court. Thatcher openly criticised Ireland's failure to comply with the demand for Ryan, and denounced growing Irish suspicion that Irish citizens would not receive a fair trial in England.

One could argue that if Doherty had been returned in 1988 he might not have been handed over to the British, but his lawyers were unable to anticipate either that possibility or the growing disillusionment in Ireland with British justice. They were only aware that within the US Administration a belief had arisen that the new extradition accord on the other side of the Atlantic would now realise British ambitions. Were Doherty's lawyers justified in defining the delays in the case as a conspiracy? There is an obvious temptation to see a conspiracy. A more accurate perception would suggest an evolving case, with very high stakes, and with very astute players on both sides of the Atlantic, who changed the rules and the nature of the game to achieve their objectives.

For the British and the United States administrations, the main objective remained constant but the tactics often changed, and their was a constant re-evaluation of the strategy, with ongoing preparation of fall-back moves to be used in the event of failure at any one judicial level. Doherty's lawyers were also involved in finding ways to protect his interests. Clever players in the legal game, they frequently outwitted their opponents, anticipating prosecution moves and introducing new tactics. A fine example was the reintroduction of an asylum application when it appeared their client might be deported to the UK

The INS responded to Doherty's attempt at seeking relief from deportation. Turning to the Attorney-General, the INS pointed out that the BIA was prepared to allow Doherty to reopen the deportation case, on the basis that his evidence represented a prima-facie case of persecution.

The year 1987 ended without any sign of a resolution of the issue, and it was not until February 1988 that the BIA referred the case to the Attorney-General, knowing that although he delegated power to it he also reserved the right to review its decisions, and was therefore the ultimate authority in matters of immigration. On 21 April 1988, Doherty filed a motion claiming the Attorney-General was not the proper person to determine the issues in his case. He argued that officers of the Department of Justice sought his return to the UK, and the fact that the Attorney-General was head of that Department logically determined there would be no fair hearing from him or any of his delegates.

On 9 June 1988 Doherty was given the Attorney-General's answer, which reversed the BIA decision to permit the Irish Republic as a designation and directed deportation to the United Kingdom. Attorney-General Meese III dismissed allegations of institutional or personal bias, impropriety or conflict in his consideration of the case. He acceded to a defence argument that, since Doherty had filed his motion with the BIA prior to his ruling, the BIA should give priority to Doherty's plea to reopen deportation hearings. The BIA agreed to do so on 14 November, but once again the INS intervened and on 5 December they requested that the decision to reopen should again be referred to Meese.

Legally the situation was ludicrous and without precedent. In June 1989 Meese, as many observers expected, reversed the BIA order to reopen and remarked that the BIA had erred in favouring Doherty's request. Doherty, he said, had not presented new evidence, and had knowingly and deliberately withdrawn his asylum application at a previous stage in favour of deportation. Reopening, he added, was unwarranted because he had no intention of using his discretionary power to grant Doherty's latest request for asylum. He ruled that Doherty was in no position to effect a change in the order to deport him, and it was exactly that which made pointless any request to reopen. Commentators wondered why, if that were truly the view of Edwin Meese III, he had not stated it without equivocation at an earlier stage.

The only option left to Doherty was to petition the United States Court of Appeals for the Second Circuit to review Meese's judgment. He also filed a bail application, once again, with an immigration judge, John K. Speer, who ruled he had no jurisdiction to consider the application. Doherty turned again to the BIA, but was informed that it too was powerless to act in his case because the Attorney-General's decision to deport him divested it of jurisdiction.

Further legal avenues were travelled by Doherty and his lawyers in 1989, but to no avail, because at each hearing the risk of flight was emphasised to justify a refusal of bail. During one of those hearings, familiar reasons were presented by prosecution lawyers, and the following verdict clearly illustrated a familiar thesis:

Nothing presented persuades us that there has been any meaningful reduction since our prior order in the likelihood that the respondent, if released, will abscond if and when his deportation becomes imminent. The respondent went to great lengths to avoid the imprisonment to which he has been sentenced. In escaping from jail he risked his life in a gun-battle. In coming to the United States, he left his family including mother, father and three sisters and he left his home and his homeland – all the community ties he developed in his life. The respondent's ties in this country are meagre in comparison to those he abandoned when he fled his homeland. In view of this history, we are unpersuaded that the respondent would voluntarily surrender for deportation, and surrender to a British jail out of a sense of obligation to his supporters in this country, or to avoid the forfeiture of someone else's money. Moreover the prospect of such deportation is closer now than when we considered this bond request in 1985, as there now exists an administratively final order of deportation to the United Kingdom that is under review in the courts.

Doherty's lawyers were convinced that their client's continual detention was aimed at furthering US foreign interests, and a Second Circuit Court panel recognised that view, when it held that the Attorney-General should not consider foreign policy while evaluating asylum applications. Doherty was held in custody because his fate was inextricably linked to British–American interests, and to the personal determination of Margaret Thatcher, a politician who was never willing to lose a battle, even a legal one. Doherty began 1990 in the Metropolitan Correction Centre having experienced seven years of litigation. Two Attorneys-General, Edwin Meese III and later Richard L. Thornburgh, had rejected his pleas, finding instead that his return to the UK would 'further the policy of the US', and that failure to deport him would 'be injurious to relations with the United Kingdom'. A lonely figure in the Metropolitan Correction Centre, he was acknowledged as an important, yet potentially dangerous, element in US–British relations. A hidden agenda had been set by the British, from which Margaret Thatcher was not prepared to move. In 1990 she sent lobbyists to Washington and made it clear to the Bush Administration that she personally wanted the return of Doherty. Her direct personal involvement was no accident of politics. From the outset the case was important to her, but other events conspired to convince her that he should be returned, whatever the cost to the US legal process. It was for the Americans to deliver him and, in her words, they 'owed' her that.

# 12

# The Battle in
# the Courts

Margaret Thatcher's preoccupation with the case of an IRA hitman did not make the headlines in the United Kingdom or Ireland, because the legal battle was being fought several thousand miles away, and obscured Doherty's relevance to US–British relations. The complexity of the litigation over seven years hid the real story of the political machinations of two major powers. He was and remains important to the British because they are protagonists in a developing conflict, which has tied their troops into urban warfare, occasionally exposed them to international criticism for undemocratic practices, brought them to the Court of Human Rights, and damaged British interests in North America. To the dismay of the British Government, the IRA, with a history of conflict and of fashioning propaganda, was often the victor in the propaganda war which the Doherty case clearly illustrated.

Until Margaret Thatcher's removal from political office in November 1990, the relentless pursuit of Doherty related not only to a British Government interest in him as a terrorist and potential *cause célèbre*, but more significantly to Thatcher's personal interest in him. Her stand on terrorism during the Reagan era was such that she expected the US Government to deliver a notorious terrorist. She was ambitious to prove there was no safe hiding place for her main enemy, the IRA, and that the United States should show an example by dealing effectively with Doherty. Her advisers convinced her of the need to win the legal battle, because it would demonstrate that the US would no longer harbour republican gunmen. They told her the US was a significant area of operations for IRA fund-raising, weapons procurement, propaganda, and an ideal hiding place for gunmen or bombers escaping British justice.

From the outset of the recent conflict in Ireland the British expressed misgivings about the 'Irish-American connection'. They regarded it as a dangerous element in IRA support and an inextricably acute dimension to the war. Margaret Thatcher viewed the return of Doherty as a symbolic gesture which would signal a change of heart in the US Government's public persona *vis-à-vis* Irish republicanism and its American characteristics. Her determination to get Doherty back to Britain never waned throughout the years of his confinement, but one event hardened her resolve to see him returned, and gave her the opportunity to use political leverage to force Reagan and the Bush Administration to support her. The bombing of Libya and, in particular, Tripoli, which was achieved by US F1-11's using British airspace, her public support for the strikes on Libyan targets, and her personal assistance, left the British public vulnerable to revenge attacks from Middle-East terror groups. The Libyan leader, Colonel Gadaffi, responded to her actions by providing the IRA with its largest-ever supply of weapons, ammunition, the deadly Czech-made explosive Semtex, and US-made SAM ground-to-air missiles. The IRA was suddenly better equipped than at any time in its history, and Margaret Thatcher rightly believed that it resulted from her publicly announced actions in support of the US air strikes. It was, she believed, Gadaffi's way of exacting revenge, because the IRA used the consignments of guns and explosives to kill British soldiers, and launch a major bombing campaign in English cities.

In 1989 and 1990 her worst fears were realised when the IRA bombed targets in England, and killed British soldiers stationed on the continent of Europe. The easily concealed explosive Semtex proved an effective terrorist weapon for blowing up British army bases in Germany, targets in central London, commercial buildings, political clubs, and the booby-trapping of cars of politicians, armed forces personnel, and business figures connected with the management of Margaret Thatcher's Tory Party. The guns used in attacks on British soldiers in Germany and Holland all came from the Gadaffi shipment.

In September 1990 the US Attorney, Otto Obermaier of the US Southern District Court of New York, was told of the British Prime Minister's personal interest in the Doherty case. He was left in no doubt about the overriding significance of the case, and the need for him to be fully cognisant of its importance to US–British foreign interests. He was also informed that it was Mrs Thatcher's view that the US 'owed her this one'.

Her support for Reagan's decision to bomb Tripoli, with the subsequent cost to British lives, was expressed as a debt which could be repaid by the US delivering Doherty. I had long known the importance attached to Doherty, but when I learned of Thatcher's personal interest I began to understand the reason for the intensity of the uninterrupted pursuit of him.

Throughout 1990, many US political figures in Washington were wined and dined and convinced of the need for their support in combating the growing bandwagon of support for his release. They were also probed for information on political colleagues who were campaigning on Doherty's behalf, or willing to provide personal money to secure a bail bond.

While the lobbying continued behind the scenes, Doherty appeared in court in April and July 1990. The latter hearings delivered a flexible principle that his continued detention would depend on a balance of four factors: (1) length of detention; (2) the extent to which the Government was responsible for the delay; (3) the strength of the evidence regarding risk of flight; (4) the strength of the evidence regarding dangerousness. At the July hearing it was the court's opinion that the Southern District Judge, not the BIA, was the correct person to assess the weight which should be given to the claim that Doherty might flee, or threaten US national security, if released on bail.

The court pointed out that Doherty would be in a stronger position if he could prove he was no longer loyal to the IRA or subject to its instructions and discipline, and if his loyalty to the IRA was now diminished. A hearing was set for 4 and 5 September 1990, in order to allow Doherty to state his case, and the Government to support its allegation that he was dangerous, and would flee if released.

Two days after the July recommendation for a hearing, the US Government wrote to the Honourable Miriam Goldman Cedarbaum, who was scheduled to preside over the September session. The Government said it had reason to believe Doherty would be testifying before her that he had had a 'change of heart' regarding the IRA, and would 'merely clarify' his former testimony dealing with his attitude to IRA orders. This was a Government ploy to require the court to seek from Doherty a statement of any new evidence he intended to offer to her. The US Attorney for the

Southern District, Otto Obermaier, and the Government were anxious to know exactly what Doherty intended to say to Cedarbaum, because it would assist the US Attorney in preparing lines of cross-examination. It was preferable for them to know in advance what their adversary intended to say, rather than reacting on the day he gave evidence. The Government argued that if the court requested Doherty to submit a summary of his intended testimony Cedarbaum would be better positioned to decide whether the hearing was really necessary.

Steve Somerstein was not vulnerable to that tactic and responded that this client would not inform the court of the 'material facts' he would present. Somerstein wrote to Cedarbaum and submitted a part of Doherty's 1984 testimony which dealt with the IRA, its rules regarding resignation and the rights of volunteers to disobey orders. That proved sufficient to block the Government's attempt to force Doherty to reveal his thoughts to Cedarbaum and ultimately Obermaier.

The Somerstein & Pike presence throughout the litigation dictated a knowledge of the history of the proceedings which was not evident in the US Attorney's Office. In 1990 Otto Obermaier and his assistant attorney, Claude Millman, were relatively new to the case, and it was incumbent upon them both to learn about it quickly.

They sought to produce arguments proving Doherty a threat to national security, still a member of the IRA and likely to flee the jurisdiction. They shaped ancillary arguments that if granted bail he would fund-raise and campaign on behalf of the IRA. They believed that his early juvenile record as an offender illustrated his propensity for criminal behaviour. In this, they were reworking tired arguments, and not searching more profoundly for flaws in the 1984 testimony, which could be used to link Doherty to the IRA while he was living in the US, and thus prove that the risk of flight did not reside with Doherty but with unknown figures in the IRA who controlled him.

The repeated argument that he was a bail-flight risk was, I believe, insufficient to have kept him in prison for so many years. The Government never produced sufficient cause to sustain its allegation, nor to overthrow Doherty's 1984 testimony that he had resigned from the IRA and was prepared to disobey instructions if ordered to flee in the event of deportation. Irrespective of whether he is to be believed, the US Government never proved its case, but to the objective eye acted vindictively against him. It never understood the need for a clear analysis of the 1984 evidence allied to a fine historical assessment of Doherty's claims. The US Government's urgency to satisfy British demands for Doherty, the cleverness of his lawyers, the constant change of Department of Justice staff working on the case, all conspired to thwart US Government intentions.

In April 1990, Steve Somerstein offered what appeared to be a reasonable deal in return for bail for his client:

It is proposed that a cash bond of 100,000 dollars be set; Mr Doherty be required to reside with Stephen A. Somerstein, one of his attorneys, in Brooklyn, New York; that he not leave the New York Metropolitan area without the permission of an immigration judge; that he be permitted to maintain gainful employment; and that he report regularly by telephone or in person, as may be required, to an appropriate official of the INS.

That offer was judged insufficient. Had the cash bond been one million dollars, would it have secured his release? I and many others, with knowledge of IRA policies, contend that Doherty was never a threat to US national security, or a danger to US citizens. The FBI clearly shared that opinion, otherwise they would have presented evidence to the contrary. If Doherty had been released, even after several years of his confinement, his value to the IRA in the US would have been limited to fund-raising, and his public prominence would have precluded any secret involvement in arms procurement simply because the FBI would have kept him under surveillance.

What seriousness attached to the fund-raising issue? A valid British argument existed, to the effect that Doherty on bail would have raised large sums of money, by appearing at functions as a celebrity figure. The British were particularly concerned about the prospect of such an eventuality when intelligence data reached them in 1990 and confirmed their suspicion that the IRA needed someone like Doherty to raise large sums of cash for a specific weapons purchase. The British knew that IRA fund-raising in the US realised a steady flow of money, but in small accumulations, not enough at any one time to purchase the coveted Redeye or Stinger missiles.

The FBI and British intelligence shared evidence that Gadaffi supplied the IRA with all the basic weaponry needed to sustain a long guerrilla war, except the most up-to-date ground-to-air missiles. British intelligence, and FBI operatives like Schulte, knew that Redeye and Stinger missiles were available on the underground arms market in North America. They reckoned that Doherty on bail would be used symbolically to raise quickly the large amount of money required to purchase one of these weapons. At that time a Stinger or Redeye would have cost the IRA $80,000 to $100,000 approximately. British intelligence told the FBI the IRA was searching for those weapons, and the SAM missiles supplied by Gadaffi were inoperative because the British army had introduced counter-measures to deal with them. The IRA response was to seek a modern equivalent for which there was no British counter-technology.

In the spring of 1990 British army helicopter pilots in the border regions of Ireland saw vapour trails; on-board photographic surveillance equipment revealed they came from ground-to-air missiles, undoubtedly of the SAM type. A decision was made not to tell the British public to avoid creating panic or disrupting normal airline routes. There was a fear that the missiles, though not effective against a helicopter, could be employed against a civilian light aircraft, especially if one of the passengers was a high-ranking politician. Military transport planes which ferried troops to Ulster would also be vulnerable. The British stressed that Doherty should not be released to facilitate the purchase of missiles, but that matter was not to be raised as part of the US Attorney's legal arguments. (In the summer of 1991 British newspapers claimed that the IRA had fired SAMs in the spring. The reports were not denied; nor did official sources reveal that missiles were being fired the previous year.)

It could be argued that if Doherty had been released on bail at the outset of the litigation he would not have become a major fund-raiser, and if he had been allowed to flee he would not have developed as a symbol of anti-British feeling within the Irish-American community. The British argument about flight was not sustainable. Surely flight was preferable to the danger he allegedly presented to national security, to the procurement of missiles and the creation of a *cause célèbre* status? Ultimately it had to be asked whether the relentless pursuit and perceived persecution of Doherty generated more problems than it solved – for both British and American interests. His incarceration could have ended at an earlier stage, and the normal process of litigation allowed its own pace. The frenetic quality of the Government line, its blurred legal thinking and failure properly to analyse Doherty cumulatively led to an embarrassing position where the cross-examination of Doherty in September 1990 did not achieve the desired result of proving the Government case. Before examining the 4 September hearing, it is worth examining Doherty's popularity, the restrictive, if not immoral, nature of his prison conditions, and how he learned to articulate his thoughts with cleverness and cunning.

Joseph Doherty had walked into the custody of the Metropolitan Correction Center in downtown Manhattan on 18 June 1983, and in 1990 he became the longest-serving prisoner ever held in that institution – which was not designed for long-term prisoners, merely short-term detainees or pre-trial accused.

His lawyers described the conditions in the MCC as 'unjustifiably punitive', and their account was disturbing. Their testimony reinforced a view among unprejudiced observers that the US Government had acted in a vindictive and uncompromising fashion. The Somerstein & Pike account of prison life was written in April 1990:

The MCC until recently has been constantly overcrowded and continuously noisy. Now, by quirk of circumstance, Mr Doherty finds himself virtually alone on the high security 9 South Wing. The constant silence is unnerving as was the previous din. The institution has no educational, vocational or recreational programs. Fresh-air is available only on the rooftop. Mr Doherty is confined to his cell for up to 23 hours per day. That cell is a tiny cubicle containing a sink and toilet, a double bunk bed, a chair and a small locker. The door is solid metal with a small window for guards to look in. The window to the outside world is covered with wire grating, is barred and does not open. Mr Doherty has frequently been made to share his cell with one other individual. He is constantly under artificial light, and must breathe recirculated air. He is taken to the roof sporadically and then for no more than an hour at a time. Weeks can pass without roof access. As a result of the absence of fresh air and natural light, he suffers dermatological distress. The cell is subjected to constant random searches by prison guards. His mail and telephone calls are monitored. On those occasions when he is taken from his cell to another location on the floor or elsewhere within the prison, such as for a visit with counsel, he is placed in handcuffs and accompanied by a guard. When he returns to the detention cell, he must undergo a humiliating nude search of his body cavities and pubic area. His life has been completely circumscribed by the regimentation of prison life. He is permitted only 3 one-hour social visits per week. He has been told when to eat, to sleep, to shower. Other than for rare court appearances he has worn nothing but the prison jump suit. The sole diversion available when he is permitted 'recreation' outside his cell is television.

Twice in 1986 he was abruptly transferred from the MCC to the Federal Correctional Institute at Otisville, New York. There he was placed in solitary confinement under 24-hour lock-up. He was let out only five hours a week for exercise in either an empty yard or an empty room. He was allowed only three showers per week. Each time he was moved from his cell he was shackled and accompanied by three guards. While acknowledging his good behaviour during his entire period of incarceration, prison officials claimed these conditions were necessary because the institution to which they had chosen to transfer him could not meet his security needs. He spent a total of 81 days at Otisville FCI under these conditions. As abruptly as he was removed from the MCC, so he was returned to it on January 20 1987.

He has established an exemplary record of behaviour during his entire period of incarceration. Although as a 'pre-trial' detainee no work is required of him, he has worked voluntarily in the prison kitchen, and on the sanitation detail responsible for cleaning the 9 South Wing.

The portrayal of the MCC was accurate when placed against the evidence of others who visited him or some of those who had the responsibility of guarding him. It was also true that Doherty twice risked damage to his person by intervening to end confrontations between guards and inmates.

He was visited by prominent politicians and churchmen, among them the late Cardinal of Ireland, Tomas O'Fiaich, and the Cardinal Archbishop of New York, His Eminence John O'Connor. Archbishop O'Connor was dismayed at the conditions and duration of Doherty's confinement, and expressed his concern to Edwin Meese III and his successor, Richard L. Thornburgh. Father Lawrence Jenco, formerly a Beirut hostage, visited him, and said he should be given bail. The Rev. Jesse Jackson interrupted his campaign for the Presidency to talk to him and offered support. Thornburgh received concerned letters from Senator Christopher Dodd, Senator Joseph L. Lieberman and US Representatives Robert Borski, Thomas Downey, Ted Weiss, Benjamin Gilman, Eliot Engel, Bruce Morrison and Thomas J. Manton. In March 1989, thirteen US Representatives asked the Attorney-General, in writing, to free Doherty on bail pending the outcome of his asylum application.

Many people guaranteed to provide employment and accommodation or to set aside personal assets to ensure he honoured a bail bond. The Westchester County Executive, Andrew P. O'Rourke, personally guaranteed to honour any bail conditions and to find Doherty a job and a home in Westchester County.

In 1989 the New York State Assembly and Senate urged that bail and political asylum be granted. Almost a hundred NY State Assembly members signed a petition for bail, and sent it to the Attorney-General.

An interesting note which arrived on the Attorney-General's desk in March 1989 clearly spelled out the view of New York Councilman Albanese: 'The Irish-American community would expect and pressure Mr Doherty to appear at court proceedings. The Irish-American community does not want its symbol to be in contempt of US law; the community would be singularly dishonoured if that were so.'

That assertion seemed to possess genuine substance and it was a position that even the IRA would not have wished to compromise, on account of the leading political figures proving willing to risk their finance and integrity. The IRA, if it controlled Doherty, could have ordered him to flee, but it would not have been in their interests to compromise republican guarantees, nor make vulnerable the position of other republicans like Doherty at a future date. The risk of flight was greater at the outset of the proceedings, but probably diminished with the passage of time, and with the growing American public commitment to Doherty's assertion that he would not flee, and that he respected the laws of a 'neutral country'. Doherty's status, and that of the republican movement, namely the IRA, was at stake, once Doherty had given public undertakings not to flee if faced with the execution of a final deportation order. If the Government and the British really wished to be machiavellian, they should have released him and allowed him to flee – which would have produced a threefold effect. First, bail would never again be granted to an Irish republican; second, Irish republican assurances would be regarded as meaningless; third, all those Irish-Americans who supported Doherty would be left feeling embarrassed and conned.

In reality, those possible effects seem not to have been uppermost in the minds of the British authorities. They regarded his continued incarceration in a punitive fashion, and remained unwilling to compromise on any of his demands: in their view Doherty was a convicted murderer. They considered his release would undermine relations between the two governments, and damage the central thesis of the prosecution case that he was dangerous, and a threat to US national security. A reversal of that position would have given impetus to Doherty's quest for political asylum. In November 1989 the AFL-CIO union, with a membership of 14 million, passed resolution no. 122 calling on the Attorney-General to grant Doherty bail and, ultimately, political asylum.

President Bush received a copy of the resolution, dated the day of the union's national convention. Attached was a covering letter from the union president, Lane Kirkwood, which stressed that every delegate of the union and the workers they represented wished the President to give the Doherty case his 'personal attention'.

The Massachusetts State Senate, the Maine State Senate and House of Representatives, the City Councils of Baltimore, Buffalo, Chicago, Glen Cove (New York), Hartford, Jersey City, Long Beach (New York), Medford (Massachusetts) and Yonkers all delivered resolutions supporting Doherty, as did boroughs, counties, political parties at county level, federations, trades councils and unions. It represented a formidable array of support.

An example of the growing political endorsement came in House Concurrent Resolution no 62, introduced by the Honourable Thomas Manton, US Representative (New York), demanding asylum for Doherty, and a bail bond in advance of his asylum application review. The resolution began with one sponsor, and soon acquired 105, with a similar resolution in the United States Senate carrying over twenty-five signatories. By the autumn of 1990 one in every four congressmen supported Doherty's right to remain in the US, and his application for bail.

His symbolic status in the Irish community was confirmed in 1988 when he was designated Grand Marshal of the St Patrick's Day parade in Philadelphia. The following year eight major centres followed suit and in New York the parade began with a dedication which sought 'liberty and justice for one particular Irish immigrant, Joe Doherty'. In 1990, San Francisco and California bestowed on him the St Patrick's Day title of Honorary Grand Marshal.

One man consistently guaranteed to honour Government bail conditions – Paul O'Dwyer, a prominent attorney and founding partner in the firm of O'Dwyer & Bernstein. His public roles included a presidency of New York City Council, and New York

City Commissioner for the United Nations and Consular Corps. He pledged $100,000 from his personal fortune towards a bond.

On 4 September 1990, O'Dwyer arrived at the Southern District Court prepared to make the same offer, joined by others such as Congressman Gary Ackerman, who was also willing to risk $100,000 from personal assets. An attorney, James Cullen from the New York City firm of De Forrest and Duer, furnished another $100,000. Paul O'Dwyer's son and Brian and Frank Durkan, both lawyers, each pledged $50,000. A Mr and Mrs Kevin Sullivan guaranteed another $100,000, bringing the cash offer to half a million dollars. In addition, a Mr Hughes from Brooklyn offered his home as security with an approximate value of $175,000. The head of the Dougherty family in the US, Jack Dougherty, offered to post his farm in Delaware with an equity of $150,000. The total figure on offer was $800,000.

The hearing on 4 September 1990 before Judge Miriam Goldman Cedarbaum began with a general outline of Doherty's history. During the proceedings Doherty explained why he had left the Irish Republic in 1982 and how he had been told to go to the United States as a civilian. He repeated his 1984 evidence that he had been instructed to remain in the US until things 'cooled down', referring to a conversation in which he had asked a member of the IRA Army Council how arrangements might be made to 'call him back' from America.

Asked by his own attorney about the resignation issue and his trip to the US, he toyed with whether he was under orders, and said he was not. Seconds later he revealed that he had 'complied with the order':

This goes back to the meeting between myself and a member of the Army Council. It was an informal meeting and I was querying him as to when and how I was to get back to Ireland and was I to be recalled. And the member of the Army Council sort of said, off the record, 'Look, Joe, just go to the United States for a year, or two, or three, and if you get settled there within the Irish community, or if you find a woman and you want to stay, if you fall in love – well, do that, it's your prerogative.'

I said, 'Is that an order?' He said, 'No, because you are not a member of the IRA, but we will get you back.' So I had no obligations to follow and there was no formal procedure set up. There was no contacts or anything. . . .

I was very apprehensive leaving my homeland, and my family, and the cause I had to leave behind, but I knew it was for the betterment of my own personal securities and the Irish Republican Army, so *I complied with the order to leave Ireland and come to the United States* [my italics].

What order to leave Ireland? In earlier comments he said there was no order and he was no longer a member of the IRA. His testimony was illustrative of an inconsistency which was a constant feature of his evidence in 1984 and was further reinforced in the September 1990 hearing.

| | |
|---|---|
| Judge Cedarbaum: | When you said that you were 'subject to recall', did you mean that if someone from the Army Council communicated to you that you should come back, that you would go back? |
| Doherty: | No, Your Honour, it was not a formal recall. When I had urged the member of the Army Council to give me some sort of a time frame to come back, he was telling me, look, just go over to the United States, you know, for a year or two years. If you want to come back between that time, or we need you, we will recall you. |

The judge quickly spotted Doherty's tendency to compromise himself by revealing that the IRA was in a position to recall him if it so wished. She detected a contradiction. She was faced with a man who, on the one hand, claimed he had left the organisation but, on the other hand, was complying with its orders:

| | |
|---|---|
| Judge: | You were told that if you were needed you would be called back? |
| Doherty: | I would be recalled. I guess it wasn't a formal order. |

Steve Somerstein tried successfully to steer his client towards a statement that resignation from the IRA was possible and that volunteers were 'free to refuse an order, or disobey an order'. Doherty replied that was so, but qualified his affirmation by de scribing a personal experience where a volunteer's wife had 'grounded her husband', and Doherty had given the man per mission to resign.

He was correct in stating that resignation was permitted within the IRA, and that volunteers were allowed to disagree with an order. However, they were certainly not allowed to disobey an order: that was a court-martialling offence. If the IRA had ever accepted the right of volunteers to disobey orders, it would not have been able to retain tight control over its members. In the IRA's 'Green Book' General Order No. 2 states:

Volunteers when making the Army Declaration promise '. . . to obey all orders and regulations issued by the Army Authority and any superior officers.'

Where an order issued by a duly accredited officer has been disobeyed, the Volunteer in question must be suspended immediately, pending investigation of the case.

Volunteers were (and remain) free to resign for a variety of motives by placing their reasons in print. Generally, men who had served prison sentences preferred to return to family life. That did not justify Doherty's claim that volunteers were free to resign if they disobeyed orders. The IRA allowed its members to resign if they were no longer committed to the cause, or to its methods; it certainly never tolerated men resigning when they refused to obey an order. Failure to comply with any orders from accredited officers resulted in suspension and probably court martial.

In 1984 Doherty had attempted to convince Judge Sprizzo that he had 'resigned' from the IRA. He was fortunate that American courts knew little of the internal workings of the IRA, and he was careful not to enlighten them. In 1990, when again faced with the lingering issue of resignation, he was careless in assuming that Cedarbaum would accept it was easy to leave the IRA, or that he could fool or confuse her by claiming that he had resigned, while at the same time admitting he had travelled to the United States under IRA orders.

Steve Somerstein elicited from Doherty a denial of membership of the IRA, that any IRA apparatus or organisation existed in the US, or that he had ever been contacted by a representative of the IRA from the moment he set foot on American soil.

| Somerstein: | Would you, Mr Doherty, know how to get in touch with the Irish Republican Army from the United States? |
| Doherty: | Certainly not! |

Sitting in court watching Doherty deliver his answer, I was reminded that before Judge Sprizzo in 1984 he had admitted that means of communication with the IRA had been established before he left Ireland. He knew who to write to in Ireland, and they knew how to get messages to him. His claim that he had never met a representative of the IRA may have been technically correct, but scarcely honest. Those people who met him at Kennedy airport hardly represented Disneyland, although, if asked, he would say they were 'sympathisers', or 'members of the republican movement'.

Somerstein asked if he would obey an IRA order to recall him if released on bail. Doherty replied with a studied eye to propaganda, but none the less an articulate account of his position:

I am not a member of the Irish Republican Army, Your Honour, I am speaking to you as an individual. If I was to be approached by the IRA on the outside and asked to go back – I could never see the day they would do that, but if I was ever asked, I would not go, because as I said, Your Honour, it is my obligation to the court and to these people here; and to the financial contribution they are willing to make for my bail bond; and also their reputations. There is so much at stake.

Doherty continued by naming some of those prominent Americans and organisations who supported him and compared his life as minuscule to the Irish community and the 'splendid individuals' who helped him. He talked of the many years spent fighting for the ideals of Irish republicanism.

Otto Obermaier began cross-questioning by abruptly changing the tone of the proceedings, from measured statements to precise, direct questions, which demanded equally brief answers. The opening cross-examination began thus:

Q:   Is lying part of the IRA training you received?
A:   Lying?
Q:   Lying!
A:   No.
Q:   Did anybody in the IRA ever tell you that you might be called upon to lie in order to fulfil a mission?
A:   In the course of a secret army . . .
Q:   Can you answer my question?
A:   Yes, sir.
Q:   Did somebody tell you that you might be called upon to lie?
A:   I'm afraid you'll have to explain the question. I don't understand.
Q:   You understand.
A:   It's the actual word lying.
Q:   You have lied as part of an IRA mission?

A:   I have used discrepancies and stuff.
Q:   Have you lied, sir, lied your tail off in connection with the ecape from Crumlin Road?
A:   I used deception.
Q:   Can you answer my question?

Somerstein interjected to protect his client and Judge Cedarbaum agreed that Doherty had answered the question. Obermaier continued:

Q:   Did you tell falsehoods in connection with that escape?
A:   Of course, as much as the American 'Seals' when they are on an operation, whether it is in Central America or Kuwait. They are going to dress up as Arabs or something, they are going to use false names and deception to get behind the lines.

The sparring between the US Attorney and Doherty persisted, without revealing anything new or particularly relevant. Watching them I felt that Obermaier achieved little, because the matters were already on the record, and Doherty had already admitted using a false passport, and so on. The public gallery was amused by Obermaier's failure to penetrate well-fashioned defences. Doherty had spent years planning defensive arguments, and Obermaier considerably less time planning his attack.

Q:   You were not a subject of the Republic of Ireland at the time you obtained that passport?
A:   Pardon?
Q:   You were not a citizen of the Republic of Ireland?
A:   Yes, I have been a citizen of the Republic of Ireland since my birth.
Q:   The Republic being the southern part of Ireland?
A:   The Republic being the whole thirty-two counties of Ireland, under articles 2 and 3 of the constitution. I am a citizen. Brian Keenan was released from Beirut this past week, Your Honour. He is from the city of Belfast, but he has an Irish passport. He is a citizen of the Irish Republic.
Q:   Are you finished?
A:   I just wanted to give you a bit of politics.
Q:   But you didn't live in the southern part of Ireland, I take it.
A:   There isn't really a southern part. If I could show you a map, the southern Ireland is more northern than Northern Ireland, because the County of Donegal is more northern than the Northern counties. I mean you are using British terms. You are being

politically biased to take the British view that there is a South and a North. But for the court's sake I will call it the South.

At that point in the proceedings the public gallery was noisy, Obermaier was happy, but no one understood what Doherty was saying. Most observers were, however, entertained by the sparring session.

Obermaier managed to augment Doherty's 1984 testimony by constantly asking the witness to clarify a word or a phrase, but he did not probe the crucial areas of IRA rules, the nature of the republican movement in the United States, and/or Doherty's status *vis-à-vis* the IRA. He continued to seek to prove that Doherty was a confirmed liar. The cross-questioning concentrated on the passport, the false social security number, the use of an alias – matters not central to the real Joseph Doherty.

Cedarbaum became exasperated, and spoke privately to both sets of lawyers out of hearing of the public. She gave them her definition of what was central to the hearing and addressed Obermaier about his line of questioning: 'To me what would be most helpful would be if you have evidence that shows that people who are sent to this country are frequently recalled, or remain under some sort of discipline.'

Her suggestion was probably the most cogent analysis of what prosecution lawyers should have been striving to prove from 1983 onwards, but Obermaier was not convinced of her logic. He returned to cross-examine, and again referred to Doherty's use of a false social security number. Steve Somerstein interrupted, and told Cedarbaum he found the exchanges between Obermaier and his client fascinating but irrelevant. She said she was not sure where the exchanges 'were going'.

Obermaier, unmoved, persisted with his singular line of thought, which only changed course when he enquired if Doherty believed he would be killed if returned to the United Kingdom. He added that such a claim appeared on Doherty's original asylum application. Doherty replied that his life would be in danger, and he would be persecuted.

During several exchanges the witness showed that his seven years in the US had equipped him with expressions which he used effectively to endear himself to his court audience. In describing the episode in which Prison Officer Kennedy was badly hurt, he reverted to vivid football imagery: 'This particular marshall, Mr

Kennedy, described by me, he must be six foot two and 255 pounds. This guy was a linebacker. It took four of us to hold him down. In doing so Mr Kennedy was hurt, but he did not lose consciousness and he was put into a cell.' Doherty cleverly packaged what was a serious assault and presented it with a casual innocence. There were also humorous asides such as when Obermaier referred to Crumlin Road prison and the escape in 1982.

Q:   Then you got out of that prison.
A:   Yes.
Q:   You haven't been back since?
A:   (*laughing*) Not to that particular prison.

At a later point Cedarbaum decided the exchanges were becoming semantic, and tried her own cross-questioning technique. She put it to Doherty that he was saying he was 'trained to kill but wouldn't call it killing'. He reiterated that he was a republican soldier who did not glorify killing, nor did he call it killing, it was merely part of 'our struggle to evacuate Ireland of the British'. Cedarbaum soon experienced the familiar problems arising from cross-questioning Doherty. He was careful about his use of language and, when cornered, preferred a semantic pursuit. None the less, she pressed on by asking him to define his 'enemy'. He said it was British law enforcement in Ireland and added: 'The enemy are British enforcers in Ireland, including Captain Westmacott. My function as a soldier was to inflict as much damage as possible, but it is the actual language I disagree with. I am not a murderer, I am a soldier.'

Otto Obermaier took heart from the judge's failure to create a crack in Doherty's verbal armour and reverted to the word 'destroy' rather than 'kill', in the expectation that the witness would be more amenable to a vague use of words.

Q:   On the day in May 1980 was it the purpose of your mission to destroy British soldiers who might come through that particular point?
A:   Yes. I mean the actual operation –
Q:   Can you answer my question, yes or no?
A:   Yes, it was to inflict as much damage on the British military force as possible.

Obermaier showed visible signs of frustration, while Doherty sat in the witness box patiently awaiting the questions as though he knew what to expect. He proved to his adversary that he was unwilling to use not only the word 'kill' but also any term which implied the same meaning, particularly 'destroy'. When Obermaier asked him if he expected soldiers to be seriously injured during the Antrim Road shooting, he refused to conform to the attorney's use of language, and said he 'expected casualties'.

Cross-examination centred for a time on the M60 machine-gun and which gang member used it. Doherty made it clear it was not 'his weapon', and that he was not trained to use it. He said he had 'read about it', and knew that it was a weapon used by American forces in Vietnam and fired 7.62 Nato standard ammunition. That issue provided little respite, and semantics once again placed Obermaier and the witness at loggerheads. Obermaier appeared for a time to have the edge in the exchanges but found himself drawn into a different type of debate, one which suited the armchair philosophy of Doherty:

Q: Do you have any remorse for the death of Captain Westmacott?
A: As a human being of course I have remorse for him, for dying, for having come to my country, for his family. As I stated to the judge, as soldiers we don't glorify killing. It is something that has to be done. Soldiers have been killed for generations and generations. British soldiers were killed in these very streets in 1776. I am sure if you asked John Adams if he liked killing, I'm sure he would have given you the same answer – we don't glorify. Somebody had to die. I didn't ask him to come to Ireland. I wasn't reponsible for his death. The British Government was responsible. Just as you were justified in 1776, or the Afghan rebels who fought against the Soviet invasion, or as your armed services are in Kuwait to defend the self-determination of the people of Kuwait. You sent several divisions with intent, to use your language, to kill. You supported the Afghan 'rebels', as you call them, and the Contra 'rebels', as you call them. You are very selective in whom you say kills and who does not, and who is a terrorist and who is not a terrorist.
Q: You would agree that you were responsible for the soldiers who fired on him.
A: The British Government was responsible.

Doherty's final reply was indicative of a sharp mind, constantly alert to verbal traps, to a word or phrase which might ensnare him. Within Obermaier's question of who was responsible was just such a trap, which sought to define him as the person in control of the

IRA unit, the shooting and, by inference, the murder of Westmacott. Doherty detected the obstacle and replied blandly that 'The British Government was responsible.'

Obermaier decided to test his response to questions about his 'resignation' from the IRA. Doherty responded by relying on his 1984 testimony with a few subtle changes (which added suspicion in my mind about his real status *vis-à-vis* the IRA). He told the attorney that in 1982 he was confused when informed that he was going to the United States, but then learned that the purpose of the trip was 'R and R', rest and relaxation. That was at variance with his 1984 evidence, in which he said he was going to America 'to avoid detection', because all but two of the escapers had been captured. He added that the IRA told him he could stay away for one, two or three years and they would 'get in touch with him'. Obermaier saw a degree of inconsistency in those statements and proceeded to seek clarification. In his mind was the hope that Doherty would relax his defences and reveal he was still under IRA control.

Q: And if they got in touch with you, you would basically go back?
A: That would be personal. I would have no formal obligation of going back, because I was not a volunteer in the IRA from February of 1982 up until my arrest.
Q: But you sympathise with their cause, don't you?
A: I still sympathise with their cause.

Just when Obermaier felt he had the witness where he wanted him, the opportunity just as quickly vanished. Within one of Doherty's replies remained scope for further questioning which Obermaier did not realise. Doherty's refusal to give a direct answer to the question whether he would return to Ireland if contacted by the IRA was in itself an admission that he was never free to answer truthfully questions related to the issue. His reason was central to his survival, in that any tacit admission that he would return if asked by the IRA implied their control over him. Instead he answered evasively, but not in a way which denied the IRA or his relationship with them; he said the question of whether he would return 'would be personal'. To undertake any options, as a volunteer he required permission, in much the same way as he sought permission to escape from prison, or to recognise, or to refuse to recognise, British courts. Obermaier also believed that to be the case but was unable to advance the evidence given by

Doherty in the 1984 Sprizzo hearing. Doherty knew how to duck and weave, how to throw counter-punches, and always how to disguise his real feelings and intent. In an unusual change of tactic, the US Attorney sought to establish whether Doherty identified with contemporary acts of IRA violence, and the central thesis of armed struggle. In an ensuing range of questions he got no closer to Doherty's real position on violence, but showed that the witness was duplicitous when reacting to certain atrocities.

Obermaier asked if he 'sympathised' with the February 1990 killing of Ian Gow, a former Conservative Cabinet Minister and a confidant of Margaret Thatcher. Doherty said he did not 'condone the death of Mr Gow', nor did he sympathise with another attempt to kill a member of the British Parliament. If one placed those admissions against a subsequent series of questions deliberately framed by Obermaier to expose what he regarded as Doherty's hypocrisy, one might conclude that Doherty was prepared to condemn the Gow murder because it offended Americans, but felt safe advocating the killing of soldiers. He knew the deaths of British soldiers did not generate the condemnation which arose from the murder of civilians. It could be said that the Sprizzo ruling in 1984 confirmed Doherty in the view that, as long as he confined his terrorist crimes to the killing of British army personnel, he would be safe on that issue in subsequent court hearings. Obermaier knew the witness was being clever but untruthful and developed a line of questions to test this thesis:

Q:   You now abhor all violence?
A:   I have always deplored the violence of British rule in my country.
Q:   Do you still believe the only way to obtain a unified Ireland is through the use of force, including killings?
A:   The use of force has always been there over the 800-year period of British rule, much as when you fought at Valley Forge and you killed British soldiers.
Q:   Mr Doherty, do you still believe that the only method to obtain a unified Ireland is through the use of force, including killings?
A:   The use of force is only a means to an end, and the IRA's armed struggle is only one of the many facets of our organisation. *We fight politically and militarily* [my italics]. The two are parallel.

In the midst of Doherty's rhetoric was an unmistakable use of 'we', which went unnoticed as Obermaier continued to concentrate on the shaping of his own questions. Again, Obermaier might have asked whether the 'we' included Joseph Doherty? Instead, he questioned the sentence 'The two are parallel', and wondered if the witness was confirming that the IRA's political struggle was an integral part of its armed conflict. Doherty replied that the political and military dimensions to the struggle were 'parallel', by which an astute observer of the history of the Irish conflict would have inferred they were 'inseparable'. It was an important admission by Doherty, and would have proved more significant if the attorney had linked it to the use of the word 'we'. Obermaier continued to probe Doherty's thoughts on the IRA, and received some interesting results which he did not pursue, as the following transcript shows.

Q: Did you ever believe that the only method by which to obtain the British evacuation of Ireland is through armed conflict?

A: As I stated before, the IRA is a means to an end, and besides the actual armed struggle there is the political struggle within the North of Ireland by Sinn Fein, the political party, and also by many individuals, including many members of the Irish-American community here who lobby Congress, who lobby city councils, the McBride Principles Campaign which was passed by several New York State legislatures and city councils. The struggle to bring about the freedom of my country comes from – it's a pervasive struggle.

Q: Can you answer my question?

A: I think I answered. I said no that the IRA campaign is the only means to get the British out of Ireland. No. There are many.

Q: Have you ever testified under oath that you believe that the evacuation of Ireland by the British could be brought about by armed conflict?

A: By armed conflict and many other fronts.

Q: Did you believe that?

A: I believed that then. I believe that now. We must force the British to the negotiation table, and this will be done through armed struggle, and also political struggle, not only in Ireland, but in Europe and the United States and Australia and Canada, any country that is close to Britain and can have influence.

Whether or not Doherty intended to mention the US in his final utterance in the above account is debatable but, irrespective of his reasoning, he compromised himself. By alluding to the use of armed and political struggle in the United States, he was contradicting his constant assertion that the US was neutral. I suspect his tendency to allow the rhetoric to flow was the reason for what was a glaring admission about IRA intentions in countries which many Irish men and women considered 'friendly', particularly the United States. I believe he intended to convey that a political struggle would be waged in countries he mentioned, though his critics would be quick to add that his own definition of the two 'parallel' roles of the IRA pointed to IRA activity in those countries which included the US.

Doherty argued that armed struggle was a permissible method, and, with that comment ringing in his ears, Obermaier returned to the killing of Ian Gow to point out that the IRA regarded such an act as part of the armed conflict. Doherty said he did not agree with many operations and actions of the IRA. He compared his attitude to that of his lawyer, Steve Somerstein, who he told the court had served as a marine in Vietnam 'fighting for his country'. 'Somerstein', he said, 'did not believe in a number of actions which his brigade was involved in, in Vietnam.' He added that he did not agree with the killing of a Member of Parliament, or bombing the London Stock Exchange, actions which took place in 1990. To further illustrate his point, he returned to a constant theme which was always central to the way in which he hoped to be perceived: 'The Stock Exchange is not an armed target. I am a soldier. My training taught me to attack British military establishments, military bases. The decision-making is with the Army Council. I am just a private first-class. I am a soldier.'

He described his training at 'military school', his term for IRA training camps, and repeated he was only trained to attack British military forces just as American paratroopers and marines were trained for their conflicts. Obermaier was not prepared to allow Doherty to deceive the court about his IRA status by claiming he was a 'private first-class'. He reminded him that he was an IRA company officer, to which Doherty replied: 'Well, a low-level officer.'

As a corollary to his enquiries about the murder of Ian Gow, Obermaier framed several questions designed to elicit Doherty's views on the IRA's attempt to wipe out Margaret Thatcher and her Government in 1984, while the Tory Party was hosting its annual conference in the Grand Hotel in Brighton. A bomb exploded in the hotel, and almost succeeded in realising the IRA's aim: eight people died including a Conservative MP. The IRA hailed the bombing as a victory, pointing out that, although they did not kill Margaret Thatcher, they 'only needed to be lucky once, she needed to be lucky all the time'. They wanted to kill Thatcher and her

Cabinet in revenge for the deaths of ten IRA hunger-strikers three years earlier. Obermaier saw in this incident an opportunity to test Doherty, to discover if he would express a view consistent with his condemnation of the killing of Ian Gow MP.

Q:        You know the IRA attempted to kill Mrs Thatcher and her Cabinet?

A:        I know they made an attack on the British Cabinet.

Q:        Was that within the terms of armed conflict, as you believe armed conflict can be used, to obtain the British evacuation of Ireland?

A:        The bombing of Gadaffi and his family, was that within –

Judge:     Mr Doherty, that is not the subject of this hearing.

Q:        Do you disavow the attempt by the IRA to inflict casualties upon the British Cabinet?

A:        I do not disagree with that particular action.

Q:        You do not. So you think that was permissible?

A:        I don't understand the question.

Judge:     Do you mean you do or do not disagree?

A:        *Your Honour, I stated that I don't agree with that particular action* [my italics].

Judge:     The question was much broader than that. Apart from your personal view do you disavow it? Is it your view that it is not part of the struggle of the IRA?

A:        I believe it is not.

As someone who has studied the IRA and its methods, tactics and philosophy, I cannot accept that Doherty was telling the truth in respect of the killing of Gow or the Brighton hotel bombing. I knew IRA men who fundamentally disagreed with the bombing of civilian targets in the 1970s and 1980s, and resigned because of those tactics, but few of them would have defined the killing of Ian Gow or the bombing of the Brighton hotel as inconsistent with the IRA armed struggle, or as comparable with the killing of civilians. In fact British politicians have always been regarded as legitimate targets throughout the history of the IRA campaign. I was convinced that Doherty, in his determination to remain within Judge Sprizzo's 'political offence exception' judgement, recognised the need to confine his role to that of a 'foot soldier', who was trained to fight other soldiers, and not kill political figures or diplomats. His self-portrayal was designed to create a sensitive and appreciative audience both in and out of court. He did not wish to be seen advocating modern methods of terror, which appalled and disturbed the sensitivities of many who would naturally understand or support a 'prisoner of conscience'. He required his audience to perceive him as a person who merely followed orders, and behaved in the way in which all soldiers are trained to respond.

Obermaier asked Doherty for his response to the 1990 killing of two Australian tourists in the Netherlands. He replied that the double killing was inexcusable, and 'the leaders of my movement' had clearly stated that the action was unintentional, had apologised and sent bereavement notices to the families of those killed. His use of the words 'my movement' went unnoticed, although it was a further example of how he identified with the republican movement, the IRA.

Obermaier enquired whether civilians were killed in IRA operations. The question appeared to offend Doherty, who reacted in a combative manner: 'And American operations. Look at the bombing of Panama City, where over one thousand civilians were killed. In all wars, civilians are killed. The Americans should know that as well as any other government.'

The US Attorney quickly returned to the issue: 'Can you answer my question?' Doherty retorted: 'You answer mine.' Cedarbaum intervened to restore order and reminded the witness that his presence in the court was solely for the purpose of replying to questions from the District Attorney.

Obermaier pursued him to establish his views on other acts of terror carried out by the IRA in 1990. These included the shooting dead of an off-duty British corporal and his sixth-month old baby in West Germany in October; the killing of ten members of the British Royal Marine Band in England; and the murder of an army major in Germany. Doherty said he could not condone the killing of the corporal and his baby, or for that matter the death of the wife of a soldier in West Germany in 1989. However, the Royal Marine musicians and the major were military targets. He added he would be concerned if the IRA mounted an operation which resulted in civilian deaths. In developing that point he made a curious admission which did not appear in his 1984 testimony: 'Members of my unit, including the leadership of the IRA, had stated quite clearly that they apologised for the killing of those innocent civilians.' I wondered which operation or operations carried out by his unit resulted in civilian casualties, because he was never forthcoming about those matters. In international law, the killing of innocent civilians removed the right of a person to claim the 'political offence exception'. Any admission that he or his unit had killed innocent civilians would have been cited as a breach of civilised behaviour, and would have made it impossible for him to fight extradition or seek political asylum.

Obermaier failed to detect the semblance of such an admission. Maybe he suspected that Doherty used language with an abandon which, if scrutinised, would simply lead to Doherty denying the import of what he said, or rephrasing an earlier reply. I was left with the dilemma of deciding whether to interpret Doherty's admission as malign or benign. I inclined to the belief that what he really intended to say was that it was general IRA policy for his – or any other – unit to apologise if civilians were killed.

Cross-examination continued, with the usual verbal sparring, until Doherty detached himself from a question and offered the judge and court a lengthy defence of IRA operations outside Ireland. He argued that the attacks on British military forces in Germany were designed 'to weigh down the troops, and to create havoc with soldiers' morale'. Such attacks, he said, 'tied up' the British Army of the Rhine and generated pressure in London for the army to demand more security, more money and political reaction from the Government. Westmacott, he added, was not killed out of malice, vengeance or hatred towards him.

The reason I was involved in that operation – his death – the pressure would come on the London Government, the soldiers going back and the amount of damage that we can inflict on the British military forces could bring the reality to the British Government that their presence in the North of Ireland is unworkable politically and militarily, that they cannot suppress the IRA, that the IRA can survive and attack back, and that targets have been selected within the Six Counties [Northern Ireland], and the IRA went outside the Six Counties to attack the British military forces in London and on the Rhine and also in Great Britain. This is to bring pressure on the British Government to force them to negotiations, not out of vengeance because they have beaten up our families or shot our people on the street.

It was a comprehensive statement of IRA thinking and policy and was more remarkable for the fact that it was spoken by a man who claimed to have left the IRA in 1982, and who at times appeared uninformed about particular acts of IRA terrorism in 1990, yet could speak with clarity about the Provisionals' general *modus operandi*.

Doherty revealed his thoughts on the hijacking of cars, the takeover of someone's home and the holding of hostages. He believed that in a war situation ordinary people were required to 'make sacrifices'. He said people understood IRA necessity even when frightened: 'I have seen people sort of look at me and they will be afraid. It's only natural.' He recalled feeling embarrassed when hijacking cars, but recognised it 'had to be done'. He believed the armed struggle was vital to bring the British to the negotiating table. He quoted John F. Kennedy: if peaceful revolution were not forthcoming, violent revolutions were inevitable. He said he was once committed to peaceful revolution but his generation became convinced that the Northern Ireland state was irreformable, and that a struggle was required to force the British to leave. His wish was to see the British and IRA talking in much the same way as De Klerk and Nelson Mandela in South Africa.

Obermaier waited patiently for Doherty to finish, aware that the court would soon bring the cross-examination to an end. Doherty ended his historical essay by pointing out that for generations war had been a way of life, and he wished it to end. Obermaier interrupted him: 'Would you do anything to support the armed conflict?' Doherty appeared to fail to grasp the text of the question and remarked that it was vague. Steve Somerstein interjected to ask the judge for a 'time reference'. She said she felt the District Attorney should be more specific with his question. He replied that he did not consider it was unreasonable that the court should permit him to continue to seek an answer to his question. Cedarbaum relented, and Obermaier asked Doherty if he was prepared to assist the armed conflict currently taking place in Ireland.

Somerstein rose to his feet to protect his client and objected to the line of questioning. The judge agreed with him and suggested that 'Mr Obermaier should break down the question'. She proposed that Doherty should first be asked if he would participate in the conflict. He replied that he would not, and the judge asked a supplementary question designed to elicit whether he would participate in armed struggle in ways other than fund-raising. Doherty said he would not, but he would continue to support the aims and objectives of the republican movement and the IRA:

I did that over the past seven and a half years by communicating with members of Congress who are here, members of state legislature who are here, members of the New York Police Department, citizens of the United States, the media and this is what I have been doing for the past seven and a half years, to continue what I believe in.

In a few sentences Doherty explained that his period of confinement was spent furthering the aims of the IRA. He was confirming exactly what the British and American Governments feared he was doing from prison. Ironically, he might not have done it so successfully if he had been freed on bail.

The armed struggle is not what I believe in, it's the British evacuation of my country, and, as I say, armed struggle is a necessity to bring that about. But there are many other fronts, political fronts in the occupied Six Counties and also within the United States and the House of Representatives, the Senate, New York State Assembly and the City Council, people marching, writing letters to President Bush, Vice-President Quayle, the Attorney-General and the Secretary of State, Jim Baker. These are all part of the struggle to force the British politically to come to the negotiating table. I did that for seven and a half years in my 12 by 6 cell. If I am to return, I will continue that politically through Congress and the media.

Doherty completed his history of his support for the IRA, and Obermaier extracted from him an admission that he believed armed conflict was a necessity. The District Attorney proceeded to ask him, again, whether he would assist the armed conflict if released on bail. Steve Somerstein objected but was overruled by the judge, who said she believed the witness was capable of speaking for himself.

Doherty paused and said he would not assist the armed conflict in any way. His obligation would be to the court if released and to the people who provided the money and resources for his bail bond. He would, however, continue his political work to force the British from Ireland but would do it politically and constitutionally within the laws of the United States.

Obermaier completed his questioning, and Steve Somerstein rose to his feet and, at the judge's discretion, was permitted five minutes to redirect his client. Somerstein was intent on seeking clarification on issues which were central to the bail application. He began by tackling the risk of flight issue and encouraged Doherty to restate his obligation to the court. The question was designed to elicit a positive response and it achieved the desired result.

Doherty repeated his commitment to the court, and to those people who supported him. He said he had spent seventeen years of his life in prison but did not regret losing so many years of freedom. It demanded sacrifices from him such as the absence of a normal existence and the lack of opportunity to have girlfriends and be married. His commitment, he told the court, was an unswerving moral one to reunify Ireland. For those principles he was willing to spend another thirty to thirty-five years in prison. He emphasised there was no personal motive which would influence him to abscond from bail.

Somerstein reminded him that his history evidenced a duty to escape from prison, and asked if such duty would encourage him to escape from an American prison or the orders of an American court. Doherty replied that from the day of his arrest in Manhattan he had obeyed, and conformed to, prison rules. He did not regard himself as a prisoner of war in the US. He wore prison uniform, even though it 'hurt him' because he was a political prisoner. The judge quickly picked the phrase 'political prisoner' and asked a rhetorical question, which Doherty, well-schooled in verbal evasion, turned to his advantage.

Judge:      You don't consider yourself a political prisoner here. You are being held because you entered the country illegally.

Doherty:    But inside me I consider myself a political prisoner and the way the Government has treated this case for seven and a half years is because of the political involvement of the British Government. They are not fighting this case on the merits of the case but rather their political alignment with the British Government. I am sure if I had to kill a Soviet captain in their army, I would not be sitting in this court. It is because it is a British soldier and Great Britain is an ally of the United States. In that sense, the way they have approached this case is political, and I do consider myself a political prisoner in my heart and mind. But as far as prison regulations are concerned, I conform. I wear a prison uniform. I do prison work voluntarily. I accept my prison number. I work as hard as any other prisoner. I am not above any other prisoner. I consider myself Joe Doherty, part of D Block, Main South, Metropolitan Correction Centre.

He added that if released he would be Joe Doherty, not a member of the IRA. He 'had no formal obligation' to the organisation. As I listened to his use of the word 'formal' I was inclined to think that, as always, he was careful in his choice of language regarding an IRA link. Did he mean that he did not have a formal association but an informal one? There was again the implicit suggestion that he could never fully or publicly distance himself from his terrorist comrades. The word 'formal' appeared as a tactical way of avoiding a denunciation of an army for which he sacrificed seventeen years of his life.

In answer to further questions, he stressed he had never been asked to 'hit a civilian target', or to operate outside Ireland or Britain. His lawyer, in prompting the latter admission, was seeking to prove to the court that his client was not a threat outside the confines of Britain and Ireland, and as a consequence was no threat to the United States.

Somerstein enquired if he would have 'disagreed' with an order to attack targets outside Ireland. The use of 'disagreed' was clever because Doherty was able to reply that he would indeed have disagreed. The fact is that if he had been given such an order he would have been permitted to disagree, but not to disobey it. Somerstein was careful to avoid the use of the word 'disobey'.

Moments later Doherty sought to exploit the word 'disagree' by telling the court that, if one disagreed with the policy of the IRA, one was entitled to resign or seek a remedy procedure by asking for the matter to be referred to the Army Council. In making that claim he was correctly stating IRA orders and guidelines. However, disagreement with IRA policy did not mean that volunteers were permitted to disobey orders. Once again Doherty had cleverly sidestepped the real issue. He completed his testimony by saying he respected the judicial branch of the US Government, which was independent from the coercion of the Justice Department. He named Judges Sprizzo and Friendly, and said they and many other jurists were 'owed his admiration'.

The day's proceedings ended inconclusively. Judge Cedarbaum ruled that the US Attorney be granted his request for an extra day to present evidence, and the hearing was adjourned until 17 September.

At 9.45 am on 17 September the same New York courtroom was again the centre of activity, with Miriam Cedarbaum the presiding judge. The Attorney-General, Richard L. Thornburgh, was represented by Claude Millman, not Otto Obermaier. In fact, Claude Millman was the lawyer with more intimate knowledge of the issue and was best suited to present the US Attorney's case.

Millman's first witness was Edmund R. Bourke, a former agent of the Immigration and Naturalisation Service, who revealed how he investigated hundreds of cases of IRA members smuggled into the United States. He had discovered that Noraid (the Northern Irish Aid Committee) was directly involved in assisting these illegal aliens, some of whom were transported into the United States from Canada, others from Mexico. Joseph Doherty was one of those illegals. Information was received from the FBI that he was working at Clancy's Bar on 53rd Street and Third Avenue, and would be there on 18 June 1983. Bourke believed that Clancy's was a location 'used by IRA members who needed assistance, housing or jobs'. On that day Bourke, and three other INS agents accompanied by FBI special agents Frank Schulte, Greg Auld and John Winslow, all of them armed, had arrested Joseph Doherty.

Bourke's evidence illustrated that nothing was simple in Doherty hearings. The INS agent, while describing his work, related an incident in which he was informed of the presence of an IRA protestor outside the British Embassy in New York: 'We set up surveillance and located Ciaran Nugent. He was subsequently arrested. One of the things that was very unusual about the arrest is that we saw the special agent who gave us the information meet Martin Galvin at the same location and point out our positions to him.'

This incident bore no relation to Doherty, but within it was a suggestion that Galvin, a New York lawyer and leading figure in Noraid, was colluding with an FBI special agent. Galvin was once arrested on a visit to Northern Ireland and was prominent in supporting the Irish republican cause in the US. Bourke was availing himself of an opportunity to damage the reputation of a leading Doherty supporter without evidence to sustain the allegation. Bourke also claimed that Galvin organised the illegal entry and transportation of IRA members into New York but had never been charged with any criminal offence.

Bourke was followed into the witness box by FBI Special Agent Frank J. Schulte, who told the court of his involvement in hundreds of cases involving the Provisional IRA, and his participation in the tracing and arrest of Joseph Doherty, alias Henry J. O'Reilly. He did not reveal that he had received assistance on the Doherty case from an informer he had recruited within the Irish community in New York City, but like Bourke he was prepared to divulge information about leading figures in New York who supported Irish republicanism and to name them, knowing he was not required to produce evidence. Under courtroom privilege, the Doherty hearing was providing excellent opportunities for damning accusations. Schulte reserved his allegations for members of the Clancy family, who owned numerous bars in New York. He mentioned the name Alan Clancy Jr, and waited for Steve Somerstein to challenge his right to talk about that person. Somerstein objected, but Judge Cedarbaum was interested in anything Schulte was prepared to say.

Judge:      Have you learned things about Alan Clancy Jr?
Schulte:    I have, Your Honour, through the normal course of my
            investigations conducting various interviews and getting
            information and published reports.
Judge:      I will permit it.

Schulte went on to allege that Clancy Sr owned the bar in which Doherty was arrested in 1983 and later sold it to Alan Clancy Jr. Alan Clancy Sr, according to Schulte, 'has 2 million Irish pounds seized by the Irish Government which they believe was destined for use by the IRA'. Clancy family bars also figured in other FBI investigations, Schulte added. In respect of Doherty, Schulte was quick to turn his evidence temporarily to the issue of IRA membership: 'I am not familiar with the term former member of the IRA. To my knowledge most individuals are either active or inactive. They don't resign.'

The FBI special agent peppered his testimony with all the issues he considered relevant, particularly the Clancy's Bar connection and Doherty's IRA status. He stressed that people with whom he dealt in various cases entered the US illegally and were members of the IRA. As he began to name them he was interrupted by Somerstein, who agitatedly told the judge he considered it improper that Schulte should lay out his numerous allegations about people unconnected with the case. Cedarbaum rebuked the attorney and reminded him it was a public hearing. Somerstein expressed his concern that the witness might express an opinion, without proof, concerning Doherty's bail-flight risk. The judge reluctantly agreed to hear Schulte's opinion but asked Claude Millman to anticipate what the witness might say. Millman seized the opportunity to point out that the FBI believed that Doherty would have all the financial and physical resources necessary to flee the US. The judge suggested to Millman that surely he was concerned not about Doherty fleeing the US but about his hiding within the jurisdiction. The Assistant US Attorney replied: 'Quite frankly, we don't know what would happen, whether Mr Doherty would go to Canada, Australia or remain in the United States.'

Millman had taken the opportunity to widen the scope of the risk posed by Doherty. Somerstein was angry and commented that he was afraid such comments would be made in open court. Cedarbaum defended her position by replying that it was difficult to deter lawyers from arguing. Somerstein reprimanded her: 'It is possible to keep them from arguing off the public record.' His rebuke was noted with a frosty stare and a reminder that he was talking to the person in charge; Cedarbaum told Somerstein: 'Let's not have any colloquy.'

Somerstein was now faced with Frank Schulte for cross-examination and reminded him that Alan Clancy Sr had initiated litigation to recover his $3,000,000 from the Irish Government and none of the Clancys had been prosecuted for any offence connected with FBI inquiries. On the bail issue, Schulte was obliged to admit that, in gun-running cases in which he was involved, bail was granted and none of those released had fled US jurisdiction.

Another day's proceedings ended, with 2 October reserved as a final day for the hearing of the US Attorney's leading witness, Professor Paul Wilkinson. His evidence and cross-examination eventually resulted in a typed transcript of eighty pages. He dealt with the history of the Provisional IRA, its actions, and its rules and regulations contained in the 'Green Book'.

In that October hearing, Wilkinson spoke at length about the crucial issue of IRA membership, in order to prove that Doherty had lied when he said he had resigned from the organisation before entering the US. His views were standard British views but none the less mostly accurate. The transcript shows that he was the most formidable witness for the prosecution owing to his knowledge of Ireland. However, he overstated the case when he said the IRA was a 'cradle-to-the-grave organisation' – an oversimplification of the recent history of the IRA. Thousands of people who joined in the early 1970s later resigned, and many who served prison sentences preferred to return to a normal life, although there were dedicated members who joined in their youth and remained bound to IRA ideals and rules throughout their lives. Wilkinson was unable to show why Doherty might be a 'cradle-to-the-grave' republican. However, he was allowed considerable opportunity to opinionate, which was exactly the reason for his having been invited.

When he faced cross-examination he was quickly made aware that Steve Somerstein intended to depict him as a stooge of the British and American Governments. Doherty's attorney tried to imply that Wilkinson's lectures to British and US defence establishments placed him in a partisan role. When this failed to achieve a satisfactory result, Somerstein asked a direct question: 'Is it your position, sir, that the IRA needs to be eliminated or eradicated?'

Wilkinson replied that he was opposed to the use of violence and supported peaceful change in Ireland. He agreed that the IRA was not alone in causing civilian deaths and that the British army, police and the locally recruited Ulster Defence Regiment, an integral part of the British services, were also responsible for civilian casualties. Somerstein was left with little scope for contesting Wilkinson's statements, and his pursuit of a clever witness served only to clarify the evidence which Millman had drawn from the professor in direct examination. Proceedings ended with an undertaking by the judge to deliver her verdict by 5 November. Few were willing to wager she would rule in Doherty's favour, and they were proved right.

In refusing Doherty bail she said the future length of his detention could not be predicted with any certainty. She admitted that no case had come to her attention in which a deportable alien had spent as much time in custody as Doherty. She rejected his claims that the length of his detention was due to the US Government's zealously pursuing its objectives to deport him to British custody.

Petitioner has not shown that the Government has improperly delayed the deportation hearings, or opposed petitioner's application for relief, for the purpose of prolonging his detention. In fact, an examination of the prior proceedings shows that substantial portions of the period of Doherty's detention. including some portions for which he seeks to blame the Government, are attributable to his own litigation strategy.

I was not convinced by the above assertion and neither were many of America's leading lawyers including a former Attorney-General, Ramsay Clark. I knew there were other forces at work determined to keep him in custody irrespective of the clever judicial arguments of his lawyers. Cedarbaum found the 'risk of flight' testimony to be 'extremely weighty'. I found it unproven and, in any event, the IRA was not prepared to damage its image in the US, or jeopardise any future court hearings, in respect of anyone arrested in that jurisdiction by allowing Doherty to flee bail. Through information from my own contacts, I have little doubt that the IRA would not have embarrassed leading political figures and lawyers in the US who were posting personal moneys for his bail. Ironically, Judge Cedarbaum's judgement suited IRA propagandists who knew the value of Doherty's constant stream of republican polemic from his prison cell.

Cedarbaum did reflect her concern about the length of his detention, which she found 'troubling'. However, in her view it did not violate 'due process, in the light of all the circumstances'. The final lines of her judgement did not deal with evidence of IRA membership or parallel cases which showed the risk of releasing Doherty on bail.

The evidence is overwhelming that petitioner, if released, would pose such a substantial risk of flight that no conditions of bail could reasonably assure his surrender for deportation. The strength of the evidence of risk of flight, combined with petitioner's failure to establish that the Government has improperly delayed deportation proceedings, shows the petitioner's detention continues to serve the valid regulatory purpose of keeping him available for deportation. The petition for a writ of habeas corpus is denied.

Doherty was returned to his cell to compose yet another article detailing his recent courtroom exploits.

# Conclusion

# Thatcher and Doherty

No one was surprised when Miriam Goldman Cedarbaum denied Doherty bail, although I felt that she sustained her judgment with unproven arguments. Irrespective of the legal outcome, there was little doubt the American system had been critically compromised by the ongoing pursuit of Doherty, and by the circumvention of the judiciary to satisfy British demands. Irish-American opinion had been hardened by the issue, and as a consequence republicanism found a bedrock of support. The nature of the alliance between Margaret Thatcher and Ronald Reagan may prove vainglorious when issues such as this are later examined by students of history. Thatcher was, as her Cabinet colleagues discovered, single-minded, and at times a narrow thinker who allowed personal ambition to cloud her judgement. She supported Reagan's foreign policy and in particular the bombing of Tripoli, but exacted a political price. Throughout the Doherty case no public mention was made about her belief that Reagan and later Bush 'owed her'. Such an admission would have angered Americans, who believed that her support for Reagan did not require reciprocal gestures which interfered with internal US politics and the American judicial process. My study of the Doherty story convinced me there was indeed a hidden agenda, and I was fortunate to observe features of the case which were obscured from public scrutiny.

Otto Obermaier and Claude Millman acted with propriety during their dealings with me and did not compromise themselves professionally. They revealed only what was on the record. Equally, the British diplomat, Sherard Cowper Coles, did not seek to influence me, but was revealing about the British position.

The two Governments analysed the issues with naïvete, and

failed to recognise Doherty as a formidable opponent who was winning the propaganda war from his prison cell. They also ignored the reluctance of the American people to allow their judicial process to be compromised. When Doherty's continued detention became a central concern of the Irish-American community, both Governments should have re-evaluated the argument that he was a 'flight risk', who should be indefinitely detained. Their attempts to 'detach him from his cause' failed, and in consequence enhanced his strategy of portraying himself as a political prisoner, a prisoner of conscience. The continued court battle internationalised the Irish conflict, which was exactly what the IRA desired. It provided Doherty with a platform to debate the nature of the war in Ireland from his own viewpoint, and exploit the Ramsay Clark statement that war was about soldiers killing soldiers. That gave him the opportunity to place his crimes in the context of other wars such as Vietnam. In so doing, he benefited from American guilt about Vietnam, and the country's ability to be forgiving about its actions in that conflict.

Astute observers in the Reagan and Bush administrations were not heeded when they warned that the pursuit of Doherty was counter-productive. Reagan admired Thatcher and her unequivocal support for his bombing of Libya. He believed she was the person to help him combat the growing terrorist campaign in Europe which threatened US interests as well as its military personnel and diplomtic staff. Thatcher's bellicose nature obviated compromise with the IRA. She was top of their hit-list, and their ally Gadaffi was her enemy and Reagan's. As she often remarked, she was 'not for turning'. She viewed the Doherty case as a symbol of her determination to pursue the IRA wherever they were found and she constantly reminded Reagan of the IRA–Libyan connection. She was not concerned about the legal or political difficulties of the Doherty case, telling Reagan and later Bush that, whatever the cost to the US legal system, Doherty's return was the repayment of a debt. She saw the IRA in much the same way as Reagan viewed Libya. The IRA was her country's main enemy and she regarded Irish-American support for it as a dangerous ingredient, which internationalised and legitimised it. Her fears increased with the 1984 Sprizzo judgement, permitting Doherty the role of a political prisoner, and threatening her ambition to ensure that no safe haven existed for terrorists within Western democracies. Thatcher's advisers warned her that Doherty's success in achieving political status would pave the way to America becoming a safe hiding place for every IRA man who killed a British soldier. A casual observation of the case would confirm that they were probably correct in that assessment.

However, in the person of Joe Doherty she was not dealing with someone who fitted neatly into her definition of a modern terrorist. He was not known to be guilty of the shooting or bombing civilians, attacks on economic targets or the murder of politicians. He had been found guilty of the killing and attempted killing of soldiers, and such crimes accorded with the activities of many British and US servicemen in recent wars. The soldier he killed was no ordinary soldier, but an officer in a highly efficient counter-terrorist regiment with a dubious history. The fact that the SAS was involved in controversial shootings, and exhibited a style of execution illustrated by the killing of three unarmed IRA personnel in Gibraltar, served to heighten Doherty's argument that his enemy was 'not without sin'. The history of the SAS permitted him to state convincingly that when he shot Westmacott he was acting to protect his own life. It was a tenuous legal argument, but evidence supported the view that if Westmacott and his men had entered number 371 Antrim Road they would have executed Doherty and his unit. Doherty used other means of wooing his American audience by describing adeptly the unfortunate circumstances of his working-class upbringing, and the plight of the Catholic community under Unionism, which, by definition, was British rule. He took full advantage of the failure of Americans to know the precise nature of the history of Northern Ireland, and subsequently many of the assertions in his 1984 testimony went unchallenged. His claim that he was tortured with electric shocks remained part of an accepted court record, and reinforced his image as a prisoner of conscience.

No one on the prosecution side of the legal battle understood the nature of the IRA, the history of internment, policies in respect of volunteers, or resignation rules. At the September 1990 hearing, Obermaier resorted to tried, tested, and inadequate and unproven arguments. To my astonishment he was proved correct in his line of reasoning because he succeeded in keeping Doherty in custody. Judge Cedarbaum's demeanour during the hearing suggested that he was not prepared to take the momentous step of releasing Doherty.

Anyone studying Doherty's life, or watching his performance in

the American courts, could not have resisted being captivated by
the story as he portrayed it, and the battle of one small man pitted
against the scheming of two Governments. Many people who
disapproved of his IRA career, and his politics, nevertheless
harboured a sneaking admiration for his bravado and cunning. His
demeanour in the witness box was that of a quiet-mannered man
employing his wits against skilled attorneys. He did not resemble
the image of the hardened, tough, uncompromising terrorist or
idealogue.

For those reasons, he posed a serious threat when the British
authorities sought publicly to convince Americans that the IRA
was a group of gangsters, racketeers, thugs, animals, men without
a conscience, who possessed no historical defence for their armed
struggle. Ironically, Thatcher and her allies presented Joseph
Doherty with the opportunity to contest and, in the minds of many
Irish-Americans and Americans with no commitment to Ireland,
defeat the arguments against him. They made him a *cause célèbre* for
Irish republicans, as well as for those who believed the US legal
system was being abused and undermined by the executive arm of
the Government. Doherty's prison cell became a symbol of one
man's persecution, and a focus of constant media attention. The
aims of the British and US Governments did not justify the means
employed to extradite Doherty: the overturning of legal judge-
ments in his favour and the interference of two Attorneys-General
transformed an 'ordinary' man into a public hero.

Thatcher's stubbornness and her influence on the weak
President Reagan obscured the complexities of the issue. It ignored
the power of Irish-American politics, the mythologised view of the
Irish conflict on the US East Coast, and it failed to take account of
the outrage many Americans felt about interference with the due
process of law. Reagan's departure changed nothing, and even in
1990 Thatcher was reminding the Bush Administration of its
indebtedness to her.

One can fully understand the need for the British to change
Irish-American attitudes to terrorism, in particular their support
for the IRA, and to seek to extradite Doherty, but the manner in
which they set about that objective seems often incomprehensible.
They failed to recognise the need for subtlety, for sensitivity.
Reagan, and later President Bush, permitted the legal process to be
railroaded into subjection. The Reagan Administration shared the
majority of the blame for the heavy-handed way it dealt with its

own court system; and Bush for allowing himself to be pressurised by Thatcher. Neither the US Government nor Thatcher understood that they were elevating Doherty to the status of political prisoner and angering public opinion by the relentless pursuit of him. Out of vindictiveness they perpetuated a problem.

I remain convinced that, had Doherty been released on bail, he would never have become such a symbolic figure. The refusal to grant him bail remained crucial to Thatcher's pressure on the US Government to deny him freedom at any price. Bail overshadowed the central objective of extradition and, later, deportation. If released and if he fled, Doherty would have damaged his credibility, and that of Irish republicans and their US backers. Everyone had become aware of that, but the legal battle continued to keep him in his prison cell where he frequently broadcast nationwide, and wrote articles for newspapers, magazines and periodicals.

When I heard the British diplomat reminding Obermaier of Thatcher's personal interest in the case I was convinced of her influence and her power over the US Administration. Thatcher made Doherty a foreign policy consideration; she determined every move in the legal battle, and ultimately her obstinacy damaged the British case. She had no wish to be perceived as 'weak on terrorism', and she viewed the prospect of Doherty on bail, walking the streets of New York, as a capitulation to terrorism. In so doing she played into the hands of the IRA, and created one of the most remarkable court sagas in US legal history. Two US Administrations, frightened of her, succumbed to her demands. She was their major ally in a changing Europe, and, as she was apt to remind them, they were indebted to her: Britain, in 1991, demonstrated its support for the US in the Gulf War.

The danger of Thatcher's 'power politics' philosophy lay in its interference with the legal machinery of another Government, and its taking no account of historical complexities or the US principle of fairness. Many people in the United States came to support Doherty, but still opposed the IRA. Anticipation of that possibility might have produced a studied approach to the problem. The naïvety of British and American officials involved with the case was astounding, as were the scenarios outlined at high-level political meetings in London. A simple study of the IRA, the Irish conflict, British–American relations and Irish-American sentiments should have convinced even the casual observer that a relentless pursuit of Doherty would only serve to reinforce mythology, and aid IRA propagandists. The Sprizzo decision was undoubtedly dangerous to US–British policy on terrorism but it should have alerted both Governments to the pitfalls inherent in the case. When Doherty agreed to be deported, even if it was to the Irish Republic, he should have been released on bail. The opportunity to review the case never became available to those handling it in the US Attorney's Office. When I sat in Obermaier's office and listened to Sherard Cowper Coles from the British Embassy in Washington, I knew that, irrespective of the merits of seeking to defuse the Doherty lobby, means were still being employed which unwittingly augmented it.

By 1991 I was convinced that, despite the outcome of the proceedings, Doherty had emerged victorious. His lawyers, Steve Somerstein and Mary Pike (who had become emotionally tied to her client), advised him well, and had enabled him to present himself as a reasonable man. They developed a constantly changing legal strategy designed to frustrate two Governments. Their role was central to shaping the Doherty persona and their commitment to him was surely not part of a financial arrangement. Estimates for his defence have ranged from $800,000 to $1,000,000. His means of paying that may remain one of the secrets of the case.

In late spring 1991 Doherty awaited a further ruling on a bail application and prepared for a Supreme Court hearing which he hoped would be scheduled for the autumn. In May he was visited by New York State Assemblymen, who helped him prepare for the Supreme Court. They told him they had a petition signed by ninety Representatives and five Senators demanding he be granted political asylum. Throughout the United States, pro-Doherty groups were devising ways of highlighting his plight in order to pressure the Bush Administration to accede to his demands. Doherty told the Assemblymen that if bail were refused he wished to be transferred to a prison in Orange County in advance of the Supreme Court hearing. It was his intention 'to breathe clean air' and to leave the narrow confines of his detention cell.

Meanwhile, Bush and his advisers were busy formulating a strategy to combat Doherty and his bandwagon of support. They were devising legislation to cope with illegal aliens, and it became apparent they intended to place proposals before Congress to deal specifically with 'alien terrorists'. The proposals were contained within a new Crime Bill and left Doherty supporters in little doubt that they were aimed at preventing the Irishman's legal plans.

Members of the American Civil Liberties Union were quick to condemn the proposals and pointed out that they had been devised to thwart Doherty's rights. The proposals included familiar justification for shaping laws to deal with international terrorist organisations who exploited the territory of the United States. In particular, there were references to infrastructures and cells which terrorists used to fulfil their aims. The US Administration believed such structures were in place in America and their members included foreign students, people holding temporary visas and permanent resident aliens. The Gulf War manifested a real possibility that terrorist cells were operating within Western democracies, and the proposed legislation was devised to eliminate threats of the type made by Saddam Hussein, who said he had terrorists in place in the US and Britain. The argument for new legislation cited sixteen examples of terrorist activity in America. Fifteen were related to people with Middle East connections, and one was identified as the IRA in Northern Ireland. The proposals were aimed at providing a means by which people suspected of being 'terrorist aliens' could be deported on the basis of secret intelligence, which could not be challenged in the courts. One of the implications was that a decision to deport someone such as Doherty would only require 'probable cause'.

Astute observers of the proposed measures argued that if the legislation had been in place in 1982 the British would only have been required secretly to confirm his IRA membership, and a belief that he was using the United States as a safe haven, with the assistance of an IRA infrastructure in the jurisdiction. Those allegations would have been sufficient to guarantee his deportation, and he would not have been permitted to contest or examine their source. On the question of deportation, the new proposals permitted the Attorney-General to detain indefinitely a 'terrorist alien' if no country accepted him. The measures also sought to remove the right of a person to choose the jurisdiction to which he or she wished to be deported.

When the proposals were made public, Doherty and his suppporters knew that if the bill became law he was in real danger of being deported before his expected Supreme Court hearing. The Bush Administration was anticipating the publicity which such a hearing might generate in the Irishman's favour. A British diplomat told me both Governments were concerned that Doherty would exploit the Supreme Court to highlight his case to an international audience:

Doherty knows the Supreme Court will be his last-ditch effort but it will also be his ultimate platform. We don't want to risk that outcome if we can avoid it. If Doherty wins, all our efforts will have been in vain.

# Postscript

On 19 February 1992, Joe Doherty was extradited to Britain, on a US Air Force jet, after the Supreme Court in America had finally ruled that his nine-year battle for political asylum there had failed.

He is now in the Maze Prison in Northern Ireland, serving the life-sentence for murder that was passed on him in 1982 in his absence, following his escape from the Crumlin Road jail in June 1981.

# Appendix:
# The Green Book

What follows is the constitution, aims, objectives and disciplinary procedures of the IRA. Known as 'The Green Book', it is the IRA's official handbook. It has not been edited or altered in any way, and is printed here in its recent edition. Any errors of grammar or of sense can be attributed to the original.

## CONSTITUTION OF OGLAIGH NA hEIREANN

### 1. Title:
The Army shall be known as Oglaigh na hEireann.

### 2. Membership:
1 Enlistment in Oglaigh na hEireann shall be open to all those over the age of 17 who accept its objects as stated in the Constitution and who make the following pledge:
'I . . . . (name) . . . . promise that I will promote the objects of Oglaigh na hEireann to the best of my knowledge and ability and that I will obey all orders and regulations issued to me by the Army Authority and by my superior officer.'
2 Participation in Stormont or Westminister and in any other subservient parliament, if any, is strictly forbidden.
3 Enlistment shall be at the discretion of the Army Authority.

### 3. Objects:
1 To guard the honour and uphold the sovereignty and unity of the Republic of Ireland.
2 To support the establishment of an Irish Socialist Republic based on the 1916 Proclamation.
3 To support the establishment of, and uphold, a lawful government in sole and absolute control of the Republic.
4 To secure and defend civil and religious liberties and equal rights and equal opportunities for all citizens.
5 To promote the revival of the Irish language as the everyday language of the people.

### 4. Means:

**1** To organise Oglaigh na hEireann for victory.

**2** To build on a spirit of comradeship.

**3** To wage revolutionary armed struggle.

**4** To encourage popular resistance, political mobilisation and political action in support of these objectives.

**5** To assist, as directed by the Army Authority, all organisations working for the same objectives.

### 5. Army Control:

**1** The General Army Convention shall be the Supreme Army Authority.

**2** The Army Council shall be the Supreme Authority when a General Convention is not in session.

**3** The Army Council, only after Convention, shall have power to delegate its powers to a government which is actively endeavouring to function as the de facto government of the Republic.

**4** When a government is functioning as the de facto government of the Republic, a General Army Convention shall be convened to give the allegiance of Oglaigh na hEireann to such a government.

**5** All personnel and all armaments, equipment and other resources of Oglaigh na hEireann shall be at the disposal of and subject to the Army Authority, to be employed and utilised as the Army Authority shall direct.

### 6. General Army Convention:

**1** A General Army Convention of Delegates (selected as set out hereinafter) shall meet every two years unless the majority of these delegates notify the Army Council that they it better for military purposes to postpone it. When a General Army Convention is postponed, it shall be summoned to meet as soon as the majority of the delegates shall notify the Army Council that they deem it advisable.

**2** An Extraordinary General Army Convention and that the urgency of the issue for the Convention does not permit of the selection of delegates as prescribed, that the delegates to the previous General Army Convention constitute the Extraordinary General Army Convention. When for any reason a delegate to the previous General Army Convention has become ineligible, or is not available, the Battalion Council shall elect a delegate in his/her stead. Every active Volunteer in the Battalion shall be eligible to stand as a delegate.

**4** When the Army is engaged on active service, no Unit or General Army Convention shall be held until a reasonable time after hostilities have terminated, unless the Army Authority decides otherwise.

**5** An Executive of twelve members shall be elected by ballot at the General Army Convention: at least eight of these members shall be delegates to the Convention. Four members may be elected from active Volunteers who are not delegates. The next six in line shall, however, be eligible as subsitutes to the Executive in order of their election. The Executive shall always have six substitutes in readiness.

**6** No member of the Executive may also be a member of the Army Council and members of the Executive subsequently elected to the Army Council will resign from the Executive. Vacant positions on the Executive arising in such a way shall be filled by those substitutes next in line from the Convention elections.

**7** The following shall be entitled to attend and vote at the General Army Convention:

Delegates selected by Battalion Convention.

Delegates selected by General Headquarters Staff and Staffs of Brigades, Divisions and Commands.

Two members of the Executive.

All members of the Army Council.

The Chief of Staff, the Adjutant-General and the Quartermaster-General.

**8** Only Volunteers on the Active List shall be eligible as delegates to the General Army Convention.

**9** A majority of the General Army Convention may invite anyone whom they wish to attend to speak.

**10** The Chairperson of the General Army Convention shall be chosen by the General Convention.

## 7. Duties and Powers of the Executive:

**1** The Chairperson of the General Army Convention or his/her representative shall, within forty-eight hours of the termination of the Conventions, summon a meeting of the Army Executive over which he/she shall preside during the election of a Chairperson and Secretary. The Army Executive shall then proceed with the election of an Army Council of seven members.

**2** The Army Executive shall meet at least once every six months. The Secretary of the Executive shall be responsible for the summoning of the members.

**3** It shall be the duty of the Executive to advise the Army Council on all matters concerning the Army

**4** The Executive shall have powers, by a majority vote, to summon an Extraordinary General Army Convention.

**5** A member of the Executive who, for any reason, ceases to be an active member of Oglaigh na hEireann shall cease to be a member of the Executive.

**6** Casual vacancies on the Executive shall be filled by co-operation after any substitutes that may be elected by the General Army Convention have been exhausted. Vacancies shall be filled within a period of one month.

**7** The Vacancies shall hold office until the following General Army Convention shall elect a new Executive.

**8** An extraordinary meeting of the Executive shall be summoned by the secretary of the Executive when a majority of the Army Council or a majority of the Executive so decide.

**9** Two-thirds of the available members shall constitute a quorum of the Executive, for co-option purposes only. Full Executive powers shall not be vested in less than five members.

## 8. Duties and Powers of the Army Council:

**1** The Chairperson of the Army Executive or his/her representative shall, as soon as possible after the election of the Army Council, summon a meeting of the Army Council, over which he/she shall preside, until a Chairperson and Secretary have been elected.

**2** The Army Council shall meet at least once a month.

**3** Vacancies occuring in the Army Council shall be filled from substitutes elected by the Executive or co-opted by the Army Council in advance. Co-options by the Army Council must be ratified by the Executive at its next meeting.

**4** Any active Volunteer shall be eligible for membership of the Army Council.

The Army Council shall have power to:

**1** Conclude peace or declare war when a majority of the Council so decide. The conclusion of peace must be ratified by a Convention.

**2** Appoint a Chief of Staff and ratify all appointments to the Commissioned ranks.

**3** Make regulations regarding organisation, training, discipline, equipment and operations, such as will ensure that the Army will be as efficient as possible.

**4** Take all necessary steps to secure co-ordination with other republican organisations.

**5** Keep in touch with all foreign organisations and countries which may help the Army in any way.

**6** Arrange for the care of wounded Volunteers and their dependants and the dependants of Volunteers killed, imprisoned or on active-service.

The Chief of Staff, Adjutant-General and Quartermaster-General shall be entitled to attend and speak at all meetings of the Army Council but not be entitled to vote unless they are members of the Army Council.

Four members shall constitute a quorum of the Army Council.

A member of the Army Council who, for any reason, ceases to be an active Volunteer, shall cease to be a member of the Army Council.

### 9. Selection of Delegates:

Delegates to the Command Conventions shall be elected by ballot as follows:

**1** At each parade called for the purpose, each unit in Command Area shall elect a delegate to attend the Command Convention.

**2** One member of the Command Staff, elected by the Staff at a special meeting called for the purpose.

**3** The Command OC shall be entitled to attend and vote at the Command Convention.

**4** Each Command Convention shall meet when instructed by the Army Authority and elect one delegate when the total number of Volunteers who parade for Unit Conventions do not exceed twenty, and two when the number of Volunteers do not exceed fifty, and one delegate for each twenty additional Volunteers on parade at Unit Conventions.

Brigade Conventions:

Where the Independent Unit is a Brigade, a Brigade Convention may be held consisting of the delegates elected by the Units, Battalion Staffs and the Brigade Staff, with the power to pass or reject any resolution brought forward by these delegates. The delegates from each Battalion shall each elect their own delegates to the Army Convention.

Election of Brigade, Divisional and Command Staff delegates to the General army Convention.

Two delegates shall be elected at a meeting of General Headquarters Staff officers, with the exception of the Chief of Staff, Adjutant-General and Quartermaster-General.

Resolutions to General Army Convention:

Command Conventions and the meetings of GHQ Staff for the election of delegates to General Army Convention shall have power to discuss any matter relating to the Army or to the Nation and to pass resolutions regarding such matters. These resolutions shall be forwarded to GHQ within the time specified by the Army Authority and shall appear on the agenda for the General Army Convention.

**10. Changes to the Constitution:**
It shall require a two-thirds majority of a General Army Convention to change articles in this Constitution.

## OGLAIGH NA hEIREANN (IRISH REPUBLICAN ARMY) GENERAL HEADQUARTERS GENERAL ARMY ORDERS (REVISED 1987)

### General Order No. 1

1 Membership of the Army is only possible through being an active member of any army Unit or directly attached to General Headquarters. Any person who ceases to be an active member of a Unit or working directly with General Headquarters, automatically ceases to be a member of the Army. There is no reserve in the Army. All Volunteers must be active.

2 The duties of a Volunteer shall be at the discretion of the Unit Commander. If for a good and genuine reason a Volunteer is unable to carry out the normal duties and routine which obtains in the Unit, the OC may allot him/her some special duties. So long as he/she performs these duties satisfactorily and makes regular reports he/she shall be considered as an active Volunteer.

3 Leave of absence may be granted to a Volunteer in the case of illness or for other valid reason.

4 A Volunteer who, for any reason, ceases to maintain contact with his/her Unit or with General Headquarters for a period of three months shall automatically cease to be a member of the Army.

5 The provision of this General Order does not apply to Volunteers in prison.

### General Order No. 2

Volunteers when making the Army Declaration promise '. . . to obey all orders and regulations issued by the Army Authority and any superior officers.'

1 Where an order issued by a duly accredited officer has been disobeyed, the Volunteer in question must be suspended immediately, pending investigation of the case.

2 Any Volunteer carrying out an unofficial operation is automatically dismissed from the Army and is liable to immidate repudiation.

Minimum penalty for breach of this order: Dismissal.

### General Order No. 3

1 All applications for re-admission by those who were dismissed or who resigned from the Army, must be submitted to the Army Council or delegated authority, who alone have the power to sanction reinstatement.

2 Where a Volunteer is summarily dismissed from the Army he/she may apply to his/her Unit OC to have his/her case tried by Court-martial. Such application must be made within seven days from the date of receipt of notification of dismissal.

3 Once a Court-martial has confirmed such a dismissal, then as in all other cases, any further appeal or application for reinstatement must be forwarded to the Army Council through the Unit Commander.

**General Order No. 4**
No member of Oglaigh na hEireann may be a member of a political party which recognises the partition institutions of government as sovereign authorities for the Irish people.

**General Order No. 5**

PART 1
A Volunteer shall not:
1 Swear or pledge allegiance or recognition to the partition institutions of government of the Six or Twenty Six County states.
2 Swear or pledge recognition of their legitimacy as sovereign governing bodies for the Irish people.
3 Swear or pledge himself/herself in any way to refrain from using arms or other methods of struggle to overthrow British rule in Ireland.
Minimum penalty for breaches: Dismissal.

PART 2
When arrested a Volunteer shall:
1 Remain silent.
2 Refuse to give any account of his/her movements, activities or associates, when any of these have any relation to the organisation or personnel of Oglaigh na hEireann.
3 Refuse to make or sign any statements.

PART 3
A Volunteer shall:
1 Refuse to obey any order issued by the partitionist authorities requiring him/her to leave Ireland or reside inside or outside a specified area in Ireland.
2 Refuse to give any undertakings about his/her future behaviour. Volunteers released from prison on ticket-of-leave are bound by this.
Minimum penalty for breaches: Dismissal.

PART 4
Any Volunteer committed to prison forfeits all previous rank and shall report into the Oglaigh na hEireann structure for de-briefing and further instructions.
A Volunteer's attitude in court shall be at the discretion of the Army Authority. Maximum penalty for breaches which are not also a breach of orders in Part 1: Dismissal with ignominy.

PART 5
No Volunteer should succumb to approaches or overtures, blackmail or bribery attempts, made by the enemy and should report such approaches as soon as possible.
Volunteers who engage in loose talk shall be dismissed.
Volunteers found guilty of treason face the death penalty.

**General Order No. 6**
Committees under Army control will have their terms of references clearly laid out for them. They will adhere strictly to these terms of reference. In case of departure from these the individual or individuals responsible will be removed from the Committee. The Army Authority has the right to remove any member of such Committees from the Committee at any time.

**General Order No. 7**
Volunteers are forbidden to undertake hunger-strikes without the express sanction of General Headquarters.
Maximum penalty for breach: Dismissal.

**General Order No. 8**
1 Volunteers are strictly forbidden to take any military action against 26 County forces under any circumstances whatsoever. The importance of this order in present circumstances especially in the border areas cannot be over-emphasised.
2 Minimum arms shall be used in training in the 26 County area. In the event of a raid, every effort shall be made to get the arms away safely. If this fails, the arms shall be rendered useless and abandoned.
3 Maximum security precautions must be taken when training. Scouts must always be posted to warn of emergency. Volunteers arrested during the training or in possession of arms will point out that the arms were for use against the British forces of occupation only. This statement should be repeated at all subsequent Court proceedings.
4 At all times Volunteers must make it clear that the policy of the Army is to drive the British forces of occupation out of Ireland.

**General Order No. 9**
Firing parties at funerals are only allowed in the case of Volunteers who die on active service or as a direct result of enemy action. General Headquarters permission must be obtained.

**General Order No. 10**
No member of Oglaigh na hEireann shall make any statement either verbally or in writing to the Press or Mass Media without General Headquarters permission. Volunteers are forbidden to advocate anything inconsistent with Army policy.
Minimum penalty for breaches: Dismissal with ignominy.

**General Order No. 11**
Any Volunteer who seizes or is party to the seizure of arms, ammunition or explosives which are being held under Army control, shall be deemed guilty of treachery. A duly constituted Court-martial shall try all cases.
Penalty for breach of this order: Death.
NOTE: As in all other cases of death penalty, sentence must be ratified by the Army Council.

**General Order No. 12**
A Volunteer with knowledge of the whereabouts of Army property which is not under Army control shall report such information immediately to his/her OC.
Minimum penalty for failure to do this: Dismissal.

**General Order No. 13**
1 Any Volunteer who attempts to lower the morals or undermine the confidence of other Volunteers in Army leadership or in any individual in the Army control shall be deemed guily of treachery.
2 Any Volunteer taking part in a campaign of slander and denigration against another Volunteer thereby weakening authority and discipline, and bringing the Army into disrepute, shall likewise be deemed guilty of treachery.

Minimum penalty: Dismissal with ignominy.

3 All Volunteers are expected to act in an honourable way so as the struggle is not harmed or undermined.

Any Volunteer who brings the Army into disrepute by his/her behaviour may be guilty of a breach of his/her duties and responsibilities as a Volunteer in Oglaigh na hEireann and may be dismissed.

### General Order No. 14

Oglaigh na hEireann is a voluntary organisation and Volunteers resign membership by giving notice to the relevant Army authority. However, no Volunteer or former Volunteer may join any other military organisation where his/her training, experience and knowledge gained in Oglaigh na hEireann could be used by that organisation.

### General Order No. 15

No Volunteer convicted by a Court-martial on a capital offence can be executed if that Volunteer can show that he did not receive instructions in the Green Book. The officer(s) responsible for recruiting this Volunteer and clearing his/her application shall be held responsible for neglect and being in breach of this order.

COURTS OF INQUIRY

**1.** A Court of Inquiry may be set up to investigate allegations against any member of the Army, any alleged irregularity, or any other matter affecting the Army.

**2.** The Court may be convened by the OC or any Unit or by the CS. The Convening Authority should supply the Court with specific terms of reference in writing, setting out the precise nature of the matters to be investigated.

**3.** The Court shall consist of three members, one of who will be appointed President by the Convening Officer of his/her representative. Any active Volunteer may be appointed to sit on a Court of Inquiry.

**4.** The powers and duties of a Court of Inquiry are: to examine all witnesses who appear before it and having considered all the evidence, to make specific recommendations to the Convening Authority. It has no power to bring in any verdict or to pass any sentence. It may recommend Court-martial proceedings, but decision on this point rests with the Convening Authority.

NOTE: The powers and duties of the Court of Inquiry should be made clear to the members of the Court and to all witnesses appearing before it, by the Convening Authority or his/her representative.

**5.** The members of the Court, should be supplied with copies of all General Army Orders, as they may be required for the drawing up of recommendations

**6.** Witnesses summoned to appear before the Court should be accommodated in a separate room to that in which the Court is held. They should be cautioned before hand that they are not to discuss the matters being investigated, among themselves. An officer should be detailed to remain in the room with the witnesses. The witnesses will be called singly before the Court to testify.

**7.** Evidence should be taken on oath which will be administered to each witness by the President. Should a witness object to testifying on oath, he/she must state the objections, to the Court. Unsworn testimony may be taken, but will not carry the same weight as sworn testimony. Once a witness has been examined, he/she may be recalled as often as the Court requires, to answer any further questions the Court wishes to put. For this reason, witnesses will not be allowed to leave the

precincts of the Court except with express permission of the Court.
8. If the Court so decided, it may call for additional witnesses to those summoned by the Convening Authority.
9. The recommendations of the Court shall be made in writing and signed by the three members of the Court. These recommendations together with a record of the proceedings and all documents connected with the inquiry, shall be forwarded to the Competent Authority by the President.
NOTE: The President appoints one member of the Court to record the proceedings unless a note-take or other means of recording is specially provided by the Competent Authority.

## OATHS FOR COURTS OF INQUIRY

To be taken by each member of the court.
I . . . swear by the Almighty God that I will conduct this Inquiry without fear, favour or affection.
And I swear that I will not disclose the vote or opinion of any member of the court unless required to do so by the Competent Authority. And I swear not to disclose the recommendations of the Court until they have disclosed by the Competent Authority.

To be taken by each witness:
I . . . swear by Almighty God that my evidence to the Court shall be the truth, the whole truth and nothing but the truth.

To be taken by the official note-taker:
I . . . swear by Almighty God that I will maintain inviolate the proceedings of this Court, and that I will not disclose its proceedings unless required to do so by the Competent Authority.

## COURT MARTIAL

1. A Court-martial is set up by the OC of any Unit or by the CS, to try any Volunteer on a specific charge or charges.
2. The Court shall consist of three members of equal rank or higher than the accused.
3. The Convening Officer will appoint one member of the Court as President.
4. When a Court-martial is set up by a Unit OC, the Adjutant of the Unit, or some members of the Unit delegated by the Adjutant to do so, will act as Prosecuting Council. When the Convening Authority is the CS, he/she may appoint any officer other than the Adjutant-General to act as Prosecuting Counsel.
5. The accused may call on any Volunteer to act as his/her Defence Counsel, or if he/she desires, may defend the case himself/herself.
6. A copy of the charge shall be supplied to the accused in reasonable time before the case is heard to enable him/her to prepare defence. The Convening Authority may either supply the accused with a summary of the evidence it is proposed to place before the Court, or arrange for a preliminary hearing at which witnesses for the prosecution will give on oath, a summary of their testimony. At such preliminary hearings, neither defence nor prosecution counsel will be present, but the accused may cross-examine the witnesses. The evidence shall be taken down in writing from each witness, shall be read over to the accused and shall be signed by him/her. If the accused wishes to make a statement or give evidence on

oath, he/she must be cautioned that anything he/she says may be taken down and used in evidence at any subsequent hearing of the case.

7. If the accused objects to any of the three officers comprising the Court, the objection will be examined by the remaining two members and, if upheld, the member objected to will be replaced.

8. The Convening Authority will supply the Court with a copy of the charges and with copies of General Army Orders.

9. The Convening Authority will ensure that the Prosecuting Counsel is in possession of all the facts relevant to the case and that all prosecution witnesses are present at the Court.

10. During the hearing of the case, all witnesses will be kept in separate rooms as in the case of a Court of Inquiry. The only persons present in the Court shall be the members of the Court, the accused, the Defence Counsel (if any), Prosecuting Counsel and note-taker (if any) and the witness under examination.

11. Evidence should be taken on oath which will be administered to each witness by the President. Should a witness object to testifying on oath, he/she must state the objections, to the Court. Unsworn testimony may be taken, but will not carry the same weight as sworn testimony. Once a witness has been examined, he/she may be recalled as often as the Court requires, to answer any further questions the Court wishes to put. For this reason, witnesses will not be allowed to leave the precincts of the Court except with the express permission of the Court.

12. At the start of the case, the President will read each charge to the accused and ask the accused if he/she pleads guilty to the charge.

13. Witnesses when called to testify will be cross-examined first by the Prosecuting Counsel and then by the Defence Counsel, or by the accused if conducting his/her own defence. Witnesses may be questioned by any member of the Court. Should either Counsel wish to recall a witness who has already testified, permission of the Court must first be obtained. The Court may recall any witness. Witnesses may not leave the precincts of the Court without permission from the Court.

14. At any time it so desires, the Court may go into private session to decide on points which may arise, such as the admissability of evidence.

15. When all witnesses have testified. Defence Counsel will sum up and make closing address to Court. This will be followed by summing up and closing address of the Prosecuting Counsel. The Court then goes into private session to consider its verdict and sentence.

16. For a breach of any General Army Order, the Court shall not have power to impose a lesser penalty than that laid down in such order.

17. The verdict and sentence of the Court shall be set down in writing and signed by the three members. This, together with a summary of the evidence must be forwarded by the President of the Convening Authority. Sentence is subject to the ratification of the Convening Authority.

NOTE: In the case of the death penalty sentence must be ratified by the A/C. (Army Council)

18. The accused may forward an appeal against the verdict or sentence or both to the Adjutant-General who will place it before the Competent Authority. The appeal should be forwarded by accused through his/her OC, who in turn will forward it to the Adjutant-General with a signed copy of verdict and sentence and

a summary of the evidence. The Competent Authority may order a new trial or reduce the penalty, but may not increase the penalty imposed by the Court.
NOTE: The President appoints one member of the Court to as recorder, unless a note-taker or other means of recording the proceedings is specially provided by the Convening Authority.

OATHS FOR COURT-MARTIAL

To be taken by each member of the court:

I . . . swear by Almighty God that I will try the accused on the issues presented to the Court without fear, favour or affection.

And I swear that I will not disclose the vote or opinion of any member of the Court or any proceedings of the Court unless required to do so by the Competent Authority.

And I swear not to disclose the verdict or sentence of the Court until they have been disclosed by the Competent Authority.

To be taken by each witness:

I . . . swear by Almighty God that my evidence to the Court shall be the truth, the whole truth and nothing but the truth.

To be taken by the official note-taker:

I . . . swear by Almighty God that I will maintain inviolate the proceedings of this Court and that I will not disclose its proceedings unless required to do so by the Competent Authority.

NOTES FOR COURT-MARTIAL

1. On the Court assembling, the Convening Authority or his/her representative reads the order convening the Court.
2. The President asks the accused if he/she has any objection to any member of the Court. Members of the Court retire and consider any objections, and decide whether objection is to be upheld or rejected.
3. If any objection is upheld, the Convening Authority or his/her representative nominates another member.
4. The President appoints one member of the Court to record the proceedings, unless a note-taker is specially appointed by the Convening Authority.
5. The President then reads the charge or charges to the accused and asks him/her to plead to each separate charge.
6. The Prosecutor presents his/her authority to the Court and makes the opening statement for the prosecution, outlining the charges.
7. The Prosecutor then calls witnesses to substantiate case for the prosecution.
8. Accused or his/her Counsel cross-examine witness for the prosecution.
9. When evidence for the prosecution is closed, the accused or his/her Counsel makes opening statement for the defence.
10. Witnesses for the defence are then called.
11. Accused or his/her Counsel makes closing statement for the Defence.
12. Prosecutor makes closing statement for the prosecution.
13. Court may ask for records as to the character and record of the accused.
14. The Court retires to consider the findings on each charge and to award the sentence.

The Court may award a separate sentence or punishment on each charge on which the accused is found guilty of, or one sentence or punishment, to cover more than one charge.

**15.** Where different sentences are proposed, the Court shall vote first on the lesser sentence proposed.

**16.** Members of the Court shall vote on sentence according to their seniority, the junior members voting first.

**17.** The President of the Court shall be responsible for forwarding to the Competent Authority.

(a) The written records or other records of the proceedings of the Court and all documents connected with the trial.

(b) The findings and sentence of the Court.

**18.** The oath to witnesses shall be administered by the President of the Court.

## CODE OF CONDUCT
### (Issued in 1987)

No serious guerrilla organisation can exist or hope to achieve victory without a number of prerequisites.

One one side of the coin these include comradeship, an internal structure (or infrastructure), rules and regulations, an ability to recruit, and a brief in achieving objectives. On the other side there has to be public support and the commanding of the admiration and respect of the public.

Where comradeship is lacking and where there are no rules and regulations one can see from past INLA feuds how disagreements can degenerate into anarchy and demoralise one's base of support.

The Irish Republican Army is one of the oldest and surviving guerilla armies in the world. It has a long tradition of struggle but at certain times in its history a number of the prerequisites for success were absent – conditions were not right, but most importantly nationalist opinion in the North was not ripe for a sustained armed struggle. All this changed in the 1960s with the attempted repression of the Civil Rights Movement and from then until now the struggle has taken on a steady momentum of its own.

The IRA's objectives are set down in a written constitution (which can only be amended by General Army Convention: the last IRA Convention was in 1986). The IRA however, is regulated by a set of General Army Orders (which can be amended at any time by an Army Council). Volunteers have always been expected to be familiar with the Constitution and General Army Orders, but in recent years familiar also with the Green Book which is a further breakdown of the aims and objectives of the organisation, the tactics of how to conduct oneself during interrogation.

### Enemy

The British government has attempted to undermine the struggle, deter people from fighting and sap the morale of Volunteers and supporters through a number of measures.

It kills people, it jails people, it consistently repeats that it will not give way to the IRA, it ridicules one's objectives as being unrealistic and unachievable. It attacks the methods such as the commandeering of cars, the taking over houses, fighting a war in the streets in which people live, the execution of informers, etc. All of this is so much hypocrisy compared to the commandeering of a country and British institutionalised violence and sectarianism. Most objective people – and not necessarily sympathetic people – can see through this hypocrisy, and only ongoing politicisation and publicity can really counter it.

It is IRA successes that demoralise the British and undermine their case. Ongoing IRA successes reinforce the belief in victory which in turn will lead to increased support.

## Behaviour

No organisation and no organisation's members are above reproach. The behaviour of Volunteers on operations and how republicans conduct themselves in their private lives will, where exploitable, be used by the British, the media, and the SDLP, and the Movement's other detractors to undermine the Movement in the minds of the general public.

When Mao's Red Army was fighting the revolution in China its Code of Conduct was summed up succinctly, (if idealistically) as follows:

*Three General Rules of Discipline*
1. Obey orders in all actions.
2. Do not take a single needle or piece of thread from the people.
3. Hand all booty over to headquarters.

*And the Eight Reminders*
1. Talk to people politely.
2. Be fair in all business dealings.
3. Return everything you have borrowed.
4. Pay for anything you have damaged.
5. Don't beat or bully people.
6. Don't damage crops.
7. Don't flirt with women.
8. Don't illtreat prisoners of war.

This is somewhat idealistic but one gets the drift about striving for the optimum in good behaviour and the necessity of avoiding scandal. Given the pervasiveness of the media in everyone's lives nowadays it is therefore even more essential for republicans to consider the effect of their attitudes and behaviour on supporters. To be conscious of how their behaviour could be used to ridicule the Movement and thus unjustifiably bring the struggle into disrepute.

The Republican Movement relies on a voluntary code of conduct (through Volunteers can still be dismissed under General Army Orders for blatant actions which bring the Movement into disrepute) and below are some of the guidelines expected of members:

1. Republican Volunteers are expected to be truthful in their dealings with other comrades and other sections of the Movement.

2. They are expected to be honest in all matters relating to the public, both in terms of official and private business. Whilst the majority of members are from working-class backgrounds, a business-person (who is also a known republican activist) who provides a poor serviced to the public or who exploits the public in business dealings is no asset to the republican cause.

3. Republicanism stands for equality and an end to sexism. Male Volunteers who mistreat or exploit their partners are flying in the face of this principle. Volunteers must practice domestically what the Movement preaches publicly.

**4.** Anyone promoting sectarianism or displaying sectarian attitudes should immediately be disciplined.

**5.** Republicanism has an international dimension which means respecting as equals other nationalities and races. Anyone who pays lip service to international solidarity and then slips into mimicking the racist attitudes which are typical of an imperialist mentality should be immediately upbraided. All people are equal and everyone has an international duty to oppose racism and oppression from wherever it emanates.

**6.** Our culture is something of which we should be proud, it is part of our identity and it can also be used, not in a chauvinistic sense, but against the British to show the separateness of our identity as an individual nation. Republicans who do not subscribe, to Irish culture, or who have no interest in promoting the Irish language, should respect those who are making progress on this front against considerable odds. It is simply laziness which prevents people from attempting to learn their native language: no-one is that busy!

**7.** The Green Book makes reference to people who take alcohol urging them to be extremely careful. Under excessive drinking people's tongues loosen, people whom one wouldn't normally trust become 'great friends', and one is vulnerable to the temptation of engaging in 'loose talk'.

Apart from the security risk, a drunken republican is hardly the best example of a freedom fighter, he or she is open to ridicule from the Movement's detractors.

The activities of republicans even engaged in innocent celebrations would be used by the enemy, so vulnerable are ambassadors of freedom struggle on this issue! So be moderate and be careful and remember what you represent. If you need to 'let off steam' then be discreet.

**8.** Alcohol affects different people in different ways, turning some aggressive people into affectionate doves, and making some normally pleasant people nasty and unbearable!

Under alcohol people's attitudes can also undergo unpleasant changes: respect towards others, one's partner, the Movement, can temporarily diminish leaving one with a lot of apologising and more than a hangover the following day. Dependency on alcohol is also a major weakness which the Special Branch will be quick to exploit.

The code set out here represents mere commonsense and is a reminder to all activists of their responsibilities. No-one has been press-ganged into republicanism. If you cannot do the struggle the honour of your service, then do not do it the dishonour of a disservice. It is as simple as that.

### Volunteer' Rights
#### (issued in 1988)

Volunteers should be well versed in General Army Orders and Court of Inquiry and Court Martial procedures. They should understand that they are aimed not only at ensuring the IRA runs smoothly within these agreed disciplinary codes, but also at protecting the rights of Volunteers. While everyone is accountabled to disciplinary process under General Army Orders, this is not their only function. They are there to protect the Army and as the Army is its Volunteers, they must serve to protect the Volunteers as well.

Communications within the Army are of vital importance. Thus all Volunteers should: be aware of how the Army structure works and of how a Volunteer can and should pass grievances or observations upwards. The onus is on the Volunteer to do this in a non-disruptive way, working through and using the proper channels all the time. All Volunteers should have access to their immediate superiors. This is through normal Army channels to GHQ. If this is unsatisfactory then there is access through GHQ to Army Council. The onus is on each tier, if requested, to pass requests upwards.

Security permitting, a Volunteer should always get an answer. Whether the Volunteer agrees with the answer is irrelevant: once Volunteers exhaust the channels, Army discipline demands that the answer be accepted. Final redress can be sought through the Army Council. Issues which are not important enough to warrant this should not be permitted to cause disruption or harmful dissensions. The onus is on the Volunteers to behave at all times in a correct, positive and responsible manner avoiding personal conflict or diversions from our main task.

Suspension of Volunteers should be conducted sparingly. Where suspensions are necessary they should not be of lengthy duration. Except in special circumstances Volunteers should not normally be suspended, unless facing charges, eg a Volunteer facing a court of inquiry should not normally be suspended. However, when a court of inquiry decided to press charges, this would normally involve suspension until the charges are adjudicated on. Special circumstances where a volunteer could be suspended by a competent senior authority could for example, include a refusal to obey an Army Order.

The above deals with suspension of membership of the Army. Suspension of a Volunteer from specific duties or a position in the Army is permissable at the discretion of a competent senior authority. Again the normal right to appeal applies. Summary dismissal of a Volunteer should be avoided except in the most extreme circumstances. Every Volunteer has the right to a court of inquiry. It should be noted that such a court, arising out of a summary dismissal, is a court, where those responsible for the dismissal will have to stand over their actions. They are not permitted to introduce new evidence other than that on which the dismissal was based. Volunteers summarily dismissed have seven days in which to appeal against the dismissal.

Courts are established by the Army Authority. Thus recommendations by courts must be agreed on by the Army Authority before they are acted on, or made known to other Volunteers.

All of the above places a heavy responsibility on those holding positions within the Army. The Adjutant General is responsible for discipline. The Adjutant General or those to whom he/she has delegated responsibility should be consulted in all cases involving the possible dismissal of Volunteers.

An organisation like ours which seeks political objectives based upon the principles of justice and freedom, must ensure that these principles are applied internally and in our dealings with one and other.

Volunteers, and this includes everyone from the CS to the Unit Volunteer, must be treated in a fair and overhand way.

# Index